CHINA

THE POLITICAL PHILOSOPHY
OF CONFUCIANISM

HISTORY, PHILOSOPHY, ECONOMICS

THE POLITICAL PHILOSOPHY OF CONFUCIANISM

An Interpretation of the Social and Political Ideas of Confucius, His Forerunners, and His Early Disciples

LEONARD SHIHLIEN HSÜ

LONDON AND NEW YORK

First published in 1932

Reprinted in 2005 by
Routledge
2 Park Square, Milton Park, Abingdon, Oxfordshire, OX14 4RN

711 Third Avenue, New York, NY 10017

Routledge is an imprint of the Taylor & Francis Group, an informa business

First issued in paperback 2016

All rights reserved. No part of this book may be reprinted or reproduced or utilized in any form or by any electronic, mechanical, or other means, now known or hereafter invented, including photocopying and recording, or in any information storage or retrieval system, without permission in writing from the publishers.

The publishers have made every effort to contact authors/copyright holders of the works reprinted in *China: History, Philosophy, Economics*. This has not been possible in every case, however, and we would welcome correspondence from those individuals/companies we have been unable to trace.

These reprints are taken from original copies of each book. In many cases the condition of these originals is not perfect. The publisher has gone to great lengths to ensure the quality of these reprints, but wishes to point out that certain characteristics of the original copies will, of necessity, be apparent in reprints thereof.

British Library Cataloguing in Publication Data
A CIP catalogue record for this book is available from the British Library

The Political Philosophy of Confucianism
ISBN 0-415-36154-0

China: History, Philosophy, Economics

ISBN13: 978-0-415-36154-5 (hbk)
ISBN13: 978-1-138-99504-8 (pbk)

[front

THE POLITICAL PHILOSOPHY OF CONFUCIANISM

AN INTERPRETATION OF THE SOCIAL AND POLITICAL IDEAS OF CONFUCIUS, HIS FORERUNNERS, AND HIS EARLY DISCIPLES

BY

LEONARD SHIHLIEN HSÜ

M.A., LL.B., PH.D., PROFESSOR OF SOCIAL THEORY AND FORMERLY DEAN OF THE COLLEGE OF APPLIED SOCIAL SCIENCES, YENCHING UNIVERSITY; BARRISTER-AT-LAW; SOMETIME MEMBER OF THE COMMISSION FOR STANDARDIZATION OF SCIENTIFIC TERMS, INDUSTRIAL PLANNING COMMISSION, AND POLITICAL SECRETARY OF MINISTRY OF FOREIGN AFFAIRS, NATIONALIST GOVERNMENT OF THE REPUBLIC OF CHINA

With a frontispiece of Confucius

LONDON
GEORGE ROUTLEDGE & SONS, LTD.
BROADWAY HOUSE: 68–74 CARTER LANE, E.C.
1932

To
MY MOTHER

CHINA: HISTORY, PHILOSOPHY, ECONOMICS

I	The Chinese Economy	*Adler*
II	A Documentary History of Chinese Communism	*Brandt et al*
III	China's Economic System	*Donnithorne*
IV	A History of China	*Eberhard*
V	The Spirit of Chinese Philosophy	*Fung*
VI	Chuang Tzŭ	*Giles*
VII	People's War	*Girling*
VIII	China's Regional Development	*Goodman*
IX	Health Care and Traditional Medicine in China	*Hillier & Jewell*
X	The Political Philosophy of Confucianism	*Hsü*
XI	Religion in China	*Hughes & Hughes*
XII	Ta T'ung Shu	*K'ang*
XIII	China's Foreign Relations since 1949	*Lawrance*
XIV	Confucian China and its Modern Fate V1	*Levenson*
XV	Confucian China and its Modern Fate V2	*Levenson*
XVI	Confucian China and its Modern Fate V3	*Levenson*
XVII	Crisis and Conflict in Han China	*Loewe*
XVIII	The Performing Arts in Contemporary China	*Mackerras*
XIX	The Rulers of China	*Moule*
XX	The Fading of the Maoist Vision	*Murphey*
XXI	The Grand Titration	*Needham*
XXII	Within the Four Seas	*Needham*
XXIII	Education in Modern China	*Price*
XXIV	Sino-Russian Relations	*Quested*
XXV	Contest for the South China Sea	*Samuels*
XXVI	The Classical Theatre of China	*Scott*
XXVII	Macartney at Kashgar	*Skrine & Nightingale*
XXVIII	The Analects of Confucius	*Waley*
XXIX	Ballads and Stories from Tun-Huang	*Waley*
XXX	The Book of Songs	*Waley*
XXXI	Chinese Poems	*Waley*
XXXII	The Life and Times of Po Chü-i	*Waley*
XXXIII	The Opium War Through Chinese Eyes	*Waley*
XXXIV	The Real Tripitaka	*Waley*
XXXV	The Secret History of the Mongols	*Waley*
XXXVI	Three Ways of Thought in Ancient China	*Waley*
XXXVII	The Way and its Power	*Waley*
XXXVIII	Yuan Mei	*Waley*
XXXIX	Confucius and Confucianism	*Wilhelm*
XL	Sociology and Socialism in Contemporary China	*Wong*

CONTENTS

	PAGE
PORTRAIT OF CONFUCIUS BY WU TAO-TZŬ OF THE T'ANG DYNASTY	*Frontispiece*
FOREWORD BY EDWARD S. CORWIN	vii
INTRODUCTION	xiii

CHAPTER
- I. THE BACKGROUND OF CONFUCIAN POLITICAL PHILOSOPHY . . . 1
- II. THE STATE AND ITS ORIGIN . . . 26
- III. DOCTRINE OF RECTIFICATION . . 43
- IV. POLITICAL UNITY AND ORGANIZATION . 61
- V. THE PRINCIPLE OF *Li* 90
- VI. THE PRINCIPLE OF BENEVOLENT GOVERNMENT 105
- VII. FUNCTIONS OF THE STATE AND GOVERNMENT REGULATION 128
- VIII. LAW AND JUSTICE 160
- IX. DEMOCRACY AND REPRESENTATION. . 174
- X. DOCTRINE OF *Chung Yung* . . . 198
- XI. SOCIAL EVOLUTION 219
- XII. POLITICAL PROGRESS 232
- SELECTED BIBLIOGRAPHY 248
- INDEX 251

FOREWORD

THE average reader's idea of Confucius is of a Chinese sage who lived several thousands of years ago, who taught reverence for ancestors, and who stated the Golden Rule negatively long before Christ stated it positively. To a mind housing this exiguous portrait of one of the three or four greatest teachers of the human race, Professor Hsü's exposition of the Confucian system will come as a revelation, and a most instructive one. Professor Hsü's general thesis is that Confucius' teaching is still relevant in many of its outstanding features, and not merely for China but for the West also. There can be no question but that he has made this thesis good.

Confucius' theory of government was at once paternal and democratic. The ruler is father of his people, and his right to rule is of the order of nature. He is moreover responsible in detail for the welfare, both material and moral, of his people. On the other hand, the highest source of human wisdom is the people themselves—they know best what is good for them—*vox populi, vox dei*. His humblest subject is the ruler's equal, and revolution against tyranny is a duty.

Probably the most astonishing feature of the Confucian teaching to the modern reader is its anticipation of the Spencerian formula of evolution, and its adaptation of this to a theory, or more precisely a programme, of progress. Things change and become more complex—so much is inevitable. But among the new forms, some are good and some are bad. So it becomes the duty of man to make a selection. Human choice thus plays its part in advancement. But this consideration does not deter Confucius from plotting the course of history. This is destined to pass through three stages. First was the period of disorder and savagery—the Hobbsian state of nature. It was followed by the stage that still persists—the age of " the small tranquillity ", which is characterized by national states and the institution of private property. In time this state will be succeeded by the period of " the great similarity ", a period of universal brotherhood, and of ownership in common. (While the terms here used are some of them modern, Professor Hsü appears to be well justified in thus adapting Confucius' thought to present-day comprehension.)

The outstanding point of contrast between Confucian and Western political thought is that between the " good ruler " idea and the idea of the " supremacy of law ". Confucianism attains its richest fruition in the wise, virtuous, and just ruler, while Western political thought culminates in the sovereign law-making body, representative of " public opinion ". Essentially the same contrast reappears in the difference between the Chinese conception of " li " and the Western notion of " positive law ". The word *li* is hardly translatable into a Western tongue, but the sense of it is perhaps conveyed with sufficient accuracy by our phrase " the right thing ". " The right thing " will, of course, for recurrent situations, find embodiment in a more or less stereotyped ceremonial usage, but for more casual or new occasions, its application is likely to vary with the personal factor and to be extremely unpredictable. Confucius always compares the requirements of *li* with penally sanctioned rules to the great advantage of the former ; and without doubt in a society centring in the family and stabilized by an ancient customary regime, both *li* and

Foreword

the good ruler idea worked very satisfactory results. Indeed, the claim of Chinese writers, that their people have in times past furnished the most happily circumstanced portion of the human family, does not smack of exaggeration. It is altogether apparent, on the other hand, that as the regime of custom weakens, social organization must find other supports, and these are only two in number, military force and law, in the Western sense, of which the former, from the nature of things, must be a temporary recourse. If, therefore, China's customary institutions are to be exposed indefinitely to the attrition of new ideas, it would seem that they must be eventually supplemented by enacted law, and the institutions through which this can be effectively elaborated and applied.

It is not without interest to ask the question how the institutional difference just described came about. A well-known Chinese writer, Chang Chih-tung (see his *China's Only Hope*, Woodbridge, Tr., p. 51) has addressed himself to this very question, and has answered it in terms which are perhaps unduly censorious of ancient China's ideals : " The dynasties following [The Chou, 1128 to 255 B.C.] had no powerful neighbours to strive against, but heaped up large treasures of literary lore at the expense of power. This accumulation produced hollowness of forms, and this in turn begat weakness. Not so the countries of Europe. These were opened up at a late period in history, fresh and vigorous. Surrounded by strong neighbours, they were always in circumstances of desperate competition, stripped for a fight, and ever striving to escape destruction. Continued apprehension produced determination, and determination begat strength."

In other words, insulated from the outside world, China had leisure to cultivate the domestic arts, to develop a subtle craftsmanship, and to create a highly refined literature, long before such things were dreamt of in Europe. Europe, on the contrary, living a dangerous life from the first, was fairly compelled to adopt efficiency as an ideal. The consanguineous family became subordinated to the competitive state, individual initiative was stirred, investion led to science ; and these divergent products emphasized still further the original differences from which they sprang. China, mother of the arts, remained quiescent for centuries on end ; in the West, the rise of modern science kept the social equilibrium unsettled at the same time that it assisted in transferring political power to a broader and more stable basis.

What, then, are the lessons that Confucianism has for us ? Foremost of these is the warning it utters against reliance on the idea of salvation by legislative process. Confucianism is the domestic virtue of China writ large. But if a people lack virtue—that is, if the individuals who make up the people lack it— they are doomed ; the legal process itself will share the common taint. Fortunately Confucius, like his near contemporary Socrates, encourages us with the idea that virtue is teachable, though it is doubtful if we yet realize the immensity of the task which this idea, with the decline of the family, puts upon publicly organized education. And a phase of this lesson is the one conveyed by Confucius' emphasis on *li*. Tolerance, mutual understanding—in a word, consideration—is the essential cement of classes in a society worth living in. If these are lacking, law will not supply the defect. Finally, Confucius teaches us that the task of government is that of good housekeeping. He at once anticipates the modern "administrative state" and supplies it with a Utopia.

All in all, the Western curriculum of social and

Foreword

political studies can no longer ignore Confucius—or for that matter, other Chinese thinkers in these fields of study. And Professor Hsü's rendition of the Great Sage's teaching will make such neglect doubly culpable.

EDWARD S. CORWIN.

PRINCETON UNIVERSITY.

INTRODUCTION

THE most difficult problem in historical research of ancient Chinese philosophy is the choice of source-material. Numerous ancient books of great prominence are not genuine productions of the time to which they are referred.[1] Some books are totally false[2]; and others are only partially genuine.[3] Many portions of the so-called "Five Classics" of the Confucian School are of doubtful authenticity. According to some writers Liu Hsin, a Confucian scholar under Wang Mang (A.D. 8–23), to satisfy his literary and political purposes, took advantage of the scarcity of books after the great fire of 213 B.C.[4]

[1] For the authenticity of the ancient Chinese literature, consult Ku Chieh-kang: *Critical Discussion of Ancient History (Ku Shih Pien)*, vols. i and ii; K'ang Yu-wei: *Research on the False Classics of the School of Hsin (Hsin Hsüeh Wei Ching K'ao)*; Chin Shou-shên: *Explanation to the Examination of Spurious Literature, Ancient and Modern (Ku Chin Wei Shu K'ao Shih)*; Hu Shih: *Outlines of the History of Chinese Philosophy (Chung Kuo Chê Hsüeh Shih Ta Kang)*, vol. i, pp. 10–33; Yü Yüeh: *Questionable Authenticity of Ancient Literature (Ku Shu I I Chü Li)*; Liang Ch'i-ch'ao: *History of Political Thoughts of the Pre-Ch'in Period (Hsien Ch'in Chêng Chih Ssŭ Hsiang Shih)*, pp. 26–32; and his *Lectures on Philosophy and Sciences (Hsüeh Shu Yen Chiang Chi)*, vol. i, pp. 1–42.

[2] Such books *Chou Kuan* (The Official System of Chou dynasty), *Kuan Tzŭ* (The Works of Kuan Chung), *Yen Tzŭ Ch'un Ch'iu* (The Chronicles of An Yen), *Lieh Tzŭ* (The Works of Lieh Yü-k'ou), and *Shang Chün Shu* (The Book of Shang Yang).

[3] Such as *Shu Ching* or the "Book of Records", *Hsün Tzŭ* (The Works of Hsün Ch'ing), *Chuang Tzŭ* (The Works of Chuang Chou), etc.

[4] In 213 B.C. Shih Huang Ti of the House of Ch'in ordered the burning of all existing literature in the country with the exception of works on astronomy, divination, medicine, and husbandry. Among

and adulterated the Confucian literature by changing the original text and by adding some spurious words, statements, chapters, and books into it.[1] Henceforth there had been the distinction between the so-called " Modern Literature " (*Chin Wên*) and the " Ancient Literature " (*Ku Wên*), the latter's authority being rejected by the more careful students. Long before this instance, adulterations, though less wholesale than Liu Hsin's, had been going on. In fact, Ku Chieh-kang maintains that there had been " professional literary counterfeiters " before the days of Mencius ; and that the authenticity of even the " Modern Literature " is doubtful.[2]

Thus students of research should be extremely cautious in accepting a book and in selecting quotations. Professor Ku Chieh-kang recognizes only a part of the *Analects* as the genuine ideas of Confucius. Dr. Hu Shih accepts only the *Book of Poetry* (Shih Ching) and the second book of the *Li Chi* or the " Record of Rites " as genuine.[3] This position is, however, criticized by Liang Ch'i-ch'ao, as being unreasonably rigid.[4] At any rate, one should avoid, on one hand, the mechanical fatalism of " Higher Criticism " and, on the other hand, such indiscrimination in the choice of material, in the determination of textual authority, and in interpretation of philosophical

the Confucian Classics, the *I Ching* or the *Book of Change* was the only book not being burnt as a book on divination. Other classics which we now have in possession were works " either saved from the holocaust by being concealed between walls or from oral quotations of survived scholars."

[1] See K'ang Yu-wei: *Research on the False Classics of the School of Hsin*.

[2] See K'ang Yu-wei: *Research on the False Classics of the School of Hsin*, and Ku Chieh-kang: *Critical Discussion of Ancient History*, vols. i, ii.

[3] See *The Development of the Logical Method in Ancient China*, preface.

[4] *Lectures on Philosophy and Sciences*, vol. i, pp. 7–8.

Introduction

systems, that the thought-systems of different schools or of different periods are confused.

One of the causes of adulteration is the desire of our ancient philosophers to refer others' name to portray their own ideas in order to borrow authority. For instance, in the *Analects*, Confucius often spoke of " Ancient sage rulers " or " Ancients ". He was, as a matter of fact, not looking backward. What he spoke of were his own ideals, maybe without any historical foundation.[1] He created these names to father his own theory on the principle that man has always idealized the past. Furthermore, by borrowing the authority and prestige of ancient kings, he could escape danger from the princes and rulers during his age of despotic militarism.

This practice of borrowing authority explains the fact that Mo Tzŭ and Confucius, though rival philosophers, both spoke of the ancient sage rulers, and both claimed to be their true representatives. Han Fei Tzŭ, living near to the Age of Confucius, queried that inasmuch as the ancient rulers could not be alive again, who could determine the truthfulness of the theories of Confucius and Mo Tzŭ![2] Chuang Tzŭ, too, frequently uses ancients' names to father his own theories. For the same reasons, the *Nei Ching* is not the work of Huang Ti, and *Chou Kuan* not the precious volume which the Duke of Chou used as his manual on public administration. Under such circumstances, the researchers should be cautious not to interpret one's idea on the basis of false books.

It is important to note, however, that spurious literature has had its influence and its place in the

---

[1] Ku Chieh-kang, for instance, maintains that Yü the Great, who has a prominent place in the *Analects*, was only a fairy-god. (See his *Critical Discussion of Ancient History*, vol. i.)
[2] *Han Fei Tzŭ*, bk. I.

INTRODUCTION

development of Chinese thinking. For instance, the false part of the *Book of Records*, the *Book of Change*, and of the *Li Chi* are inseparably read with the part of the true classics. No one will doubt that *Hsiao Ching* or the " Book of Filial Piety " was not written by Confucius ; yet this book has been read by even literate Chinese at childhood. *Chou Kuan* or the " Official Systems of Chou " is doubtlessly one of the most wonderful books on ancient political thinking China possesses. Likewise, *Kuan Tzŭ*, *Lieh Tzŭ*, *Han Fei Tzŭ*, and numerous other works of philosophy are rare beauties of the ancient, and may be interpreted as the thinking of the time when these books were written, though not of the persons in whose names they appear. After all, the world does not have much great literature or great pieces of art. If they are to be rejected on the ground of falsehood, indeed there would be little left for Chinese philosophy ! [1]

For the present study the author tries to be careful in the use of original materials. He has left out all spurious passages and books, however interesting to modern readers they may be. He makes no attempt, however, to give extensive explanations of the authenticity of ancient classics, as the latter belongs to the field of textual criticism and Chinese archæology. He understands that Confucianism is a more or less misleading general term for the teachings of the so-called Chinese Classics upon cosmology, the social order, government, morals, and ethics ; and that Confucius is not the founder of the system, but largely the transmitter of the teachings of antiquity. In this study the author is primarily interested in presenting in a somewhat systematic way the political and social ideas of early thinkers of the Classical school as well as those ideas of Confucius and of his early disciples which are widely scattered in the Confucian Classics and other ancient books.

[1] See Liang Ch'i-ch'ao : *Lectures on Philosophy and Science*, vol. i, pp. 1–42.

INTRODUCTION

The importance of a scientific study of Confucian political philosophy could hardly be overstated. By the Chinese people Confucius has for centuries been regarded as their greatest teacher. Even though the Confucian Classics might not have been written or edited by Confucius, but they have been cherished, studied, and applied in practical life and in politics. They have, in fact, constituted a sort of unwritten constitution for China.

In preparing this monograph the author has had two purposes in view. In the first place, it is hoped that this study may help students both in the Orient and in the Occident to understand the social and political pyschology of the Chinese people in relation to their social and political developments. Politics has its root in psychology and ethnology: to study a people socially and politically, two factors must be reckoned with—human nature in general, and the racial temperament of the people in particular. The significance of these factors is best revealed in the philosophies of the great scholars of the nation, for they are the makers and interpreters of the national psychology. The Confucian Classics are at once a record, a history and a landmark of the early developments of Chinese civilization. They have also had tremendous influence in shaping subsequent developments in Chinese politics. Confucius has been the national ideal of the Chinese people, and the Classics have been a mirror in which has been reflected the national mind of China.

In the second place, the author hopes that this study may furnish some new viewpoints in political philosophy. It is frequently questioned by Western writers whether or not the Chinese people possess a system of political philosophy. Ignorance of the facts and lack of scientific study of Chinese political philosophy have led Western scholars to deny that

INTRODUCTION

the Chinese people have any such philosophy. The results of the author's study do seem to indicate that the Confucian School advanced a rather distinct type of political speculation. Some of the ideas as presented in the Confucian Classics, which have heretofore been overlooked by modern students, may yet come to be generally recognized as valuable contributions to politics.

At the very outset the author wishes to warn the readers against identifying "Confucian" political philosophy with "Chinese" political philosophy as a whole. China has had a great number of schools of political thinking besides the Confucian School. Indeed, in China there are about a dozen different systems of political speculation. Each has had its independent development and each has had a certain amount of influence upon the political and social development of the Chinese people. There are anarchists such as Lao Tzŭ, humanitarian socialists such as Mo Ti, legalists such as Hsün Tü and Han Fei Tzŭ, ceremonialists such as Hsün Tzŭ, political economists such as Kuan Chung, progressive absolutists such as Shang Yang, co-operativists such as Hsü Hsin, practical socialists such as Wang An-shih, imperialists such as Wang Yang-ming, and constitutional monarchists such as Tung Chung-shu.

As far as the science of politics is concerned, sometimes the theories of these scholars surpass the political philosophy of the Confucianists in the brilliancy of ideas, consistency of system, modernness of methods of approach, and vividness of speculation.

While the Confucianists combined both ethics and politics, the legalists, the progressive absolutists, and the political merchantilists, accused Confucianists in most effective language of confusing practical politics with theoretical morality, for a lack of discrimination between expediency and principle, for

Introduction

maintaining an abstract impracticable doctrine of a government of virtue. They themselves advocated, and to a great extent actually practised, the principle which Machiavelli restated 1,500 years later, namely, the separation of ethics and politics. They advocated many financial and political policies that are aggressive, militarstic, and imperialistic in nature. They instituted a number of unethical political and diplomatic schemes, based on expediency and policy rather than on morality and justice.

Of the non-Confucian schools, some were extremely materialistic, advocating the doctrine that the end of the state is wealth and power and that the life of the individual be subjected to that external vanity which sacrifices its own happiness and lets the crafty few dominate the innocent many. In other words, China has had political thinkers of the Machiavellian, the Nietzschian, and the Hegelian type. On the other hand, there were anarchists who demanded the abolition of all government and all existing " artificial cultures " and a return to a state of nature ; political transcendentalists who preferred a passive, individual, happy life to a progressive, active, social life ; humanitarianists who demanded absolute equality, universal fraternity, and sometimes a communistic order. The others were either too practical or too idealistic. They engaged at one time in a sharp conflict with the Confucian School. This happened during the period of Feudal Disintegration, dating from the fifth century to the first century B.C.

Seeing that public opinion was controlled by false propaganda, that the minds of the people were confused with one-sided doctrines, either too radical or too conservative, either too materialistic or too idealistic, that human lives were sacrificed mercilessly in the search for power and wealth, that the empire fell into hopeless anarchy, recognizing the authority

Introduction

of no sovereign or the existence of no family relationships, and that governments were feeding fat battle-horses by starving men, Confucius and his followers waged life-and-death battles with the "false" philosophies. Confucius and his disciples aimed to preach the true doctrine of good government, and to show the people the dangers of militarism, imperialism, and merchantilism on the one hand, and those of anarchisms, indiscriminating humanitarianism, extreme individualism, and idealistic communism, on the other. He and his disciples worked to cultivate a public opinion based upon intelligence, truth, and fairness; and hoped to maintain the golden mean between the extremes of political speculation.

Such was the spirit of Confucius and his early disciples! It was, however, only after long and painful political experience that the Chinese people accepted the Confucian philosophy as the guiding principle in their politics—adopting at the same time some of the political teachings of other thinkers in so far as they were practical, reasonable, and unharmful. On the whole, when compared with the results in Western countries, the situation in China is not altogether unsatisfactory. The Chinese have outlived the rise and fall of the Egyptians, the Chaldeans, the Assyrians, the Medes, the Persians, the Phœnicians, the Carthaginians, the Greeks, the Romans, and many other peoples. Their civilization stands out as the evergreen pine-tree towers above the hillside flowers which blossom and wither away with seasons.

At last, after two centuries of suffering from industrial and political turmoil and from dreams of world empires, the nations are beginning to think that a mixture of politics and morality is not altogether an undesirable thing. The aim of all human association is humanity—not wealth and power. Western civilization, which has been seeking after power and wealth, has been described as a semi-pagan civilization, not wholly Christian.[1] If the West desires to realize the highest ideals of Christianity, it must practise something like unto the Confucian teachings of political morality, and be restored to consciousness from the chloroform of Machiavellian politics. Otherwise, this world-wide social, political, and moral paralysis will continue until the final disappearance of art and learning—which are too beautiful and too precious to be destroyed.

It is also to be noted that Confucius lived twenty-five centuries ago. The social and political conditions of his day were very different from present-day conditions. Many of his ideas, ideas of antiquity which Confucius once considered important, and the ideas of early Confucian disciples, are no longer applicable to modern society. Still, the fact remains that Confucianism has had immense influence in having shaped the political organization of the Chinese people, as well as in having cultivated their political psychology. No matter how perfect the Western system may be, the theoretical foundations of the new China will necessarily be drawn not so much from the West as from her own resources. Moreover, as already discussed, the Westerners themselves begin to realize that their political philosophy and system of corporate living are defective and they are seeking for means of improvement. If China has anything to contribute to the world, Confucianism will be a part, not a small part indeed, of this contribution.

Some portions of Chapters V and XII appeared in the *China Journal of Arts and Sciences* and the *Chinese Social and Political Science Review*, and I gratefully acknowledge my obligations to them, particularly to Dr. J. C. Ferguson and Dr. M. T. Z. Tyau, editors of these journals respectively. In the course of my

[1] Ellwood, *Reconstruction of Religion*, ch. iv.

INTRODUCTION

study and in the preparation of this volume, I am deeply indebted to the valued suggestions and assistance of my former teachers, colleagues, and friends, particularly to Professors Benjamin F. Shambaugh and Jacob Van der Zee of the State University of Iowa, Professors Hsieh Wei-yü and late Liu Jên-hsi of Hunan Chüan-shan Seminary, late Professor Liang Ch'i-ch'ao of Ch'ing Hua University, Professors Hu Shih and Liang Shu-ming of the National University of Peking, and Professors Lucius Porter, Philip de Vargas, and Ku Chieh-kang of the Harvard-Yenching Institute of Chinese Studies. I am very thankful to Professor E. S. Corwin of Princeton University for the Foreword, to Professor Porter for help in romanizing Chinese names, and to Col. Egerton for editorial correction. Throughout my wife has been a constant help and inspiration in the work. The book was largely completed in 1923 when I was in America, but after I returned to China, owing to heavy academic work and poor health, the writer has not been able to get the book through the press until such a late date. The writer will of course assume complete responsibility for inaccuracies and demerits in the book.

LEONARD S. HSÜ.

CHAPTER I

THE BACKGROUND OF CONFUCIAN POLITICAL PHILOSOPHY

Three factors to be considered :—
Life of Confucius : Biographies not reliable—His ancestry and his early life—His love for learning—His administration in the State of Lu—Anti-Confucius movements and the resignation of Confucius—Travelling and teaching—His death and postmortem honours.
Political and Social Conditions of the Confucian Era : Disintegration of the feudal empire—Political tyranny and economic exploitation, social unrest—The Observations of Confucius and his disciples—Domination of militarism, mercantilism, and legalism, and their influence on Confucianism, Anarchism, and political transcendentalism.—Taoist influence on Confucianism—Attitude of Confucius toward irresponsible hermits.
Basic literature of Confucianism : The Orthodox interpretation—Various groupings of the *Classics*—The attitude of the higher critics in the Sung and Ch'ing dynasties—The discoveries of modern researches in ancient Chinese history—Conclusions of Professor Ch'ien.
Summary.

Three factors must be considered in studying the background of the political philosophy of Confucianism, namely, the life history of the founder, the social and political conditions of his time, and the basic literature of the Confucian School.

LIFE OF CONFUCIUS

K'ung Ch'iu or Confucius was born in 550 or 551 B.C.[1] in the State of Lu, which is now part of

[1] According to Ssŭ-ma Ch'ien in the *Historical Record*, Confucius was born in 550 B.C. But according to Kung-yang and Ku-liang, two earlier commentators on the *Spring and Autumn*, Confucius was born in 551 B.C.

Shantung Province. Although a life history full of romance has been painted for the great teacher by Chinese historians, a large part of the story is doubted by modern critics. In order to make the story as reliable as possible without being unduly influenced by traditional scholarship, the author's story here has to be very sketchy.

According to *Tso's Commentary*, Confucius was of noble ancestry. One of his ancestors, who was an official under the Prince of Sung, was murdered by a court plotter; and his son escaped to the State of Lu.[2] Confucius's father, Ts'e Shu-he, was once a city major who distinguished himself as a brave soldier.[3] He probably died before Confucius was born; but his mother was then a young lady. Her name was Yen Chêng-tsai. She was well educated and of good character.[4]

When Confucius was young, he was very poor; and had to do a variety of manual work.[5] Mencius said that Confucius was once a keeper of stores and at another time a superintendent of parks and herds for a wealthy family.[6] At fifteen he decided to be a student.[7] The truth of the traditional story that Confucius studied philosophy under Lao Tzŭ, music under Chang Hung and Su Hsiang, and politics under Tang Tsu has been doubted, but it was probable that Confucius was very industrious and eager to learn from great masters in different subjects. He said of himself:—

" I was not born with knowledge. I am only one who has given himself to the study of antiquity,

---

[1] For instance, a part of the biography of Confucius by Ssŭ-ma Ch'ien in his *Historical Record* (*Shih Chi*) is not reliable.
[2] The 7th year of the Duke of Chao.
[3] The 10th year and 17th year of the Duke of Hsiang.
[4] *Li Chi*, bk. 11, sec. i, pt. i.   [5] *Analects*, bk. ix, ch. vi.
[6] *Mencius*, bk. v, pt. ii, ch. v.   [7] *Analects*, bk. ii, ch. iv.

and is diligent in seeking for understanding in such studies."[1]

"He (Confucius himself) is simply a man who, in his eager pursuit of knowledge, neglects his food : and in the joy of its attainment forgets his sorrows of life ; and who thus absorbed does not perceive that old age is coming on !"[2]

"When I walk along with two others, they may serve me as my teachers. I will select their good qualities and follow them ; and single out their bad qualities and avoid them."[3]

"To meditate in silence ; patiently to acquire knowledge ; and to be indefatigable in teaching it to others ; which one of these things can I say that I have done ?"[4]

"Even in a small commune of ten families, there must be men who are as conscientious and sincere as myself ; only they may not be so fond of learning."[5]

Judging from his own words and the words of his pupils, Confucius was recognized not only as a good scholar, but also as a great teacher. But Confucius was strongly inclined to enter into political service. At first he went to the kingdom of Ch'i and discussed politics with the Prince of Ch'i ; but the latter did not employ him.[6] He returned to Lu where he remained in teaching for a number of years. Later on he held several official positions in the State of Lu.

The administration of Confucius in Lu was evidently quite successful. Some historians recorded that the success of Confucius as a public administrator had even aroused the fear of its neighbouring

---

[1] *Analects*, bk. vii, ch. xix.   [2] *Analects*, bk. vii, ch. xviii.
[3] *Analects*, bk. vii, ch. xxi.   [4] *Analects*, bk. vii, ch. ii.
[5] *Analects*, bk. v, ch. xxvii.
[6] *Analects*, bk. xii, ch. xi ; bk. xviii, ch. iii.

State, Ch'i, lest Lu would arise to a position of military and moral supremacy in the Empire and thus endanger the balance of power among the feudal States. It was thought that if Lu were to become excessively powerful Ch'i would be the first to be annexed by Lu. A plot was laid to bring pressure to bear upon the Prince of Lu to dismiss Confucius. The Prince of Ch'i invited the Prince of Lu to a friendly conference, and the invitation was accepted. Confucius, however, suspected the plot and was prepared to meet any emergency.

On this occasion, Confucius accompanied his Prince to the conference as a substitute for another official. During the meeting, suddenly an armed force consisting of rough peoples from the uncivilized border-regions of Ch'i mutinied and attempted to seize the person of the Prince of Lu. However, these mutineers were suppressed immediately. Arising before the conference, Confucius said : " Our two Princes are having a friendly conference. How dare the sons of these barbarous regions attack them by force. . . . It is a recognized rule of international usage that no uncivilized subjects, knowing neither law nor order, should be admitted to a royal conference ; no military forces should be disguised in a friendly meeting. Otherwise, it is profane to God ; it is a violation to virtue ; and it is discourteous to men. No Prince should be justified in doing so ! " In spite of this and other malicious attempts on the part of the Prince of Ch'i, Confucius was able to defeat the plots and the conference ended in strict observance of the rules of international propriety. Not only Lu preserved her national dignity and honour, but the Prince of Ch'i was obliged to apologize, and as a mark of friendship, to restore the former conquests which Ch'i had taken from Lu.[1]

[1] The story was taken from the *Tso's Commentary*.

Background of Confucian Thinking

At the time of Confucius there were a number of barons who were disobedient and disloyal to the sovereign. Confucius remarked :—

"It is now five generations since revenues of the State has left the ducal house. It is now four generations since the powers of government have passed into the hands of the great officers. Therefore the descendants of the Three Huan have lost all power and are now living in obscurity!"[1]

"When good government prevails in the Empire, the initiative and final decision in matters of religion, education, and the declaration of war form the supreme prerogative of the Emperor. When bad government prevails in the Empire, that prerogative passes into the hands of the princes of the Empire; in which case it is seldom that ten generations pass before they lose it. Should that prerogative pass into the hands of the great officers, it has rarely happened that these officers do not lose their power in five generations. When the subsidiary ministers of the great officers have the power of government in their hands, it is seldom that they do not lose their authority in three generations.

"When right principles prevail in the kingdom, government will not be in the hands of the great officers. When right principles prevail in the kingdom, the common people will have no discussions about the government."[2]

The spirit of Confucius that rights and duties of individual officers in the hierarchy of government must be strictly observed was at once put into practical affairs.[3] In connection with his official duties he ordered that the walls of the cities of three disobedient powerful noble families be torn down; and thus

---

[1] *Analects*, bk. xvi, ch. iii.   [2] *Analects*, bk. xvi, ch. ii.
[3] See *Analects*, bk. xiii, ch. xv, quoting the conversations of Confucius with his Prince concerning this governmental policy.

greatly strengthened the authority of the central government.[1]

Then a movement to oust Confucius came both from the nobles in the country and from foreign diplomats. At about the same time the Prince of Ch'i presented to the Prince of Lu a number of dancing girls. The Prince of Lu was so infatuated with his pleasures that he did not preside over the Court for three days.[3] Confucius, finding the very head of the State indulging in the vices which he was punishing in others, was obliged to resign in order to preserve his self-respect. He left the capital city very reluctantly, hoping that the ruler would come to himself and recall him to his post.[4] But the ruler remained absorbed in his pleasures, and Confucius left his native State. He was in office only three months; and he was already fifty-five when he left his native country.

Confucius spent the next fourteen years in travelling from State to State, seeking office, but finding none. He knew that the times were out of joint. Seeing that Chinese civilization was drifting into decadence, he did his best to find entrance into public service.[5] He believed himself to have been commissioned by God to lead the people back into the paths of justice and safety.[6] Many times he was exposed to danger, want, starvation, and pursuit; but trusting in God and himself, he

---

[1] The *Tso's Commentary* recorded that this expedition of Confucius was not altogether successful. See *Tso's Commentary*, 12th year of the Duke of Ting.

[2] Kung-po Liao's attempt to oust Tzŭ-lu, a disciple of Confucius, from government service was an example. See *Analects*, bk. XIV, ch. xxxviii.

[3] *Analects*, bk. XVIII, ch. iv. [4] *Mencius*, bk. v, pt. ii, ch. i.

[5] *Analects*, bk. XIV, chs. xxxiv, xli, xlii; bk. XVIII, chs. vi, vii; bk. VII, ch. x; bk. IX, ch. xii; bk. XIII, ch. x.

[6] *Analects*, bk. XIV, chs. xxxvii, xxxviii; bk. VII, ch. xxii; bk. IX, ch. v.

went on travelling.[1] Explaining the failure of Confucius to get into power, Bishop Bashford says: " We wonder at his failure, and yet his terms were hard. He was willing that the ruler of the State should remain nominally sovereign, with the supreme power of dismissing him at any time. But Confucius insisted that, as prime minister, the reins of the government must be placed in his hands. Even modern kings have been slow in learning this lesson, and it is not strange that Oriental sovereigns were loathe to surrender their rule to a prime minister who wanted the kingdom ruled according to puritanical ideals."[2] In other words, what Confucius desired was a responsible ministry with an unhampered hand, which accounts partly for his unpopularity among the sovereigns. Having spent fourteen years in travelling abroad, Confucius returned to his own native State. The ruler who had been carried away by singing girls was dead, and a disciple of Confucius had become a successful military general under the young ruler. The general sought to have Confucius restored to power; but Confucius, seeing that the movement was not spontaneous, declined to consider the matter. He spent his remaining years with his disciples in literary labour. He died in 478 B.C.

After his death the highest honours were bestowed upon him. The prince of his native State came to pronounce eulogy upon him, and he was buried in what is now called the " Forest of K'ung ", to which trees were originally brought from other States by his pupils. His pupils stayed near his tomb until the

[1] *Analects*, bk. VII, ch. xxii; bk. IX, ch. v; bk. XI, chs. ii, xxii; bk. XV, ch. i.
[2] James W. Bashford: *China, An Interpretation*, p. 201. In connection with Mr. Bashford's statement one should note that writers on Confucianism disagree whether or not Confucius actually held as high an office as that corresponding to the premiership in a modern state.

end of three years' mourning, and Tzŭ-kung stayed there three additional years.[1] Later, over 600 families moved to the vicinity of his tomb, forming what was called "The Confucian Village". His house was converted into a Memorial Hall in which his clothes, hats, musical instruments, carriages, and books were stored. In later centuries emperors, princes, high officers, as well as common visitors, from all over the Empire paid tribute to this great Chinese sage.[2]

The Time of Confucius

Political and social conditions determine the type of philosophy of a period. Philosophy in turn influences subsequent developments. Thus a survey of the life environment of Confucius and his disciples will enable us to understand the sources of their political ideas. Confucius lived during the time of the decline and downfall of that magnificent feudal system which had been highly developed in China during the Western Chou dynasty (1122–771 B.C.). The central government became weaker, many feudal princes began to grow in power by annexing small feudal States and by conquering undeveloped tribes in the South and in the West. Ignoring orders from the Imperial Government, the feudal princes usurped powers and titles and called themselves kings or dukes as they pleased. War was prevalent, and people were massacred by cities. The Empire fell into hopeless anarchy; and there was anything but order and organization.

To describe the political conditions of that period, Mencius said : " Again, the world faced decay and

[1] *Mencius*, bk. III, pt. i, ch. iv.
[2] Ssŭ-ma Ch'ien : *The Historical Record*, bk. xlvii.

principles of right government faded away. Perverse speaking and oppressive deeds again became rife. There were instances of ministers who murdered their sovereigns, and of sons who murdered their fathers."[1] During the period of "Spring and Autumn" (770–484 B.C.) there were thirty-six regicides. There were also numberless dominicides, parricides, assassinations, murders, and usurpations for the sake of wealth or power or pleasure. There were instances in which the minister abducted the queen, killed the king, and seized the throne. There were instances in which the ruler, habituated to court effeminacy and indulgence, murdered the queen and neglected State affairs.

Needless to say, political corruption was prevalent. False propaganda led public opinion astray. The evils of the rule of political bosses were notorious. Furthermore, political bosses and landlords had formed combinations contrary to the interests of the mass of the people, most of whom were petty farmers. Political tyranny and economic exploitation went hand in hand. During the latter part of his life Confucius accompanied by a number of his disciples spent fourteen consecutive years in travelling, and came into personal contact with many scores of princes and political leaders. They witnessed revolutionary movements on every hand. Public grievances against tyrannical governments were being expressed throughout the Empire. It was from those first-hand observations that Confucius and his disciples drew many of their political principles.

The dominance of a "dangerous" political philosophy was another factor. There were men who propagated the theory that virtue as a basis for the State was not practicable; that is, the State was not bound by ordinary moral rules. The world

[1] *Mencius*, bk. III, pt. ii, ch. ix.

was a practical one, leaving no room for moral ideals. A government of ethical ideals was only an ideal; the State which attempted to achieve such ideals would thereby only commit suicide. What these men desired was military glory, territorial expansion, commercial domination, practical efficiency, thorough expediency, and an overflowing public treasury. They favoured a strict enforcement of the laws with heavy punishments for those who violated them. They sought political and economic domination over other States and absolute obedience from within their own State. The test of a State was its military strength: war was the inevitable means of reuniting the Empire.

These people exerted both a positive and a negative influence upon Confucius and his disciples. On the positive side the Confucianists acquired from them a practical way of thinking, and so they became thoroughgoing nationalists. Likewise, the early Confucianists advocated materialism, maintaining that economic well-being was one of the important aims of all governments. They were imperialists, and constantly associated themselves with the idea of establishing a great Empire that would have a commanding influence, moral as well as material, upon all other nations.

At the same time, Confucius and his disciples advanced the theory of a government of virtue in opposition to the theory of a government by force as advocated by the early militarists or progressive absolutists. They proposed that the government should not interfere with competition among the common people—a policy quite at variance with the ideas of the early Chinese mercantilists. Opposing the early jurists' idea of the supremacy of law, Confucius definitely said that morality should be the basis of law.

At the same time, there flourished a large number of political nihilists. For instance, Lao Tzŭ, a pioneer of Chinese anarchism, was one of the most influential teachers of his time. He advocated the abolition of State and government, the overthrow of the existing social order, the destruction of all morality, and a return to the state of nature.[1] Taoism had no little influence on the development of the political philosophy of Confucianism. For instance, the Confucian theories of natural and social evolution, of the essentials of the State, of government of virtue, and of passive resistance, showed distinctly Taoist origins. The doctrine of rectification, of political unity, and of political paternalism were but direct antitheses of Lao Tzŭ's ideas. Lao Tzŭ maintained that the fundamental remedy of social chaos was to be found in the surrender of all discriminations between good and bad, right and wrong, beautiful and ugly, proper and improper, just and unjust, long and short, rich and poor, and high and low. Confucius held, on the other hand, that the business of government was to make these distinctions more clear, so that the people might be able to choose. Lao Tzŭ proposed the abolition of all government and all civilization, including all literature, class distinctions, money, and political honours. Confucius believed that government, civilization, and literature should be developed to a higher degree ; that property was essential, though it should be regulated ; and that political honours and class distinctions were essential to induce the wise and the capable to render service to the society.

Still another group of the contemporaries of Confucius may be classed as undesirable citizens. These were the hermits and world-haters who, seeing the demoralizing conditions of the time, became hopeless pessimists. They withdrew from ordinary society and retreated to remote primitive regions.

[1] See Lao Tzŭ's *Tao Tê Ching* or the *Book of Reason and Virtue*.

Willing to live under such primitive conditions, they refused to become interested in what was happening in the world. Quite different was the spirit of Confucius. He set out to improve society rather than to withdraw from it and seek refuge in a Utopia.[1]

One day Confucius lost his way in the country. Seeing two farmers working in the field, he sent one of his disciples to inquire the road. The two farmers, who were hermits, insulted the disciple and criticized Confucius for being so restless in his endeavour to get into office and to improve existing political conditions. One of them said : " Disorder, like a swelling flood, spread over the whole empire, and who is he that will change the State for you ? " Then the farmers continued to work, paying no further attention to the questions put to them. When the disappointed disciple related to Confucius what had transpired, Confucius remarked sorrowfully : " I cannot associate with birds and beasts. If I associate not with my fellow-beings, with whom shall I associate ? If peace and order were prevailing in the empire, I would not care to change it."[2]

On another day the same disciple while walking with Confucius happened to fall behind. Meeting an old farmer who was cutting weeds he inquired of him if he had seen the master. Whereupon the old man replied with scorn : " Your limbs remain idle ; you cannot distinguish the five kinds of grains. Who is your master ? " He proceeded to cut weeds, paying no further attention to the disciple, who offered no defence and stood before the old man respectfully. Finally, the old man invited the disciple to pass the night in his house and prepared a chicken dinner for him ; and he introduced the disciple to the members of his family. On the following day the

[1] *Analects*, bk. v, ch. vi.   [2] *Analects*, bk. xviii, ch. vi.

disciple reported his adventure to Confucius, who said that this old farmer was a recluse ; and he sent the disciple to visit him again. But when the disciple reached the place the old man was gone. Voicing the sentiments of Confucius and indicating his principle, the disciple then delivered the following message to the man's family : " Not to take office is a denial of righteousness. If the relations between old and young may not be neglected, how is it that he sets aside the duties that should be observed between the sovereign and minister ? Wishing to maintain personal purity, yet he allows that great relation to come to confusion. A superior man takes office, and performs the righteous duties belonging to it. As to the failure of right principles to make progress, he is aware of it ! "

Such was the attitude of Confucius towards the hermits and recluses of his time. The hermits thought that the world was in a hopelessly chaotic condition ; that efforts for political and social reform were all useless since no improvement could be expected ; and that Confucius was foolish in going from country to country seeking office. Confucius clearly saw the dangers of such an attitude of mind. If all good men refused office, who was there to take the responsibility of improving the existing conditions ? If the empire were peaceful and prosperous, the service of wise men would not be needed. His attitude is well expressed by the words : " If I associate not with my fellow-beings, with whom shall I associate ? "

Such was the political and philosophical background of Confucianism. The next question is : Where can we get materials to study the political ideas of the Confucian School and what are these ideas ?

[1] *Analects*, bk. XVIII, ch. vii.

Political Philosophy of Confucianism

Basic Literature of Confucianism

The *Ching* or " Confucian Classics ", according to orthodox interpretation, were originally six in number, namely, the *Book of Poetry*,[1] the *Book of Records*,[2] the *Book of Rites*,[3] the *Book of Change*,[4] the *Book of Music*,[5] and the *Spring and Autumn*.[6] After the fire of 213 B.C., the *Book of Music* was almost completely destroyed. What was left was made a chapter of the *Book of Rites*, called *Yüeh Chi*, or the " Record of Music ". Hence there was the name of *Wu Ching*, or " Five Classics " of the Confucian School.

During the later Han dynasty, the incorporation of the *Analects*[7] and the *Book of Filial Piety*[8] into the " Five Classics " made up the " Seven Classics ". The scholars of the T'ang dynasty combined the so-called *San Li* or the " Three Rites " and *San Chuan* or the " Three Commentaries " to the *Spring and Autumn*, with the *Book of Poetry*, the *Book of Records*, and the *Book of Change*, thus forming the so-called " Nine Classics ". The " San Li " included

---

[1] In Chinese, *Shih Ching*, a collection of three hundred and five rhymed ballads in various metres. With two exceptions, all were written by different authors in the Chou dynasty (about 1182–598 B.C.).

[2] In Chinese, *Shu Ching*, a collection of historical documents from Yao the Great (2757–2258 B.C.) to Duke Mu of Ch'in (659–621 B.C.).

[3] In Chinese, *I Li*, a book treating of the ceremonial observances of everyday life in feudal China.

[4] In Chinese, *I Ching*, a book dealing with the principles of cosmic and social evolution. Since Change is the most fundamental factor in evolution, the book is called the *Book of Change*.

[5] In Chinese *Yüeh Ching*, a book on music. It was lost during or before the Han dynasty (after A.D. 85).

[6] In Chinese, *Ch'un Ch'iu*, a historical critique of practical politics during the reign of twelve dukes from 722 to 481 B.C.

[7] In Chinese, *Lun Yü*, a work of twenty short chapters or books, retailing the views of Confucius on a variety of subjects, and expressed so far as possible in the very words of the Master.

[8] In Chinese, *Hsiao Ching*.

BACKGROUND OF CONFUCIAN THINKING

the *Chou Li*[1] or the " Official System of Chou ", the *I Li* or the " Book of Rites ", and the *Tai Li*[2] or " Tai's Records of Rites " ; and the " San Chuan " included the *Tso Chuan*[3] or " Tso's Commentary ", the *Ku-liang Chuan*[4] or the Ku-liang's Commentary, and the *Kung-yang Chuan*[5] or Kung-yang's Commentary. Lou Teh-ming, a scholar of the T'ang dynasty (618–907), in his notable book, *Ching Tien Shih Wên* or " Explanations of Classical Literature ", gave a different classification of the " Nine Classics " ; the latter included the *Book of Poetry*, the *Book of Records*, the *Book of Change*, the *Spring and Autumn*, the *Analects*, the *Book of Filial Piety*, and the " San Li ".

During the Sung dynasty (960–1279), the " Thirteen Classics " were formed by adding the *Êrh Ya*,[6] the " Mencius ",[7] the *Analects*, and the

[1] A book that deals with constitutional matters in the Chou dynasty.

[2] The *Ta Tai Li*, or the " Elder Tai's Record of Rites ", was compiled by Tai Tê, a scholar of the Han dynasty. The number of its original books is disputed. It has thirty-nine books now. The *Li Chi*, also called the *Hsiao Tai Li*, the " younger Tai's Record of Rites ", was compiled by Tai Shêng, second cousin of Tai Tê. It has forty-nine books now ; but its original number is also disputed.

[3] The *Tso Chuan* or the " Tso's Commentary ", is said to be an interpretation of the *Spring and Autumn* written by Tso Ch'iu-ming, a disciple of Confucius. But this is doubted ; it is probably a production which appeared toward the end of the former Han dynasty. It is a book formed from the *Kuo Yü* or the " Narrations of Nations ", with many spurious passages added ; and aimed at interpreting the *Spring and Autumn*.

[4] The *Kung-yang Commentary* and the *Ku-liang Commentary* are said to be oral interpretations or detailed explanations of Confucius of his own book, *Spring and Autumn*, translated by the disciples of Confucius, and reduced to writing during the Han dynasty. This is not a reliable story. Especially the latter is a book of comparative inferior quality.

[5] See footnote above.

[6] The *Êrh Ya* has been considered the oldest dictionary in China. It is probably a product of the Han dynasty.

[7] The *Mencius* is a collection of the sayings of Mencius, probably gathered by his disciples.

Book of Filial Piety to the original " Nine Classics " of the T'ang dynasty. The Sung's classification has been seriously criticized for its confusing the *Ching* or " Classics " with *Chuan* or " Commentaries " and *Tzŭ* or " Works of Philosophy ". For instance, the " San Li ", the " San Chuan ", the *Book of Filial Piety*, the *Analects*, the *Mencius*, and the *Ĕrh Ya* were either books of philosophy or commentaries to the *Ching* ; and therefore they should not be classified as *Ching*.[1] The real *Ching* in existence, according to the more critical scholars, were the *Book of Change*, the *Book of Poetry*, the *Book of Rites*, the *Book of Records*, and the *Spring and Autumn*.

The famous " Four Books " or *Ssŭ Shu*, a classification made by the philosophers of the Sung dynasty (A.D. 960–1277), included the *Analects*, the *Mencius*, the *Ta Hsüeh* or the " Great Learning ", and the *Chung Yung* or the " Doctrine of the Mean ". The latter two books, which remained originally as two of the forty odd books in the *Li Chi* or the " Younger Tai's Record of Rites ", were singled out from the collection by Ch'êng Hao and Ch'êng I to form part of the " Four Books ". The " Five Classics ", which we may purchase from ordinary book stores, include, together with the other four Classics, the *Li Chi*, instead of the *I Li*, or the " Book of Rites ". The reason is that, although the *Li Chi* appeared late in the Han dynasty (206 B.C.–A.D. 220), it contains, however, passages of the Confucian era. Furthermore, the *Li Chi* did not, like the *Chou Li*, treat of mere matters peculiar to one dynasty, but matters important in all time : not like the *I Li*, of usages belonging to one or more of the official classes, but of those that concerned all men. Thus the *Li Chi*

---

[1] The traditional classification of books in China is : (*a*) *Ching* or Classical Texts ; (*b*) *Shih* or History ; (*c*) *Tzŭ* or Philosophy ; and (*d*) *Chi* or General Literature. Strictly speaking, a *Chuan* belongs to *Shih*, although it is a historical commentary of a *Ching*.

has taken a higher position than the *I Li* and the *Chou Li* : ranking with the *Book of Change*, the *Book of Records*, the *Book of Poetry*, and the *Spring and Autumn*, as one of the " Five Classics " of the Confucian School for common reading. These " Five Classics " and the " Four Books " together constituted the so-called *Wu Ching Ssŭ Shu*.

The classifications discussed above are tabulated on page 18.

The next question is : What is the relation of Confucius to this basic classical literature. According to traditional scholarship, the *Spring and Autumn* and a part of the *Book of Change* were written by Confucius ; and the *Book of Poetry*, the *Book of Records*, the *Book of Rites*, and the *Book of Music* were edited by the Master. The *Analects*, the three *Commentaries*, the *Records of Rites*, the *Mencius*, the *Hsün Tzŭ*, the *Doctrine of the Mean*, and the *Great Learning* were writings of the early disciples of Confucius and have been constantly associated with the Confucian Classics.

The authenticity of some of these books, however, has long been doubted by thinkers of the Sung dynasty (960–1279), such as Ou-yang Hsiu, Ssŭ-ma Kuang, C'hêng I, and even more seriously by thinkers of the Ch'ing dynasty (1644–1911) such as Yen Jo-chu, Yao Chi-hang, and K'ang Yu-wei. Although there were individual differences among these various thinkers, most of the writers maintained that the *Ku Wên* or the " Ancient Literature " in the Classics was adulterated by scholars of the Han dynasty (206 B.C.–A.D. 220). Prior to Ch'ien Hsüan-tung, Professor of Chinese at Ch'ing Hua University, and Ku Chieh-kang, professor of History at Yenching University, the attitude of the criticists may be described generally as follows :—

(I) The *Book of Poetry* was accepted in its entirety.

(II) The *Book of Records* had twenty-eight acceptable books, namely, books of the Modern Literature.

	Original six classics.	Five classics of the early Han dynasty.	Seven classics of the later Han dynasty.	Nine classics of the T'ang dynasty.	Nine classics of Lu Teh-ming.	Thirteen Classics of the Sung dynasty.	Four books and Five Classics.
Book of Poetry	*	*	*	*	*	*	*
Book of Records	*	*	*	*	*	*	*
Book of Change	*	*	*	*	*	*	*
Book of Rites	*	*	*	*	*	*	*
Chou Li				*	*	*	
Tai Li { Ta Tai Li / Li Chi }				*	*	*	*
Book of Music	*	⊙	⊙	⊙	⊙	⊙	⊙
Spring and Autumn	*	*	*	⊙	*	⊙	*
Tso's Commentary				*		*	
Kung-yang's Commentary				*		*	
Ku-liang's Commentary				*		*	
Analects			*		*	*	*
Book of Filial Piety			*		*	*	
Êrh Ya						*	
Mencius						*	*
Great Learning (originally in the *Li Chi*)							*
Chung Yung (originally in the *Li Chi*)							*

The twenty-five books of the Ancient Literature were universally rejected.

(III) The *Book of Rites* or *I Li* was considered acceptable.

(IV) The *Book of Change* contained *Shih I* or " Ten Appendices ", which traditional scholarship attributed to Confucius ; but modern students doubted that they were all written by Confucius. These appendices were :—

1. *Shang T'uan Chuan* or sixty-four explanatory notes on the sixty-four Kua-tz'ŭ. Part I.

2. *Hsia T'uan Chuan* or same. Part II.

3. *Shang Hsiang Chuan* or sixty-four explanations of the *Hsiang*.

4. *Hsia Hsiang Chuan* or 384 explanatory notes on the 384 Yao-tz'ŭ.

5. *Hsi Tz'ŭ Shang Chuan* or the Great Appendix. Part I.

6. *Hsi Tz'ŭ Hsia Chuan* or the Great Appendix. Part II.

7. *Wên Yen* or Remarks on the first two Kua.

8. *Shuo Kua* or Remarks on some of the Kua.

9. *Hsü Kua* or On the Order of the Sixty-four Hexagrams.

10. *Tsa Kua* or Miscellaneous Remarks. The general belief was that Appendices 1, 2, 3, and 4 were written by Confucius himself, that Appendices 8, 9, and 10 were not reliable, and that Appendix 7 contained a few genuine sayings of Confucius. Appendices 5 and 6, " though not free from frequent interpolations, form on the whole an invaluable collection of many undoubtedly genuine views of the Master, some of which were probably of his own writing, while others were recorded, in all probability, by his disciples." [1]

---

[1] Hu Shih, *The Development of the Logical Method in Ancient China*, pp. 30–1. In turn, Dr. Hu accepted here the critical views of Ou-yang Hsiu, of the Sung dynasty, as presented in his *I Tung Tze Wên*.

(V) The *Spring and Autumn* was a genuine book written by Confucius.

(VI) The *Analects* was written by the disciples of Confucius; and it is quite reliable, though the last five chapters are doubtful.

(VII) The *Book of Filial Piety* was written neither by Confucius nor by his disciples; but by some scholar during the Han dynasty.

(VIII) *The Family Sayings of Confucius* was not reliable.

(IX) *The Official System of Chou* or *Chou Li* was undoubtedly not the work of the Duke of Chou, but was compiled by a scholar of the Han dynasty.

(X) *Elder Tai's Record of Rites* was compiled by Tai Tê, a scholar in the Han dynasty.

(XI) *Li Chi* or the *Younger Tai's Record of Rites* was compiled by Tai Shêng. Liang Ch'i-ch'ao was of the opinion that these two *Records of Rites*, Elder Tai's and Younger Tai's, were good references for the study of Confucian philosophy, provided students would exercise a great discretion.[1] On the other hand, Hu Shih accepted only the second book of the *Li Chi*.[2]

(XII) The *Ta Hsüeh* (The "Great Learning") and the *Chung Yung* (The "Doctrine of the Mean") were considered of great importance, the former as the "gateway to the true principles of Confucius" and the latter as "the nucleus of Confucian teachings handed down from one to another in the Confucian School". Both Books, being written by Confucianists before the time of Mencius were considered very reliable.

(XIII) *Tso's Commentary* was not the work of Tso Ch'iu-ming, who is said to be a disciple of Con-

---

[1] *History of Political Thoughts of the Pre-Ch'in Period*, p. 109.
[2] *Development of the Logical Methods of Ancient China*. Preface; also *Outlines of the History of Chinese Philosophy*, vol. i, p. 14.

fucius, but a production which appeared toward the end of the former Han dynasty (206 B.C.–A.D. 6). It is a book formed from the *Kuo Yü* or "Narrations of Nations", with many spurious passages added; and aimed at interpreting the *Spring and Autumn*. The *Kuo Yü*, which seemed to have appeared during the Period of Warring States, contained valuable historical data concerning the Chou dynasty. In fact, it was considered the only reliable basis of study of the political philosophy of the period between 771 and 522 B.C.[1] Meanwhile, the materials of the *Chou Li* and the *Tso's Commentary* were drawn from the *Kuo Yü* and other old books. Although they were products of the Han period, they gave much information about old customs, institutions, and facts. They are useful as references in spite of the fact that students must exercise discrimination.

(XIV) *Kung-yang's Commentary* was considered a reliable work, and *Ku-liang's Commentary* was of inferior quality.

(XV) The *Mêng Tzŭ* (The "Mencius") was considered a genuine product of the disciples of Mencius; and a large part of the book was probably edited by Mencius himself.

(XVI) The *Hsün Tzŭ* (The "Works of Hsün Ch'ing"), it was thought, contained partly interpolations of later writers.

(XVII) The *Érh Ya* ("Encyclopædia of Confucian Literature") was a product of the Han period, not of early Ch'in dynasty, although the author of this book might have drawn materials from ancient books. It was considered absurd to attribute this book either to Confucius or to the Duke of Chou. It was nevertheless a good reference for the study of Classics.

In 1926 Professor Ku Chieh-kang published his

[1] See Liang Ch'i-ch'ao: *History of Political Thoughts of the Pre-Ch'in Period*, p. 30.

first volume of the *Ku Shih Pien* or "The Discussion on the Ancient History", which contained a number of essays and letters written by Professors Ku Chieh-kang, Ch'ien Hsüan-tung, Hu Shih, and others discussing the authenticity of ancient classics and literature. In one of the letters Professor Ch'ien Hsüan-tung gave the following conclusions which were very revolutionary in nature :—

(*a*) That Confucius had nothing to do with the writing or editing of the "Six Classics", although they were important literature of Confucianism ;

(*b*) That what Confucius said about *Li* and *Shu* were not the same texts known to-day as the *I Li* or the "Book of Rites" and the *Shu Ching* or "The Book of Records" ;

(*c*) That there never was the "Book of Music", although there is evidence to show that Confucius might have edited some articles on music ;

(*d*) That Confucius read a large number of the poems in the present collection known as the *Book of Poetry* ;

(*e*) That Confucius had ever seen the *Book of Change* is to be seriously doubted ;

(*f*) That the *Spring and Autumn* was but a collection of news reports during the years of 722–481 B.C., and that it never was even read seriously by Confucius ;

(*g*) That the *Book of Poetry*, a collection of unknown authorship, already existed before the time of Confucius, although it was not free from interpolations ;

(*h*) That the *Book of Records* was originally a collection of government documents during the so-called "Three dynasties" ;

(*i*) That the *I Li* came into existence probably during the period of Warring States (491–249 B.C.) ; that the *Chou Li* was attributed to Liu Hsin and that nine-tenths of the two *Tai Li* were written by philosophers during the Han dynasty (206 B.C.–A.D. 220) ;

BACKGROUND OF CONFUCIAN THINKING

(*j*) That the appendices to *Book of Change* were written after the time of Confucius ; and

(*k*) Finally, that the *Analects* was the only reliable source in the study of the ideas of Confucius ; and even then it contained a large number of spurious statements.[1]

While the books above referred to may not be written or edited by Confucius himself, they have, nevertheless, formed the basic literature of Confucianism for 2,000 years. Indeed, we should be careful not to include spurious passages and books as those written by scholars of Han and later dynasties. The following list of books are valuable in studying the social and political ideas of Confucianism, if not that of Confucius :—

(*a*) The *Book of Poetry*.
(*b*) The *Book of Records*—The twenty-eight books of the " modern literature ".
(*c*) The *Analects*.
(*d*) The *Book of Rites*.
(*e*) The *Book of Change*, especially the " Great Appendices ".
(*f*) The *Spring and Autumn*.
(*g*) The two Tai's *Records of Rites*.
(*h*) The *Tso's Commentary*.
(*i*) The *Kung-yang's Commentary*.
(*j*) The *Mencius*.
(*k*) The *Hsün Tzŭ*—in part.
(*l*) The *Great Learning*, and
(*m*) The *Chung Yung*.

In conclusion, it is to be noted that the first fifteen books of the *Analects* are the only reliable sources in the study of the ideas of Confucius himself. It is also to be noted that many books mentioned above, such as the *Book of Poetry*, include materials existing long before Confucius and that they are by no means

[1] Ku Chieh-kang : *Discussion on Ancient History*, vol. i, pp. 67–82.

products of Confucius or his disciples. They are, however, important material in the study of political and social ideas of Confucianism because of being subsequently incorporated into what we call the Confucian Classics, and of their influence over Confucius and his disciples.

SUMMARY

When we study the political philosophy of Confucianism, we ought to know :—

(1) What was the life history of Confucius, the founder of the School?

(2) What was the social and political conditions in feudal China that determined the type of philosophy of the Confucian School?

(3) What are the basic materials in the study of the political ideas of the Confucian School?

Confucius was born in 551 B.C. in the State of Lu. He was a great teacher and had a large number of disciples. He was, however, strongly inclined to enter into political service since he thought that government was the greatest institution to bring social salvation to his Empire. He held several public offices in his native State. Although his term of office lasted only three months, he seemed to have proved himself a successful administrator and a wise diplomat. After his resignation, he travelled throughout the different feudal States for fourteen consecutive years, hoping that he might be used by a wise ruler. But he failed and returned to his native State at the age of sixty-eight. He died at the age of seventy-two.

The age of Confucius was marked by political chaos, revolutionary movements, moral degeneration, the influence of corrupt demagogues in office, the grievances of common people against powerful

The State and its Origin

used to designate the State; the character *chêng* to designate government or politics; and the character *wei* to designate government offices.[1]

As to the essentials of the State, Confucius and his disciples point out *min* or the people, *chêng* or the government, and *ti* or the territory; that is, a State is a group of people inhabiting a certain territory with a government.[2] The State also has its symbols, namely, the *shê-chi* or the Altars to the Spirit of Territory and Grain, the *tsung-miao* or the Ancestral Temple, and the *ch'ao-t'ing* or the Court. Like the national flag of a modern State, the *shê-chi* represents the State and its government. It should be respected and honoured. Sovereigns may die or the people may sacrifice their lives and property in order to defend the honour of the *shê-chi*.[3]

The "ancestral temple", according to Confucius, represents respect for the authority of the ruling family. Because of the fact that the family is the foundation of the State, proper discharge of sacrificial functions in the ancestral temple by the ruling family serves as a model of order, and duty to the people.[4] The "court" refers to the relationships between the sovereign and the minister, the superiors and the subordinates, the officials and the people. Throughout the Classics, Confucius and his disciples emphasize

---

[1] See the *Analects*, bk. I, ch. v; bk. II, chs. i, xxi; bk. IV, chs. xiii, xiv; bk. VIII, ch. xiv; bk. XI, ch. xxv; bk. XIV, chs. i, iv; bk. XV, chs. v, vi, ix; bk. XVI, ch. i.

[2] The *Analects*, bk. I, ch. v; bk. II, chs. i, iii, xxi; bk. III, ch. xxi; bk. V, ch. vii; bk. VIII, ch. xiv; bk. XI, chs. xxiv, xxv; bk. XII, chs. vii, ix, xi, xix, xx; bk. XIII, chs. i, ii, iii, vi, xi, xiii, xv; bk. XIV, ch. xxxix; bk. XVI, chs. i, ii.

[3] The *Analects*, bk. III, ch. xxi; bk. X, chs. i, xii, xiv; bk. XI, chs. xxiv, xxv; bk. XVI, ch. i.

[4] The *Analects*, bk. III, chs. x, xv; bk. X, chs. ii, vii, xiv; bk. XI, ch. xxv.

the fact that good government means the maintenance of proper relationships in the court.[1]

Indeed, the entire volume of the *Spring and Autumn* is devoted to a critical interpretation of such proper relationships. Mencius says:—

"The world fell into decay, and principles faded away. Perverse speakings and oppressive deeds waxed rife again. There were instances of ministers who murdered their sovereigns, and of sons who murdered their fathers.

"Confucius was afraid, and wrote the *Spring and Autumn*. What the *Spring and Autumn* contains are matters proper to the emperor. On this account Confucius said, 'Yes! It is the *Spring and Autumn*, which will make men know men, and it is the *Spring and Autumn* which will make men condemn me.'"[2]

Relating the greatest deeds in history, Mencius continues:—

"In former times, Yü repressed the vast waters of the inundation, and the empire was reduced to order. Chou Kung's achievements extended even to the barbarous tribes of the West and North, and he drove away all ferocious animals, and the people enjoyed repose. Confucius completed the *Spring and Autumn*, and rebellious ministers and villainous sons were struck with terror."[3]

The *Spring and Autumn*, in fact, is a book on public law. This book does not set forth a philosophical scheme of public law, nor is it a code of statutes or a text-book on common law. But it re-states the law as existing facts. Its laconic sentences or phrases, the peculiar position of words, striking omissions of titles, and the employment of unusual terms to denote

---

[1] The *Analects*, bk. III, chs. ii, v, xix, xxii; bk. x; bk. xi, ch. xxv; bk. xiii chs. ii, xi, xvii, xix; bk. xvi, chs. i, ii, iii.
[2] *Mencius*, bk. III, pt. ii, ch. ix.
[3] *Mencius*, bk. III, pt. ii, ch. ix.

The State and its Origin

certain events, etc., are susceptible to double interpretation. For this reason, in studying the book commentaries on it are used.[1]

Place of the State in Social Development

Having determined the essential characteristics and symbols of the State, we now proceed to discuss the Confucian conception of the State in social development. In Chinese philosophy, the character *lun* or "relationship" is a keyword in the discussion of social justice as well as of individual virtue. The polity refers to the relationships between the governor and the governed; the family refers to the relationships between parents and children, husband and wife, older and younger brothers; the society refers to the relationships between friend and friend. Thus there is the theory of *wu-lun* or "five relations", which is of very ancient origin.[2] In a word, *wu-lun* constitutes a general term denoting social phenomena as contrasted with natural phenomena.

Though without mentioning specifically five relations, Confucius, in his discourses, emphasizes the idea of "relations", especially the relations between the governor and the governed, relations between parents and children, and relations between friends. It is safe to state that Confucius interprets social phenomena in terms of relationships and that political relationships, namely, relationships between the governor and the governed, is only one phase of our manifold social relationships. In other words, State is only a part of society.

---

[1] The *Kung-yang's Commentary*, the *Tso's Commentary*, and the *Ku-liang's Commentary* are used.
[2] In the "Canon of Yao" and the "Counsels of Kao Yao", of the *Book of Records*, the term *wu tien* is used to denote the five relations.

Political Philosophy of Confucianism

The Evolutionary Origin of the State

Inasmuch as the State is a part of society, it is also created by the general process of evolution; and its influence is constantly expanded by the achievements of social geniuses [1] to make the State most useful for the improvement of corporate life. Thus we can see that Confucius and his early disciples would sanction no social contract theory nor would they accept the notion that government was instituted by any one person. It is significant to note that the "Great Appendix" of the *Book of Change* which gives a survey of the growth of the Chinese civilization, merely mentions that certain ancient sage rulers, observing the phenomena of heaven and earth, the life of birds and animals, the faculties of man's own mind and body, and the existence of other matters in the universe, instituted fishing, cooking, housing, clothing, domestication of animals, navigation, transportation, marital systems, funeral ceremonies, systems of bargaining and marketing, and systems of government.

It says: "Anciently, when Pao-Hsi had come to the rule of all under Heaven, looking up, he contemplated the brilliant forms exhibited in the sky, and looking down he surveyed the patterns shown on the earth. He contemplated the ornamental appearances of birds and beasts and the different suitabilities of the soil. Near at hand, in his own person, he found things for consideration, and the same at a distance in things in general. On this he devised the eight trigrams, to show fully the attributes of the spirit-like and intelligent operations working secretly, and to classify the qualities of the myriads of things.

"He invented the making of nets of various kinds by knitting strings, both for hunting and for fishing.

---

[1] In Confucian terminology, "Ancient sages."

The State and its Origin

The idea of this was taken, probably, from *Li* (the third trigram, and thirtieth hexagram).[1]

"On the death of Pao-Hsi, there arose Shên-nung in his place. He fashioned wood to form the share, and bent wood to make the plough-handle. The advantages of ploughing and weeding were then taught to all under Heaven. The idea of this was taken, probably, from *I* (the forty-second hexagram).

"He caused markets to be held at mid-day, thus bringing together all the people, and assembling in one place all their wares. They made their exchanges and retired, every one having got what he wanted. The idea of this was taken, probably, from *Shih Ho* (the twenty-first hexagram).

"After the death of Shên-nung, there arose Huang Ti, Yao, and Shun. They carried through the necessarily occurring changes, so that the people did what was required of them without being wearied; yet, they exerted such a spirit-like transformation, that the people felt constrained to approve their ordinances as right. When a series of changes has run all its course, another change ensues. When it obtains free course, it will continue long. Hence it was that 'these sovereigns were helped by Heaven; they had good fortune, and their every movement was advantageous'. Huang Ti, Yao, and Shun simply wore their upper and lower garments as patterns of the people and good order was secured all under Heaven. The idea of all this was taken, probably, from *Ch'ien* and *K'un* (the first and eighth trigrams, or the first and second hexagrams).

[1] Each "hexagram" represents a principle of social or cosmic evolution which is discussed in the "Text" and "Appendices" of the *Book of Change*. The number of trigrams and hexagrams designate the order of those principles as arranged in the "Text". Everyone of these principles is supposed to be drawn from the observation and interpretation of a particular class of phenomena.

"They hollowed-out trees to form canoes; they cut others long and thin to make oars. Thus arose the benefit of canoes and oars for the help of those who had no means of intercourse with others. They could now reach the most distant parts, and all the people were benefited. The idea of this was taken, probably, from *Huan* (the fifty-ninth hexagram).

"They used oxen in carts and yoked horses to chariots, thus providing for the carriage of what was heavy, and for distant journeys—thereby benefiting all under the sky. The idea of this was taken, probably, from *Sui* (the seventeenth hexagram).

"They made the defence of the double gates, and the warning of the clapper, as a preparation against the approach of marauding visitors. The idea of this was taken, probably, from *Yü* (the sixteenth hexagram).

"They cut wood and fashioned it into pestles; they dug in the ground and formed mortars. Thus the myriads of the people received the benefit arising from the use of the pestle and mortar. The idea of this was taken, probably, from *Hsiao Kuo* (the sixty-second hexagram).

"They bent wood by means of string so as to form bows, and sharpened wood so as to make arrows. This gave the benefit of bows and arrows, and served to produce everywhere a feeling of awe. The idea of this was taken, probably, from *K'uei* (the thirty-eighth hexagram).

"In the highest antiquity they made their homes in winter in caves, and in summer dwelt in the open country. In subsequent ages, for these the sages substituted houses, with the ridgebeam above and the projecting roof below, as a provision against wind and rain. The idea of this was taken, probably, from *Ta Chuang* (the thirty-fourth hexagram).

"When the ancients buried their dead, they

covered the body thickly with pieces of wood, having laid it in the open country. They raised no mound over it, nor planted trees around; nor had they any fixed period for mourning. In subsequent ages the sages substituted for these practices the inner and outer coffins. The idea of this was taken, probably, from *Ta Kuo* (the twenty-eighth hexagram).

"In the highest antiquity, government was carried on successfully by the use of knotted cords to preserve the memory of things. In subsequent ages the sages substituted for these written characters and bonds. By means of these the doings of all the officers could be regulated, and the affairs of all the people accurately examined. The idea of this was taken, probably, from *Kuai* (the forty-third hexagram)."[1]

Each of the sixty-four hexagrams represents the development of a certain phenomenon, as quoted above, each historical achievement derives its origin from some hexagram. That is, each achievement, such as the invention of fishing, housing, clothing, agriculture, or the development of commerce, transportation, and navigation, or the institution of rituals, law, and government, is the result of imitating a certain phenomena. The State, like any other aspect of civilization, is created through the process of phenomenal imitation.[2]

THE STATE AND THE DEVELOPMENT OF CIVILIZATION

The *Book of Change* goes on discussing the development of society, saying :—

"Heaven and earth existing, all material things then got their existence. All material things having existence, afterwards there came male and female.

[1] *Book of Change*, The Great Appendix, bk. II, ch. ii. Legge's translation, in Müller, F. Max, *The Sacred Books of the East*, vol. xvi, pp. 382–3.

[2] For detailed explanation of their theory, see chapter xi.

From the existence of male and female there came afterwards husband and wife. From husband and wife there came father and son. From father and son there came sovereign and subjects. From sovereign and subjects there came high and low. Following the distinction between high and low came the arrangements of propriety and righteousness."[1]

There is no clearer expression as to the origin of the State. To begin with, there were heaven and earth. The term "heaven and earth" indicates the formation of the earth in the universe. Thus the evolutionary theory of the Confucian School begins with the formation of heaven and earth, that is, it begins where modern geology begins, making no excursions into realms in which scientific data are not ascertainable. No attempt is made to fathom the absolute origin of life. After the earth had been formed, material things were created. Material things include both animate and inanimate objects. Then the different sexes appeared. Man is the highest type of animal. The beginning of the relationship of husband and wife marks the beginning of civilization; it is the primary phase of social relationship. The term "husband and wife" indicates the existence of the family institution, moral and ritual. The birth of children gave rise to the relationship between parent and child and to that between elder brother and younger brother. This led to the increase of population and, consequently, to the relationship between friend and friend.

As between husband and wife, between parent and child, between elder and younger brothers, and between friend and friend, there are certain ethical codes. There is authority on the one side and obedience on the other. There is a need for

[1] *Book of Change*, orderly sequence of the hexagrams, ch. ii.

mutual confidence to maintain these principles. In family ethics, family education, obedience and authority, and mutual confidence, there is to be found the bases of political relationships. Confucius, as well as his disciples, think of the State as a great family, and of the individual family as a miniature State. Family code are the bases of government codes. Family education becomes essentially public education. Authority and obedience are necessary to the existence of political order. Popular confidence in the government and confidence of the government in the people are fundamental in the State. And so also the relationship between parent and child is followed by the relationship between ruler and ruled.[1]

Thus it is clear that the State is a phase of social life, a product of natural evolution built upon patriarchal foundations. In the State there are ruler and ruled; there are high officials and low officials. There are official ranks and differences of power and authority. Each official is provided with proper powers and duties, and each officer has his own distinct official rank in the political hierarchy. Thus the distinction of high and low exists in the political State. When the distinction between high and low is made, the existence of propriety and righteousness is possible. By propriety (*li*) Confucius means an ethical code enforced by social tradition on one hand and by public law on the other.[2] It is really a body of unwritten constitutional laws founded upon an ethical basis. By righteousness (*i*) Confucius means justice or virtue consisting of benevolent activities that will secure the greatest social harmony and the greatest advantage to the life of man![3]

So much for the steps or stages in the origin of

[1] *Infra*, chs. iii, iv, and vi.   [2] *Infra*, ch. v.
[3] *Infra*, ch. v.

POLITICAL PHILOSOPHY OF CONFUCIANISM

the State. As already noticed, from the " Heaven and Earth " to " Propriety and righteousness ", there are eight different stages. They are as follows :—

Relationships.	The Stage.	Position to family.
(1) Heaven and Earth	Physical Stage ⎫	
(2) Material things	Animal Stage ⎬	The causes of family.
(3) Male and Female	Stage of Man ⎭	
(4) Husband and Wife	Social Stage	The family.
(5) Father and Child	Patriarchal Stage ⎫	
(6) Sovereign and Subject	Political Stage ⎬	The sequences
(7) High and Low	Constitutional Stage	of family.
(8) Propriety and Righteousness	Moral Stage ⎭	

The first column are the *I Ching* terms ; the second are terms suggested by the author to explain Confucian ideas. The first stage is the stage of heaven and earth. In this stage there were only physical or inanimate things. It was in the second stage of material things that life appeared. In the third stage, man and the relationship of male and female appeared. Due to the co-operation of the two sexes, the human race was perpetuated and civilization was developed. Thus arose society in which the family was included, with the relationship of husband and wife. In this connection the *Book of Change* recognizes the words " male " and " female " as biological terms, and the words " husband " and " wife " as sociological terms.

The next stage is the stage of father and son, or the patriarchal stage which led to the development of political relationships. The seventh stage, the stage of high and low, is called the constitutional stage because in that stage some sort of organic law, written or unwritten, determines the government organs and political authority. The highest stage is the stage of propriety and righteousness, or the moral stage. In this stage man is more rational. He recognizes to a greater degree ethics, justice and reason in political life than he does in the next earlier stage.¹ We see also that the family is the central scheme in the eight stages. The first three stages lead to the creation of family. The last four stages are direct sequences of the family. The family, therefore, is the foundation of all political relationships.² These eight stages explain the origin of the State and the development of political life down to the day of Confucius. In a later chapter will be discussed the idea of the Confucian School concerning the further evolution of political life.³

Justifications of the Existence of the State

Having inquired first into the Confucian conception of the State, the place of State in social development, and the idea of the natural evolution of the State, we may now inquire into the Confucian idea of the value of the State; that is, the justifications for the existence of the State.

A disciple on one occasion inquired of Confucius what was essential in the government of a country. The Master answered: "There must be sufficient food for the people, an efficient militia, and confidence of the people in their rulers." ⁴ Among these three essentials of government, the first two really refer to two very important functions of the State, namely, the promotion of economic well-being of the group, and the protection of the group from external and internal dangers.

In primitive times the most common danger to men was natural calamities. The *Book of Records* gives numerous historical instances illustrating the

---

[1] Compare with the three stages of political progress. *Infra*, chap. xii.
[2] See *Analects*, bk. I, chs. ii, vi, ix. [3] *Infra*, chap. xii.
[4] *Analects*, bk. XII, ch. vii.

necessity of political organization in overcoming natural calamities and in the securing of a peaceful life.¹ In other words, the State came into existence as a result of the necessity of driving out wild animals, controlling floods, etc., so that the people might pursue peaceably their routines of livelihood.

The way to promote economic welfare of the people is efficient utilization of nature which constitutes another justification for the existence of the State and political authority. The *Book of Records*, the *Book of Rites*, and the *Book of Change* praise highly the wise administration of ancient rulers who caused rapid progress of material civilization of ancient China such as the development of agriculture, domestication of animals, cooking, weaving, housing, trading, invention of boats and oars, and the like, thus nature being subjected to the use and pleasure of man.

The State, furthermore, is a vitally important institution in adjusting human and natural phenomena for the good of man. Throughout the "Great Appendix" of the *Book of Change*, the idea that the State should be organized according to the laws of nature is emphasized. The State will prosper if its organization and activities are in conformity with natural forces; otherwise it will perish.²

The "Great Appendix" goes on to say: "Heaven and earth set up the forms, and the sage rulers complete the process of evolution. Man acts in consulting with God, even the common people are capacitated."³ This statement is interpreted as this: Heaven and earth set up natural phenomena which should serve as models or forms for the human phenomena. The wise men teach the world with fundamental principles of natural and social evolution, namely, the doctrine of *I*: thereby men comprehend the source and

[1] Especially pt. i and the first three books of pt. ii.
[2] Bk. I, chs. i, xi.   [3] Bk. II, ch. xii.

principles of evolution and render their rational judgment in the processes of transmutation and phenomenal imitation. In this way the wise men complete the process of evolution; for, first, nature furnishes certain natural phenomena and natural laws; second, the wise men study them and tell the common people; third, men achieve civilizations by following the natural law; and fourth, they use rational selection in the course of evolution—thereby social and political progress results. By "Man acts in consulting with God" is meant that man should act in accordance with the will of God and the law of nature: the latter are revealed in the principles of *I*. Teaching the principle of *I* to the world, therefore, would enable even the most ignorant people to participate in the great work of achieving social and political progress.[1]

Lest man does not understand natural phenomena, says the authors of the *Book of Change*, and, as a consequence, that he blindly runs his government contrary to the laws of nature, the wise men wrote the doctrine of *I*, telling the fundamental principle of "heaven, earth, and man" as the guiding philosophy of political control.[2] When they are in office, they regulate the life of the State as well as individual

[1] *Book of Change*, The Great Appendix, bk. I, ch. xii. In the chapters of the Great Appendix, the words *t'ien hsia* are sometimes used to designate the "state" instead of the "world". When *t'ien hsia* is used to mean the state, the term refers to a political organization with a supreme authority. When *t'ien hsia* is used to mean the world, the term refers to a universal community of human minds. The term "wise men" refers to geniuses, philosophers, and leaders of men. The term is used by Confucius and his disciples at one time to mean men of the past and at other times to mean the ideal leaders of the future. Similarly the term "ancient sage rulers" refers, at one time, to the best sovereigns of the past, and at other times to the ideal sovereigns or the sovereigns ought-to-be.

[2] *Book of Change*, The Great Appendix, bk. I, chs. ii–iv, vii–viii; bk. II, ch. i–ii, v–viii, x–xi.

actions in accordance with the laws of nature.[1] In this way, the State becomes the central agency for rulers to adjust human phenomena with natural phenomena for the good of man. Thereby, the existence of the State would, on one hand, prevent the peril of human civilization by risking conflicts with nature ; and on the other hand, promote social and political progress by keeping harmony with natural forces.[2]

Lastly, the State is important in the adjustment of human relationships. Confucius thinks that the State is the greatest of all institutions in the preservation of proper social relations. The family is the cradle of all virtues ; and the State is only a family writ large. When a people is politically organized, genius may come into power. By using his power and position he may display his virtue and wisdom and have much influence with the masses. In the State, the genius, therefore, can benefit not only his own family but other families as well. Here the influence of virtue and wisdom is wider. Furthermore, it is through the State that universal education may be carried on ; that authority may be exercised to preserve the good and eliminate the bad ; that co-operation may secure safety and peaceful living ; and that many other things may be done which could not be done by individuals or by small groups.[3]

In short we may safely state that Confucius and his disciples point out two uses of the State, one is economical and the other educative. The economic

---

[1] *Book of Change*, The Great Appendix, bk. i, chs. ii–iii; bk. ii, chs. ii, vii, viii.

[2] *Book of Change*, The Great Appendix, bk. i, chs. vii–xi; bk. ii, chs. ii–iii, xi–xii.

[3] Discussions on this point are given in the *Book of Records*, pt. i, bk. i ; pt. ii, bk. i–iii ; throughout the *Analects* ; and the *Book of Change*, the Great Appendix.

use includes overcoming natural calamities, opening natural resources, inventions, building up industries, and seeking protection against external dangers. The educative use includes the conscious attempt of geniuses to solve such problems as those pertaining to the adjustment of natural and human phenomena for man's benefit, and to the adjustments of social relationships.

Summary

The distinction between State and government is observed in the *Classics*, although no formal definition of the State is given. The State has three essentials, namely, people, government, and territory. It also has its symbols, namely, the altars of the Spirits of the Land, the Ancestral Temple, and the Court.

The State is only one phase of social life. It is only a part of society. It is a product of natural evolution. The State, like any other aspects of civilization, is created through an evolutionary process of phenomenal imitation. Ancient kings, who were epoch-makers in the development of the Chinese State, achieved their success by imitating some external phenomena.

The State is based upon a patriarchal foundation; that is, the family is the basis of the State. From the formation of earth to the development of the ethical State there are eight steps of evolution, namely: (1) Heaven and earth; (2) material things; (3) male and female; (4) husband and wife; (5) father and son; (6) sovereign and subjects; (7) high and low; and (8) propriety and righteousness. They signify in order, the physical stage, the dawn of life, the dawn of man, the dawn of social life, the age of patriarchalism, the political stage, the constitutional stage, and the moral stage.

The state exists for two uses, economic and educative. The first use embodies conquests of natural dangers and utilization of natural resources. The educative use refers to adjustments of man with nature and to adjustments of social relationships.

CHAPTER III

THE DOCTRINE OF RECTIFICATION

The three principles of social phenomena : (*a*) The principle of spontaneous development ; (*b*) The principle of imitation ; and (*c*) The principle of discrimination between tendencies.

The doctrine of rectification : Definition—Rectification as the greatest function of government—The fundamental concept of Confucian political philosophy—The three stages of rectification.

Practical programmes of rectification : Moral education : the seven principles and three extremes—Rule of virtue—Universal free education—Social constitutionalism—Civil service—The teaching of history and political science—The conclusion from functions of the Spring and Autumn —Conclusion.

Summary.

The Three Principles of Social Phenomena

Three principles of social phenomena which should be observed in public administration are stressed by the Confucian School.[1] In the first place, all developments are spontaneous. Things change from matters of little moment to matters of large extent and of great significance. Moreover, these things develop from very simple to very complicated situations. Likewise troubles in society and in government begin from very simple and very insignificant causes that frequently escape one's attention. In the course of time, through spontaneous development, they are aggravated into great troubles which may become uncontrollable. A small cause of dissatisfaction may lead to revolt. When revolution develops

[1] For detailed discussion on the principles of social evolution, consult ch. xi of this book.

a dynasty may be overthrown. Accordingly the public administrator must constantly guard against small troubles at their very beginning. It is easier to control them at their source than after they have developed into graver situations. Although the work of the public administrator is great in extent, he must nevertheless give much attention to the development of matters of minor importance in the community, as it is really upon these smaller developments that the peace and prosperity of society rests. Thus it is the root of the matter that calls for the attention of the genius in public administration.[1]

In the second place, all phenomena take place by the process of phenomenal imitation—which goes on continuously. There is a model in imitation of which things are created. So if there is a bad model, the resulting products are bad. They in turn create others of like nature, and the bad will prevail. On the other hand, if there is a good model the products will be good. Thus, goodness will prevail. Hence the importance of selecting the model cannot be over-emphasized. The conclusion of this line of thought is that in the State the sovereign and high officials are models, which the mass of people and smaller officers are likely to imitate. Thus, the personal character of the sovereign and high officials determine the destiny of the whole State. As in a family, if the father is good and virtuous the wife and children are so influenced and the family will be good and happy. If the father is bad and immoral, the wife and children are likewise influenced and the whole family will be bad.[2]

It follows that the sovereign and the high officials

[1] *Book of Change*, *T'uan Chuan*, pt. i, hex. ii.
[2] Such ideas are expressed throughout the Confucian Classics. See especially *Li Chi*, bk. xxiv, ch. viii; *Analects*, bk. i, ch. ii; bk. xiii, chs. iv, vi, xiii.

must first develop their own personalities before they are fit to govern other people's. No one can govern the Empire well if he cannot manage himself and his family in a virtuous manner. Consequently, the government of virtue is emphasized. The government of virtue is a government by moral influence, by positive example, by reason and justice, while government by force is the negation of these principles. By government of virtue is meant a polity in which the rulers themselves are virtuous and strive to secure peace and order in the Empire through the proper education of the people, and not through their subjugation by force. The government of virtue is possible only when the sovereign and the high officials themselves are virtuous and wise; that is, when the models are good. Thus according to the teachings of Confucius the government of virtue is the only sound foundation of public administration.[1]

In the third place, public administrators should study the tendencies of all phenomena and discriminate between them. As already indicated, things change according to the process of phenomenal imitation. Some changes exhibit tendencies that are profitable and good, while others exhibit unprofitable and harmful tendencies. The public administrator should study all these tendencies and define each clearly. He should determine which are good and which are bad, so that the people may know what course to pursue. Thus, in their practical political and social conduct, they are able to follow the good and avoid the bad. Through such ideas we are introduced to the famous Confucian doctrine of rectification.[2]

If all things develop from the simple and

---

[1] *Analects*, bk. I, chs. ii, xii; bk. II, chs. i, xx, xxi; bk. XII, chs. xi, xvii, xviii, xix, xxii; bk. XIII, chs. ii, iii, vi.

[2] The *Book of Change*, The Great Appendix, bk. I, chs. ii–iv; bk. III, chs. v–vi.

insignificant to the complex and significant, and if the public administrator were to guard against troubles at their beginning, we wonder: How may these evils be detected in their earlier stages? We are told that the selection of models is important; but how can good models be selected? The answer is that the public administrator should study the tendencies of phenomena and discriminate between them. But how can he know that certain things will produce good tendencies? These questions point to the need of a workable standard in the application of these principles. These questions are answered by the doctrine of rectification.

The Doctrine of Rectification

One day a Confucian pupil asked his Master what he should do first if employed in the government. Confucius replied that, "What is necessary is to rectify names.... If names be not correct, language will not be in accordance with the truth of things. If language be not in accordance with the truth of things, business cannot be carried on with success. When business cannot be carried on with success, proprieties and music will not flourish. When proprieties and music do not flourish, justice and law will disappear. When justice and law disappear, people will suffer from anarchism and warfare.[1]

The absence of correct names will lead to moral degeneration, to the disappearance of law and justice, and to political anarchism. What, then, is meant by "correcting names" or "rectification"? Rectification may be defined as giving to things names which truthfully describe them in order to distinguish between right and wrong and to set up a universal standard that will distinguish the true from the

[1] *Analects*, bk. XIII, ch. iii.

untrue, the right from the wrong, the beneficial from the harmful, the logical from the illogical, the just from the unjust, and the proper from the improper. This standard will be the standard of rational judgment in collective achievement and social control.[1]

"If names be not correct, language will not be in accordance with the truth of things." The use of language or words is two-fold—to describe a certain fact and to bring out human thoughts. Each fact and each idea should have a distinct proper name. If the name is confusing, the fact and the idea will also be confused. Then the language loses its original utility. If the truth of facts and thoughts are confused, there will be a confusion of right and wrong. White appears as black, and black as white. Thus, in an ill-governed state moral integrity is destroyed, and laws are wrongfully applied. The right appears as wrong, and wrong seems to be right. The public does not learn the truth, and so permits itself to be influenced by false propaganda. The people do not know what to do in private and public affairs. Even law-abiding officers and learned scholars are unable to escape from the pressure of falsehood. There is a state of indecision, and the people grope in the darkness. In other words, there is a hopeless psychological and political anarchy.[2]

Confucius says that "if language be not in accordance with the truth of things, business cannot be carried on with success". By business is meant the business of the State. The success of public administration depends upon the support of public opinion. When public opinion points toward a benevolent government, benevolent government will then be possible. Where there is a will, there is a way.

[1] *Li Chi*, bk. xxiv, ch. vii.
[2] This idea is very well interpreted in the *Hsün Tzŭ*, ch. xxii.

Crystallization of the group will is essential to the carrying out of public policies. In the time of Confucius " the principles of right government faded away. Perverse speakings and oppressive deeds became rife again ".[1]

Thus the fundamental cause of corrupt government is the lack of correct names. Inability to carry out the public business successfully results in that state of affairs where " proprieties and music do not flourish ", " justice and law disappear," and " anarchism and warfare " prevail. The term " proprieties and music " refers to moral integrity, development of art, culture, and social happiness. In short, lack of correct names is the root cause of political chaos and the decadence of civilization.[2] Thus, what the chaotic world needs is a standard whereby right and wrong and good and bad can be distinguished and tested " in the minds and thoughts of the mass of people ".[3]

Who is to set up this standard ? Confucius answers: the government. " To govern means to rectify." [4] When the government sets a standard of correctness, the people dare not do wrong. Then public opinion will be in accordance with the truth of things ; art and culture will flourish, justice and law will be effectively applied, and social happiness will result.

But some people may object, declaring that if the " name " is not correct, then the government will be bad, as the former is the cause and the latter is the effect. How, then, can the government correct the name ? What Confucius really meant is that the wise and virtuous men should first obtain control of the government ; and then by means of government they

---

[1] *Mencius*, bk. III, pt. ii, ch. ix.   [2] *Hsün Tzŭ*, ch. xxii.
[3] Hu Shih : *Outlines of the History of Chinese Philosophy*, vol. i, bk. IV, ch. iv.
[4] *Analects*, bk. XII, ch. xvii ; *Li Chi*, bk. XXIV, vii.

The Doctrine of Rectification

should proceed to " rectify " the attitude of mind of the people. Confucius and his disciples invariably emphasize the point that the attitude of mind of the people is the root of all public actions. In other words, *the Confucian School advocates political and social reorganization by changing the social mind through political action*.[1]

And so, according to the political philosophy of the Confucian School, the greatest function of government is rectification. Through various agencies, such as education and civil service, it should set up a correct standard which will determine right and wrong, just and unjust, proper and improper, good and bad. Let the people see these distinctions that they may pursue the right, the just, the proper and the good, and prevent the wrong, the unjust, the improper, and the bad. *The Great Learning* points out three steps in the performance of this function. The first step is " to illustrate virtue ", which is rectification itself. Illustration means demonstration. The demonstration of virtue is through practical administration, universal education, civil service, and teaching of history and political science. The second step is " to renovate the people ". When the work of rectification is established, the people are educated and enlightened through political and moral teachings. This is of the highest excellence, which is the ultimate purpose of rectification. It is an ideal—the highest moral excellence with the happiest social life.[2]

Practical Programmes of Rectification

Here and there in the Classical Literature of the Confucian School, many practical programmes of rectification are suggested. The most important of

[1] *Li Chi*, bk. xxiv, vi, vii, viii.
[2] *The Great Learning*, Text, sec. i. See also ch. xii of this volume.

these programmes is found in the theory of moral education. The *Ta Tai Li* says: "Reason is to illustrate virtue. Virtue is to respect reason. Without virtue, reason will not be respected. Without reason, virtue will not be illustrated. Education is the means of attaining virtue and of illustrating reason. The best horse in the nation, if not trained, could not be used to run for a thousand *li*.[1] Although a state possesses immense territories and a large population, it can not be prosperous and powerful if it is not enlightened. Therefore, wise rulers in ancient times internally cultivated seven educational principles and externally achieved three political extremes. When these seven principles were cultivated, the internal affairs of the empire were secure. When the three extremes were attained, it secured mastery abroad." The seven educational principles may be briefly stated. If the rulers respect the old, the people will be filial. If the rulers maintain harmony with others, the people will be fraternal. If the rulers extend philanthropic work, the people will be generous. If the rulers employ wise ministers, the people will keep good associates. If the rulers respect the virtuous, virtuous people will seek public services. If the rulers despise covetousness the people will cease quarrelling. If the rulers are courageous and strong the people will possess a sense of shame.[2] The last point means that when a government is patriotic and is able to defend its own dignity, the people will be ready to recognize their own rights, duties, and honours.

The three extremes follow: When the extreme of propriety is attained without modesty, the empire will be well-governed. When the extreme of reward is given without being excessive, the people will be

---

[1] The Chinese *li* equals to 358/1,000 of an English mile.
[2] *Ta Tai Li*, ch. on "Words of the Master" (Chu Yen).

delighted. When the extreme of music is enjoyed without voice, the people will be in perfect harmony.[1]

Ta Tai Li further remarks that " in the ancient times the wise ruler knew the names of all the wise scholars in the Empire. Knowing their names, he knew the exact number of wise scholars. Knowing the number, he knew where they were located. The wise ruler, using the honour of the Empire, honours the scholars of the Empire. This is what I mean by ' when the extreme of propriety is attained without being modest, the Empire will be well-governed '. With the salaries of the Empire the scholars of the Empire are enriched. This what I mean by ' when the extreme of reward is given without being excessive the people will be delighted '. When the people are delighted, the Empire will be enlightened and happy. This is what I mean by ' if the extreme of music is enjoyed without voice the people will be in perfect harmony '."[1]

In short, the first step toward rectification is the practical example of virtuous administration shown to the people by the rulers. In turn the people, morally influenced, will arise to do good. This is part of the programme of universal education. The Empire is a great university ; the people are the students ; and the rulers are the instructors. Practical policies and administration are the lessons.[2]

In addition to the moral influence and practical examples, Confucius emphasizes universal free education as an agency of rectification. Thus, " when the man of high station is well instructed, he loves men; when the man of low station is well instructed, he is easily ruled."[3] Again, " where there is instruction, there will be no distinction of classes."[4] Government

---

[1] *Ta Tai Li*, ch. on " Words of the Master " (Chu Yen).
[2] See *Li Chi*, bk. XVI.   [3] *Analects*, bk. XVII, ch. IV.
[4] *Analects*, bk. XV, ch. XXXVIII.

and education are closely related. Confucius calls it cruelty when the government punishes the people without having educated them first.[1] In a later chapter will be discussed the Confucian system of public education and its democratic and representative features.[2]

Another idea which is essential to the process of rectification is that in the state all persons should keep their own proper place. The state is simply a society with authority, organization, and unity. It is a complex organization, in which there is a division of labour, and in which each person has his proper place with proper duties to perform. Each then should keep his " proper " place and perform his duties properly. If the situation is confused, and one man goes beyond his proper sphere of action, there will be disturbance throughout the entire society. When the situation is aggravated, the result will be revolution, anarchism, and political chaos.

One day a prince asked Confucius about government. Confucius replies " There is a government, when the prince is prince and the minister is minister, when the father is father and the son is son ". " Good ! " said the prince, " if, indeed, the prince be not the prince, the minister be not minister, the father be not the father, and the son be not the son, although I have my revenue, can I enjoy it ? "[3] Confucius meant that in the state the sovereign and the subjects, and in the family the father and the son, should keep their proper places and exercise their duties properly. Otherwise there is usurpation and chaos. When the condition of prosperity is maintained there will be in the state both order and efficiency. Then " the business of government can be carried on successfully ".

[1] *Analects*, bk. xx, ch. ii.   [2] *Vide infra*, ch. ix.
[3] *Analects*, bk. xii, ch. xi.

The Doctrine of Rectification

Civil Service is another important means of rectification. Government is a human institution. When there are good men, there is good government. Never is there good government without good men. Confucius says that "the principles of the government of Wên and Wu [1] are always displayed in the records—the tablets of wood and bamboo. But, when there are the right men, such a government flourishes, while without such men such a government decays and ceases. When there are good men, the growth of government is rapid, just as vegetation is rapid in land of good quality. A government is like an easily-growing rush. Therefore, the administration of government depends upon men".[2]

It is through Civil Service that good men may be employed in government. "Employ the upright and put aside the crooked; in this way, the crooked may be made to be upright." [3] If all public officers are upright, honest and efficient, there will be good government. When there is good government, the people will be contented with the government and obedient to it.[4]

The teaching of history and political science is also a powerful means of rectification, and so it is emphasized by the Confucian School. The *Book of Records*, the *Book of Poetry*, the *Book of Rites*, the *Book of Change* and the *Spring and Autumn* have been therefore considered since the Han dynasty by the Confucianists as the primary texts for all scholars. The *Spring and Autumn* is particularly regarded as a book on rectification.

In regard to the value of *Spring and Autumn*, Mencius says: "Again the world fell into decay, and principles faded away. Perverse speakings and

---

[1] Two "sage rulers" in ancient China.
[2] *Chung Yung*, ch. xx.   [3] *Analects*, bk. xii, ch. xxii.
[4] *Analects*, bk. ii, ch. xix.

oppressive deeds again became rife. There were instances of ministers who murdered their rulers, and of sons who murdered their fathers. Confucius was afraid and wrote *Spring and Autumn*. *Spring and Autumn* contains matters proper to the Son of Heaven. On this account Confucius said, ' It is the *Spring and Autumn* which will make men know me, and it is the *Spring and Autumn* which will make men condemn me.' "[1]

Again Mencius says, " Formerly, Yü repressed the vast waters of the inundation, and all under the sky was reduced to order. The Duke of Chou's achievements extended to the wild tribes of the east and north, and he drove away all ferocious animals, so that the people enjoyed repose. Confucius completed the *Spring and Autumn*, and rebellious ministers and villainous sons were struck with terror."[2]

The volumes of the *Spring and Autumn* contain the practical applications of the Confucian doctrine of rectification. Mencius, therefore, remarks further that " the traces of true royal rule were extinguished, and the royal odes ceased to be produced. When these odes ceased to be produced, the *Spring and Autumn* was written. The *Shêng* of Chin, *T'ao Wu* of Ch'u, and the *Ch'un Ch'iu* of Lu were books of the same character. The subjects of the *Spring and Autumn* are Huan of Ch'i and Wên of Chin, and its style is historical. Confucius said, ' Its righteous decisions I ventured to make.' "[3]

The *Spring and Autumn* together with the Commentaries has rendered four distinct services, which may also be said to be the four services of history and political science as advanced by the Confucian School.[4]

[1] *Mencius*, bk. III, pt. ii, ch. ix.   [2] *Mencius*, bk. III, pt. ii, ch. ix.
[3] *Mencius*, bk. IV, pt. ii, ch. xxiii.
[4] Three of the four points are suggested by Dr. Hu Shih with a few changes by the author. See his *Outlines of the History of Chinese Philosophy*, vol. i, pt. IV, ch. iv.

The Doctrine of Rectification

Its first function is to give names and definitions to phenomena. An eminent Chinese scholar who lived about the first century B.C., said that " the book of *Spring and Autumn* defines the nature of things and corrects their terminology. Thus the names and the things conform to the truth without the least misrepresentation ".[1] Red is red and green is green. Horse is horse, and cattle is cattle. There can be no interchangeability of terms. The terms " sovereign ", " people," " duke," " baron," " prince," " minister," " war," and " government " have their distinct proper meanings, and no confusion can be tolerated. It is the duty of historian and political scientist to give names correctly describing phenomena without the possibility of confusion. Not only nouns, but also verbs, adjectives, adverbs, prepositions, and conjunctions should be carefully studied. It is the function of language to represent thought in the course of social intercourse. If language fails to perform this function properly, society will fall into a state of confusion. Thus, definitions and terminology are essential in discriminating between social forces; and such discrimination is essential to successful public administration.[2]

The second function of *Spring and Autumn* is to define the fundamental principles of the organization of the state and outline the limits of individual spheres of action in the political and social organization. As already stated, in the state each individual has his own duties to be performed. One who goes beyond his proper sphere of action is an usurper and is antisocial. Who shall determine the extent of one's sphere of action in society? The sovereign, the minister, the

[1] Tung Chung-shu: *Many Dewdrops of the Spring and Autumn* (*Ch'un Ch'iu Fan Lu*), ch. xxxv.
[2] *Park of Narrative* (*Shu Yüan*), ch. on " Essentials of Government ".

people, or the father of the family? No, not they; but the historians and the political scientists who are more learned in philosophy, history, and politics, should determine social positions; and the sovereigns, the ministers, and the common people should follow their ideas. The sovereign, the subjects, the father, the son, the scholar, the farmer, the artist, and the merchant should keep within their own respective fields, and should not perform duties or exercise rights which do not properly belong to them.[1]

The second function of *Spring and Autumn* is different from the first function in that the giving of definitions amounts to a discrimination of types, while to determine the sphere of action is a discrimination of authority. The former deals with similarity and dissimilarity, the latter deals with high and low. The former is philosophical and juristic, the latter is constitutional and organic. It is the latter function which has given the book of *Spring and Autumn* its reputation as the greatest document on the public law in ancient China.

The third function of this book is to pass judgment upon the actions of men. *Spring and Autumn* assumes the position of the chief justice of a supreme court deciding upon the actions and laws of sovereigns, princes, and ministers. " It historically illustrates the royal doctrines of the ancient sage rulers. It clears up doubts and suspicions. It shows the distinctions between right and wrong. It avoids indecisions. It points out the good as good, the bad as bad, the worthy as worthy, and the unworthy as unworthy . . . It is the keynote to the royal doctrine!"[2]

Spring and Autumn performs the function of rational judgment. To point out the good as good and the

[1] *Hsün Tzŭ*, ch. ix.
[2] Ssŭ-ma Ch'ien, *Historical Records, Shih Chi*, vol. i, preface.

bad as bad means, in modern terminology, the final judgment as to whether or not the law is constitutional, whether or not the action is legal, or whether or not the man is a criminal. It eulogizes those who obey the law and it condemns those who violate it. This is rectification. Thus, on the one hand, the people are prevented by the words of *Spring and Autumn* from committing wrongs or crimes. On the other hand, they are encouraged to do positive good. For instance, the book records thirty-six regicides. In some instances the act of assassination is recorded as "shih" or murder. In other instances it is recorded as "sha" or mere killing. The work "shih" (murder) implies the presence of guilt, while the work "sha" (killing) implies that the act, being legally justified, is not murder. This is a valuable contribution to public law. The book of *Spring and Autumn* teaches the people that it is not murder to kill a sovereign or a father if the latter is worthy of the death penalty. The spirit of this revolutionary principle was expressly stated by Mencius more than one hundred years later, when he declared that to kill a tyrant is no murder.[1]

The fourth function that the book of *Spring and Autumn* has performed in the process of rectification is the illustration of the possible tendencies of various phenomena.[2] As already stated, things develop from the simple to the complex, from the insignificant to the significant. This book records numerous grave political changes, and shows their causes and effects. By reading this book one is able to comprehend the tendencies of various political and social phenomena, and he will know better how to institute social and

---

[1] *Mencius*, bk. i, pt. ii, ch. viii.
[2] Tung Chung-shu: *Many Dewdrops of the Spring and Autumn*, ch. xvii.

political control. In short, this book teaches the art of statecraft.[1]

Voicing the value of the *Spring and Autumn* to statesmen and students of politics, Tzŭ-hsia, a disciple of Confucius, declares that " One who has the control of government, must read *Spring and Autumn*. If he does not read it, he will not know the dangers of political phenomena, the fundamentals of Government, and the responsibility of administration. If the principles of *Spring and Autumn* are carried out on a small scale, the nation will achieve its supremacy over other nations. If they are practiced on a large scale, the whole world will be at peace and in royal order.[2]

Why is *Spring and Autumn* of such unique importance ? Tung Chung-shu, a leading Confucianist and a renowned statesman during the Han dynasty, states that the book is a product of practical observations on the affairs of man. It explains the control of human nature and feelings in daily social and political life. Its broad principles are deduced from facts drawn from the " ordinary " habits and customs of men and communities. The book is valuable as a true interpretation of human politics.[2]

The four functions of political science just mentioned are really essential steps in the process of rectification, for through the teachings of historical and political sciences the standard of rectification is established in philosophy. Then, through universal free education, the philosophy of rectification is taught to the people. By means of the moral leadership of wise scholars, a well-developed system of civil service, and a benevolent public administration, the philosophy of rectification is carried out in practical politics. These steps constitute the practical programme " to illustrate illustrious virtue ". The results will be

[1] Tu's preface to the *Spring and Autumn*.
[2] *Many Dewdrops of the Spring and Autumn*, ch. xvii.

The Doctrine of Rectification

"to renovate the people", and "to rest on the highest excellence"—in other words, the perfection of social and political organization and the realization of supremely good political life.[1]

Summary

Rectification is the chief function of government. It means the making of distinctions between right and wrong, the setting up of a universal standard that will show how the true differs from the untrue, the right from the wrong, the beautiful from the ugly, the logical from the illogical, the just from the unjust, the proper from the improper. Thus Confucius places government on a purely ethical and educative basis. This is important because the political state itself is governed by the attitude of mind of the mass of people. If their mind tends in the right direction, the state will be sound; but if their mind tends in the wrong direction, the state will be unsafe.

Thus, successful public administration requires the application of three principles. First, the rulers should study the causes of social and political unrest. The human mind is small, while the political state is large. But things spontaneously develop from small to large, from simple to complex, from insignificant to significant. The dissatisfaction of one mind may lead to the overthrow of a dynasty. Public administrators, therefore, should pay attention to the small, simple, and significant matters.

Second, the rulers themselves should be wise and virtuous before they attempt to govern others. They should personally set the model of rectification, and the people will follow them according to the process of phenomenal imitation.

Third, public administrators should study the

[1] *The Great Learning*, text, ch. i.

tendencies of political and social phenomena. Some tend to do good, others tend to do harm to society. Public administrators who can interpret the tendencies should discriminate between the good and the bad phenomena, so that the people may follow the good and avoid the bad. These three principles are prerequisites of the process of rectification.

The practical agencies of rectification consist of a government of virtue, universal education, proper political organization, a well-developed civil service, and historical and political science. The latter has four functions which are essential to rectification. They are: to give definitions and names describing the truth of things; to settle the proper sphere of action of individuals in the political and social organization; to pass critical judgment upon the actions of men, and to describe the causes and tendencies of political and social phenomena. The result of the successful practice of rectification will be an improvement of the social and political organization, and the realization of a happy and good life.

CHAPTER IV

POLITICAL UNITY AND ORGANIZATION

Social disorganization and the solution of Confucius.

Nature and Political Organization : Reasons for conforming to natural laws—The Confucian concept of nature—Methods advanced—Confucius sensitive to natural phenomena.

Family and the State : Husband and Wife the bases of human Society—Family as the foundation of the State : Reasons—The principles of family organization should be applied to the State—Political significance of ancestor worship.

Political Unity : The Confucian concept of unitary sovereignty—The location of ultimate sovereignty—Mencius' interpretation of the patriarchal theory of government—The concept of popular sovereignty—Centralization of power.

The King : As the model of the nation—The organic theory of Kingship—As the maker of laws—The theory of revolution—The ideal qualities of the king—The Declaration of Chou.

The Minister of State : His position in the political organization—The principle of ministerial responsibility—His duties.

Summary.

In discussing the ideas of Confucius and of his disciples as to how the state should be organized, one should bear in mind the fact that Confucius lived in the age of feudalism. At that time, class distinction was strong even though hereditary nobility was not so prevalent in early China as in Europe of the middle ages. The society was built upon patriarchal basis, and so the king was regarded as the parent of the people. He was, in fact, the sire and his officers the responsible elders of his provinces and districts. Under the sovereign was the great body of the people. They were divided into (1) *shih* (officers), (2) *nung* (agriculturists), (3) *kung* (artisans), and (4) *shang* (merchants). The first class, namely, the *shih*, consisted of (*a*) " officials " who carried on the governmental administration and some of whom belonged to classes of nobility, and (*b*) the " scholars " or " literati ". The *nung*, the *kung* and the *shang* were distinctly separated and a very marked gulf existed between them and the *shih* class next above them. There were, however, not a few instances where a *nung* or a *kung* or a *shang* reached a higher rank.

Political duties and rights of individuals in the Empire varied according to their own rank. There were peace and order as long as each class of people observed faithfully the duties and rights that were assigned to that particular class. During the days of Confucius this gigantic system of feudalism began to break down. Usurpations and murders happened daily, and the Empire fell into complete chaos. Confucius came to believe that the most fundamental solution of the existing problems was for the different grades of officials as well as the different classes of common people to perform their proper duties and to act in accordance with law and the doctrine of rectification. He made clear that not only rectification is the main function of government, but government is the principal institution to carry out the function of rectification.

Nature and Political Organization

The next question is : How should the State be organized so that rectification may be best carried out ? This is a question of political unity and organization.

In this connection, the establishment of a government

Political Unity and Organization

in accordance with examples furnished by nature is urged throughout the classics.[1] For instance, the *Book of Change* says that the ancient sage rulers established political and social institutions in imitation of some natural phenomena ; and that similarly all rulers in later times should follow the examples of these ancient sages.[2]

But why should human institutions be operated in conformity with the laws of nature ? The first reason is that nature furnishes the example of rectification. "He who exercises government," says Confucius, "by means of virtue may be compared to the north star which keeps its place while all the other stars turn toward it." [3] In other words, nature has a system, a unity and an order ; and this example of system, unity and order should be followed by man, especially in government. In the second place, nature is a complex, but harmonious whole composed of unequal differentiated forces ; and only by creating harmony of dissimilar forces in human life, can social progress be made possible.[4] The *Book of Change*, however, warns at the same time that excessive harmony disregarding the principles of virtue, should not be encouraged.[5] In the third place, nature has the great quality of universal nourishment and production. Nature is nourishing and so things can grow. In government the principle of nourishment should be observed in order to make possible the healthy growth of the people and their civilization.[6] Finally, nature's

---

[1] *Book of Change*, Hsiang Chuan, pt. i, hexs. xiv, xvi ; pt. ii, hexs. xlv, lviii.

[2] *Book of Change*, Hsiang Chuan, pt. i, hex. xxii.

[3] *Analects*, bk. ii, ch. i ; *Book of Change*, Hsiang Chuan, pt. i, hex. xi ; pt. ii, hex. xxxiv.

[4] *Book of Change*, Hsiang Chuan, pt. i, hexs. xi, xii, xvi, xxii ; pt. ii, hex, xxxviii.

[5] *Book of Change*, Hsiang Chuan, pt. i, hex. xvi.

[6] *Book of Change*, T'uan Chuan, pt. i, hex. xxvii, pt. ii, hex. xxxi.

great quality of constancy should be applied in public administration. Constancy means regularity, truthfulness and long-endurance. "The way of heaven and earth," says the *Book of Change*, " is constancy without end—The everlasting shine of the sun and moon and the regular changes of seasons cause things to grow and flourish. The sage influenced the world morally by holding on constantly their great principles."[1]

Analysing the Confucian ideas of nature, the *Chung Yung* says:

"The way of Heaven and Earth may be completely declared in one sentence . . . They are without any doubleness, and so they produce things in a manner that is unfathomable.

"The way of Heaven and Earth is large and substantial, high and brilliant, far-reaching and long-enduring."[2] *Chung Yung* goes on to explain the greatness of nature:

"The sky now above us is only a little bright shining spot. But when viewed in its inexhaustible extent, the sun, moon, stars and constellations of the zodiac are suspended in it, and things are overspread by it. The earth before us is but a handful of soil. But when regarded in its breadth and thickness, it sustains great mountains without their weight, and contains the rivers and oceans without their leaking away. The mountain now before us appears only a stone. But when contemplated in all the vastness of its size, we see how the grass and trees are produced on it, and birds and beasts dwell on it, and precious things which men treasure up are found in it. The water now before us appears but a ladleful, yet extending our view to its unfathomable depths, the largest tortoise, iguanas, iguanadons, dragons, fishes, and

[1] *T'uan Chuan*, pt ii, hex. xxxii.
[2] Ch. xxvi, sec. 7–8.

turtles are produced in them, articles of value and sources in wealth abound in them." [1]

Thus according to Confucius and his disciples the government which endeavours to keep in conformity with natural laws, will make the people happy and prosperous, and so it is a good government.[2] Confucius and his disciples point out also many ways as to how one can conform to natural law. First, nature furnishes such political ideals in the exercise of benevolent government as justice, efficiency, equality, etc., and all governments should work toward these ideals.[3] Secondly, the element of time should be observed in government administration. Confucius points out " the employment of the people at proper seasons " as an essential of good government.[4] Mencius, stressing the idea of Confucius, warns the rulers of his time, that the people should not be taxed in service during the farming season in order that the people may be freed from famine.[5] Thirdly, the nature of man such as racial temperament, traditions and customs, group desires, and public opinion should be understood by the rulers.[6] Fourthly, the nature of animate and inanimate things should be studied.[7]

Confucius was so sensitive to natural phenomena that a sudden clap of thunder or a violent wind or a shower would cause him to change countenance, and at night he would get up and dress if already in bed.[8] Since he was anxious to study nature, he " studies

[1] Ch. xxvi, sec. 9.
[2] See *Book of Change*, Great Appendix, pt. i, ch. iv.
[3] See *Book of Change*, Hsiang Chuan, pt. i, hexs. iv, xiii, xiv, xvi; pt. ii, hexs. xxxi, xxxii, xlviii, lxiii; also the Great Appendix, pt. ii, ch. i.
[4] *Analects*, bk. I, ch. v.
[5] *Mencius*, bk. I, pt. i, chs. iii, vii.
[6] *Book of Change*, the Great Appendix, pt. i, chs. xi, xii; *Analects*, bk. XII, ch. vii.
[7] *Book of Change*, Great Appendix, pt. ii, ch. v.
[8] *Analects*, bk. x, ch. xvi.

extensively all learning ",[1] and he was so earnest in studying that he sometimes " neglected his food ".[2] He was fond of the *Book of Change*,[3] music, poetry, history and the *li* of different nations, as by virtue of these studies he could understand the nature of cosmic evolution, the psychology of man, and the laws of social development.[4] For instance, Confucius once encouraged his pupils to study poetry, for : " Poetry calls out the sentiment. It stimulates observation. It teaches sociability and regulates the feeling of resentment. It not only has lessons for the duties of serving one's father and of serving the sovereign, but also makes us acquainted with the names of birds, beasts, and plants."[5] Using modern terms, poetry covers lessons in psychology, sociology, political science and natural science. It explains the nature of mind, society, government and the nature of organic and inorganic matters. Thorough knowledge of these factors, mind, society, government, and nature . . . is important to all who prepare themselves for public service.

Family and State.

Referring to the system of nature, the Confucian School maintains that heaven and earth are the bases of the universe. Heaven is high, and earth is low . . . such is the cosmic system. Through the interaction of heaven and earth, all things are created and all phenomena take place.[6] Likewise in human society, husband and wife are the bases. The family, therefore, is the foundation of social organization. Since State is a part of the society,

[1] *Analects*, bk. vi, ch. xxv. [2] *Analects*, bk. vii, ch. xviii.
[3] *Analects*, bk. vii, ch. xvi. [4] *Analects*, bk. vii, chs. viii, xvii.
[5] *Analects*, bk. xvii, ch. ix.
[6] *Book of Change*, the Great Appendix, pt. i, chs. i, xi.

family is also the basis of political organization. The *Book of Change* says: "The Rectification between man and woman is the great law of the nature . . . When the relationships between parent and son, between brothers, and between husband and wife are rectified, universal tranquillity will be recalled.[1] In the *Great Learning*, the position of family in political progress is mostly clearly defined. It says: " Everything has its root and its branches. To know what is first and what is last will lead near to the Royal Doctrine. The ancients who wished to illustrate illustrious virtue throughout the kingdom first governed well their state. Wishing to govern well their state, they first regulated their families. Wishing to regulate their families, they first cultivated their personalities. Wishing to cultivate their personalities, they first rectified their minds. Wishing to rectify their minds, they first sought to be sincere in their thoughts. Wishing to be sincere in their thoughts, they first extended to the utmost their knowledge. The extension of knowledge is by the investigation of things. Things being investigated, knowledge became complete. Their knowledge being complete, their thoughts were sincere. Their thoughts being sincere, their hearts were then rectified. Their hearts being rectified their persons were cultivated. Their persons being cultivated, their families were regulated. Their family being regulated, their States were rightly governed. The States being rightly governed, the whole kingdom was made tranquil and happy."[2]

This is the order of different tasks in securing universal peace and political progress. Indeed the regulation of the family is a pre-requisite for a well governed state.

The Confucian theory that the family should be

[1] *T'uan Chuan*, pt. ii. hex. xxxvii.   [2] The text of Confucius, sec. 3–6.

the foundation of the State is logical. In the first place, the family is a social unity. The family, as already said, is the basis of social organization. The State is only one aspect of social phenomena. Thus the family is also the basis of political organization. In the second place, the family is an educational unit. A government of virtue is the only form of government that can assure political progress. A government of virtue is possible only when the sovereign and the officers are able to influence the people to be virtuous and wise.[1] The family is the best institution for the training of individual character, virtue, and wisdom. In the family, good will, self-control, honesty, moderation, righteousness, earnestness, kindness, prudence, economy, love, propriety, filial piety, and fraternity are emphasized. Similar virtues should be emphasized in the State. Family virtues may be transformed into political virtues. For instance, filial piety toward parents may be transformed into loyalty to the sovereign; and fraternal duty to the elder brother may be transformed into kindness to fellow-citizens.[2] To rightfully fulfil duties as a member in the family is to teach one how to rightfully fulfil the duties of citizenship. To know how to govern well a family is to know how to govern a State. And so, if the family is virtuous and benevolent, the whole State will become virtuous and benevolent. If the family is undermined by covetousness and perverseness, the whole State is in danger of rebellions and disorder.[3]

In the third place, the family is an agency of rectification. Rectification, which is the main function of government, should begin with family. If the parent is kind to the child, and the child is filial to the parent;

---

[1] See *Analects*, bk. XIII, chs. i, vi, xiii.
[2] See *Analects*, bk. II, ch. xx.
[3] *Great Learning*, Commentaries, ch. ix.

if the elder brother is fraternal to the younger, and the younger respects the elder ; if the husband is just to the wife, and the wife is devoted to the husband, and all keep their proper place in the family, then the family is rectified. If the family is so rectified, the entire state will be rectified.[1]

In the fourth place, the family is the primary school for training in political organization. Confucius was asked why he was not engaged in the government. He replied : " What does the *Book of Records* say of the duties of a good son. ' Be dutiful to your parents, be brotherly to your brothers. These qualities are displayed in government.' This, then, also constitutes the exercise of government ! Why then must one take part in the government of the country in order to discharge the duties of government."[2] Indeed, the administration of one's family and the state are different only in degree. In both family and state there is government, and this government should be based upon virtue. In both there is the presence of authority . . . some one to command and others to obey. In both, efficiency and discipline are emphasized. In both, codes of behaviour or regulations are developed. In both, the controlling authority is to be responsible for the welfare of general group. The controlling authority is to exercise judgment, discretion, and wisdom in his administration, while the general group is to follow. In both there is an organization of work and a distinction of superiors and inferiors. The regulation of the family, therefore, offers much valuable political experience ; and so the wise man learns his statecraft within the doors of his own home.[3]

[1] *Book of Change, T'uan Chuan,* pt. ii, hex. xxxvii ; Tso's Commentary to the *Spring and Autumn,* 16th year of the Duke of Wên.
[2] *Analects,* bk. ii, ch. xxi.
[3] The *Great Learning,* Commentaries, ch. ix.

In the fifth place, the family is the smallest economic unit, having the closest economic relation to the individual. As long as the family exists, the individual can never make his economic life absolutely independent. The economic importance of the family to the state is based, first, upon the reproduction of population and the perpetuation of race. The Confucian School regards this as the most important function of the family. Secondly, the family furnishes a division of labour; and the advancement of civilization is thereby made possible. Having furnished the fundamental necessities of life, man then has a surplus of time and energy for the cultivation of art, learning, and literature. Thirdly, the family is a property-holding unit. The family should be regarded as the smallest unit in the distribution of the social wealth; and within the family there should be absolute communism. For these three reasons the family is the most important economic unit of the state; and in turn the national state is simply a larger economic unit.[1]

So much for the reasons which explain the family as the foundation of the state. The *Book of Change* maintains that the organization of the family should follow that of the cosmos. In the universe, the heaven represents the *yang* (male) force, and earth represents the *yin* (female) force. So in the family man represents the *yang* force and woman the *yin* force. Man is by nature strong, dynamic, active, and firm; and woman, weak, static, inactive, and tender.[2] In the universe heaven is the directing force, and so in the family the father should have the directing authority.[3] The *Book of Change* also describes three types of social

---
[1] A detailed discussion on this point is found in Dr. H. C. Chen's "The Economic Principles of Confucius and his School" in *Columbia Studies*, vols. xliv and xlv.
[2] *Book of Change*, the Great Appendix, pt. i, ch. i.
[3] *Book of Change*, T'uan Chuan, pt. ii, hex. xxxvii.

relations in the family, namely, between father and son, between brothers, and between husband and wife.[1] As between father and son, the father is the controlling authority; and so intelligent obedience is a virtue of filial piety.[2] As between brothers or friends, the elder one is the controlling authority; and the virtue of respect should be cultivated between them.[3]

As between husband and wife, the husband should be the controlling authority on external affairs, and the wife should have in charge the affairs within the home. The husband should respect the wife, and the wife should be devoted and obedient to the husband.[4] If in the home the wife dominates, such a home will be ruined. Likewise in a society where woman occupies a dominant position and man a subordinate position, that society is contrary to nature, is abnormal, and will soon perish.[5]

The same principle of organization is used in the government of the state as in the government of the family.[6] The sovereign and the people are the bases of the state. In the state there are relationships between the sovereign and the people, between the sovereign and the ministers, between the officials and the people and between the higher and lower officials. The position of the sovereign corresponds to that of heaven in the universe, and father in the family. Thus he is called in the Classics the son of heaven and the parent of the people. Such is the famous Confucian patriarchal theory of government.[7]

[1] *T'uan Chuan*, pt. ii, hex. xxxvii.   [2] *Analects*, pt. ii, ch. v.
[3] *Analects*, pt. i, ch. vi.
[4] *Book of Change, T'uan Chuan*, pt. i, hex. ii; pt. ii, hex. xxxvii.
[5] See *Book of Change, T'uan Chuan*, pt. i, hex. ix.
[6] *Analects*, pt. ii, ch. xxi.
[7] This theory probably originated long before the days of Confucius, and it was well established in the Chinese system of political thinking when it was re-stated in the *Book of Records* and the *Book of Poetry*. One hundred years later Mencius further explained it with his characteristic effectiveness.

In order to emphasize the importance of family relationship and the virtue of filial piety as means of securing political tranquillity, Confucius becomes an ardent advocate of ancestor worship. Ancestor worship is advocated by Confucius not on religion's ground, but on ethical ground ; not because it is good for the soul, but because it is an extension of human sympathy.[1] Filial piety is the chief virtue of the Confucian moral system. By it, as explained by the *Li Chi*, the son may return the love and care which his parents rendered to him. When the parents are dead, the son of course does not cease his affection and respect for them, and so the principle of filial piety should continue to be observed. To make this possible, ancestor worship was instituted. It is by ancestor worship that one may serve the dead as if they were alive, and respect the departed as if they were still abiding in the family.[2]

Ancestor worship, therefore, is not based upon the belief that the departed parents have authority to control the destiny of the family ; nor is it practised with the idea that any good or blessing may come from the spirits. It is based upon devotion and affection to parents, and on the continuance of such devotion and affection after their death.[3] Politically speaking, ancestor worship cultivates the virtue of filial piety which in turn cultivates the love of the people for their sovereign and their nation. Moreover, ancestor worship increases the sense of propriety and righteousness. This high sense of propriety and righteousness cultivates respect for law and order on the part of the people. Furthermore, ancestor worship teaches patriotism. When people devotedly love their parents, they naturally love their fatherland, and cherish the

---

[1] See *Analects*, pt. ii, ch. v ; also for the statement of his disciples, see *Analects*, pt. i, chs. ii. ix.
[2] *Li Chi*, bk. xxii, 1–4.   [3] *Li Chi*, bk. xxii, 3.

civilization and institutions which have been handed down by their forefathers. For these reasons the State should encourage ancestor worship.[1]

Having discussed the family as the foundation of political organization, it is logical to proceed with a consideration of the Confucian idea of political organization, the essence of which is political unity.

Political Unity

There must be a unity in the State for two reasons: first, to protect it from external danger and, second, to carry on its business efficiently. Confucius declared that the internal disintegration of a nation is more dangerous than its external aggression, because internal disintegration is decadence from within and undermines the foundation of the State. Furthermore, internal disintegration is likely to invite aggression from without, and in that case the State is defenceless for there is no unity within. The rulers, therefore, must first maintain order within the nation; and having secured this internal order, the influence of the State may then be extended beyond the seas.[2]

Oneness of political authority is essential to the promotion of political unity.[3] Confucius believes in unitary sovereignty. "There are not two suns in heaven," he says, "nor two sovereigns over the people."[4] Inasmuch as the State is a complex organization, the absence of a central authority would bring about confusion and chaos—just as a family without a father or a man without a head. For this

[1] See *Li Chi*, bk. xiv, 19; bk. xxi, sec. i, 13–15; and sec. ii, 19–20.

[2] *Analects*, bk. xvi, ch. i.

[3] This idea is expressed throughout the *Book of Records*.

[4] Quoted by Mencius, pt. v, bk. i, ch. iv, sec. i. See also *Li Chi*, bk. xxvii, 5.

reason, the king should address himself as " the one man ". Although this designation is supposed to be a modest one for the king, it includes that the king is the one man who represents the entire nation. Everywhere Confucius and his disciples emphasize the oneness of the State.[1]

The king, according to the Confucian terminology, is called *Yüan Shou* (the source and the chief) ; for he is the chief of the nation and the source of all political authority.[2] It is in his name that all orders and laws are issued, and all power and authority are granted. Any law, order, power, or authority which does not emanate from him is not legal. Thus kingship is a sign of the source of all political power.

The king, however, is not the absolute source of political authority. Although the officers receive their authority from the king, the king himself receives his authority from God. It is God who possesses ultimate authority. Having created men on earth, God would not turn them loose without control. Men have senses, desires, ambitions, and wishes ; and each individual pursues his ambitions and desires without regarding the welfare of others. If there is no control, there would be constant strife among mankind. For this reason, God appoints men of virtue and wisdom to be the rulers and teachers of the mass of the people ; to educate them and lead them into the good life. The sovereign so appointed is called *Tien Tzu* or the " Son of Heaven ".[3] It is sometimes called *Yüan Tzu* or the " First Son of Heaven ".[4] One historian interprets that the king

[1] *Shu Ching*, pt. iv, bk. IV ; *Li Chi*, bk. I, sec. 11, pt. i, 16.
[2] *Shu Ching*, pt. ii, bk. iv.
[3] The term may be found throughout the *Shu Ching*; and later the term is used to address kings. See pt. vi, bk. x.
[4] *Shu Ching*, pt. v, bk. xii ; pt. v, bk. I, vii ; also quoted by Mencius : See *Mencius*, pt. i, bk. ii, ch. iii.

is the "first" son of heaven because all people are sons of heaven and because the king is the head among the people.[1]

The king, therefore, is the son of heaven and the parent of the people. He is commissioned by God to assist his work on one hand, and becomes the ruler of the people on the other hand. Although he possesses divine authority, he himself is quite human and is merely an individual from the mass. In other words, his position and his authority are relative only. If he is not virtuous or does not work for the welfare of the people, he will be dismissed from his high position by God, and another person may be put on the throne.[2]

In interpreting this patriarchal theory of government, Mencius quotes the following statement from an ancient wise man: "When God has created this people, he allows those who are first educated to teach those who are later in being educated; and those who first apprehend principles to instruct those who are slower in doing so."[3] Mencius goes on to say that it is God who gives the Empire to a ruler, not by any express or written appointment, but by "showing its will by his personal conduct and his conduct of affairs". "The emperor to be retired," says Mencius, "can recommend a man to God to succeed him, but he cannot make God give that man the empire. A prince can recommend a man to the emperor, but he cannot cause the emperor to make that man a prince. A great officer can recommend a man to his prince, but he cannot cause the prince to make that man a great officer. Yao

---

[1] Liang Ch'i-ch'ao: *History of Political Thoughts of the Pre-Ch'in Period*, p. 51.
[2] *Shu Ching*, pt. v, bk. IV; pt. iv, bk. I; pt. iv, bk. v, sec. I; pt. iv, bk. iii; *Tso's Commentary*, 14th year of the Duke of Hsiang.
[3] Pt. v, bk. II, ch. i.

the Great presented Shun to God, and God accepted him, and he exhibited him to the people, and the people accepted him. Therefore I say, 'God does not speak. It simply indicates its will by his personal conduct and his conduct of affairs.'"

Mencius was asked how Yao the Great could present Shun to God and God accepted him, and how he could exhibit Shun to the people and the people accepted him? He replied: "He caused him to preside over the sacrifices, and all the spirits were well pleased with them; thus God accepted him. He caused him to preside over the conduct of affairs, and affairs were well administered, so that the people reposed under him; thus the people accepted him. God by virtue of the action of the people gave the Empire to him. Therefore I said, 'The emperor cannot give the empire to another privately.'

"Shun assisted Yao in the government for twenty and eight years; this was more than man could have done, and was the will of God. After the death of Yao, when the three years' mourning was completed, Shun withdrew from the son of Yao to the south of South River. The princes of the Empire, however, went not to the son of Yao, but they went to Shun. Litigants went not to the son of Yao, but they went to Shun. Singers sang not the son of Yao, but they sang Shun. Therefore I said, 'God gave him the Empire.' It was after these things that he went to the Middle Kingdom, and occupied the emperor's seat. If he had, before these things, taken up his residence in the palace of Yao, and had applied pressure to the son of Yao, it would have been an act of usurpation, and not the gift of God.

"This sentiment is expressed in the words of the Great Declaration: 'God sees according as my

Political Unity and Organization

people see; God hears according as my people hear.'"[1]

When the king has been duly chosen, he should have an effective control of his government. In other words, centralized government is indispensable to political unity and proper government organization. Being alarmed at the breaking down of political unity, and predicting, therefore, the inevitable ruin of the empire, Confucius remarks: " When good government prevails in the Empire, ceremonies, music, and punitive expeditions proceed from the Son of Heaven. When bad government prevails in the empire, ceremonies, music, and punitive military expeditions proceed from princes. When these things proceed from the princes, as a rule, the case will be few in which they do not lose their power in ten generations. When they proceed from the Great Officers of the princes, as a rule, the cases will be few in which they do not lose their power in five generations. When the subsidiary ministers of the Great Officers hold in their grasp the orders of the State, as a rule, the cases will be few in which they do not lose their power in three generations. When there are order and justice in the government of the kingdom, the supreme power of the government will not be in the hands of the Great Officers. When there are justice and order in the government, the common people will not meddle with government."[2]

The King

The personal qualities of the sovereign are of vital importance to political unity and proper political organization. In the first place, the king is the

[1] *Mencius*, pt. v, bk. i, ch. v.   [2] *Analects*, bk. xvi, ch. ii.

model for the nation and so the people are likely to imitate him. Confucius was asked whether or not it is possible to obtain a good government by "killing the crooked for the good of the honest". Confucius replied: "Why should you use killing in carrying on your government. If yourself be good, the people will be good. The relation between the rulers and the ruled is like that between the wind and the grass. The grass must bend when the wind blows across it."[1] On another occasion, the same person asked Confucius about government. Confucius said: "To govern means to rectify. If you lead on the people with correct examples, who will dare not to be correct?"[2]

The *Li Chi*, interpreting this idea of Confucius by pointing out negatively the effect of personal non-rectification on political unity and organization, says that if the ruler is not virtuous, the government will not be rectified. As soon as the function of rectification breaks down, the great ministers will attempt to control illegitimately the powers of government, and small officers will attempt to steal. On the one hand the law will not be effectively enforced; and on the other hand severe punishment, cruelty, and injustice will be imposed upon the people. The people will be demoralized in their spirit and in their customs; and the bounds of the *Li* will vanish. In the end chaos will prevail.[3]

Again it says: "To the people the rulers is as their heart; to the ruler the people are as his body. When the heart is composed, the body is at ease; when the heart is reverent, the body is respectful; when the heart loves anything, the body is sure to desire it. The body is the complement of the heart, and a wound in the body makes the heart

[1] *Analects*, bk. XII, ch. XIX.   [2] *Analects*, bk. XII, ch. XVII.
[3] *Li Chi*, bk. VII.

suffer. The ruler is preserved by the people and perishes also through the people."[1] And so the king is a sort of ceremonial example of virtue. If the example is good, the people will be good ; if not, the nation will be in trouble. The *Li Chi* even points out that self-government of the people will be promoted only by imitating the ruler's being capable of self-rectifying.[2]

There is another reason why the personal character of the sovereign is important to political unity and organization ; that is, the king is the maker of law. All laws emanate from the king ; and most of the laws, whether prohibitory or commanding, are concerned with the action and conduct of the people. If the spokesman of the law is corrupt, how can one expect to enforce that law effectively among the people ? "When a ruler's personal conduct," Confucius says, " is correct, his government is effective without the issuing of orders. If his personal conduct is not correct, he may issue orders, but they will not be followed."[3]

As already indicated, only a virtuous man is qualified to become the " Son of Heaven " by receiving the authority from God and approval from the people. If the king is not virtuous, he naturally loses his authority that was bestowed upon him by God. In other words, he receives no more authority from God. When the authority of the king himself does not come from the proper source, the authority of all officials beneath him is illegal. In such a case the entire government rests on an illegal foundation.

---

[1] *Li Chi*, bk. xxx.
[2] The *Li Chi* says : " The ruler is he to whose brightness men look; he does not seek to brighten men. It is he whom men support; he does not seek to serve men . . . Therefore, the people imitate the ruler, and we have their self-government." (Bk. vii.)
[3] *Analects*, bk. xiii, ch. vi.

Thus, the *Li Chi* says: " The Son of Heaven receives his authority from God; and the officers receive their authority from the king. If, therefore, the king has legitimate authority, the officers have legitimate authority. If the king has illegitimate authority, the officers have illegitimate authority." [1]

When the government does not rest on a legitimate foundation, its name at the outset is not correct. " If names be not correct," says Confucius, " language is not in accordance with the truth of things. If language be not in accordance with the truth of things, affairs cannot be carried on to success. When affairs cannot be carried on to success, *li* and *yüeh* will not flourish. When *li* and *yüeh* do not flourish, law and justice do not attain their ends. When law and justice do not attain their ends, the people will be at a loss to know what to do." [2] In short, when the ruler does not possess virtuous qualities, political unity and proper governmental organization are impossible.

In the Classics, Confucius and his disciples discuss extensively the ideal qualities of a king, a thorough study of which cannot be entered upon in this connection. Furthermore, the study of the virtuous qualities of the king belongs to the field of ethics, rather than political science. It is proper, however, to mention briefly some of the most important virtues of an ideal king that are directly concerned with political unity and effective governmental organization. First, the king should love the people, respect them, and employ them in accordance with the proper rules.[3] Social justice should be observed in conducting the affairs of the

---

[1] *Li Chi*, bk. xxix.   [2] *Analects*, bk. xiii, ch. iii.
[3] *Analects*, bk. xv, chs. i, xxxiv, xxxv; bk. ii, ch. xx; bk. xiii, ch. iv; bk. iii, ch. xix.

government.¹ "I have taught to believe," says Confucius, "that those who have kingdoms and possessions should not be concerned that they have not enough people and territories, but should be concerned that wealth is not equally distributed; they should not be concerned that they are poor, but should be concerned that the people are not contented. For with equal distribution there will be no poverty; with mutual goodwill, there will be no want; and with contentment among the people there can be no downfall and dissolution."²

This principle of social justice leads to another virtue required for an ideal king, that is, the king should promote the economic welfare of the people, not his own riches. Confucius remarks: "When the people have plenty, the king will not be in want. If, on the other hand, the people are in want, the king will not have plenty."³ A noble was distressed at the frequency of robberies in the country, and so he asked Confucius what should be done. "If you yourself," answered Confucius, "show them that you do not wish for wealth, although you should reward them for stealing, the people would not steal."⁴ Covetousness of the ruler, therefore, is itself a cause of poverty and crime among the people.⁵ At the same time Confucius praises highly the economy of Yü's government as a worthy example.⁶

To employ and trust virtuous and wise ministers in the administration of State affairs, according to Confucius, is fundamental to good government. While talents are difficult to find,⁷ the proper way is "to advance those whom you already know: there then will be no fear that those whom you do not know

---

[1] See *Analects*, bk. XIII, ch. iv.   [2] *Analects*, bk. XVI, ch. i.
[3] *Analects*, bk. XII, ch. ix.   [4] *Analects*, bk. XII, ch. xviii.
[5] *Analects*, bk. xii, chs. ix, xviii; bk. XIII, ch. xvii.
[6] *Analects*, bk. viii, ch. xxi.   [7] *Analects*, bk. viii, ch. xx.

will be neglected ".[1] Moreover, by employing the upright and putting aside the crooked, " the crooked can be made to be upright."[2]

In conclusion, we may quote from the *Analects* a statement on the government of the Chou emperors to illustrate the Confucian concept of the ideal king. The statement is as follows :—

" With the inauguration of the Chou dynasty, the country was greatly prosperous ; but only the good were rich.

" The emperors guided themselves by the principles contained in these words : ' Although there are relatives, yet we do not consider them equal to the virtuous men. If the people fail in their conduct, it is we alone who are to blame.'

" The emperors set themselves to adjust and enforce uniformity in the use of weights and measures, examined the body of laws, restored the discarded offices ; in this way, good government was resulted.

" Then they revived States that had been extinguished, restored families whose line of succession had been broken, called to office retired men of virtue and learning ; thus the people throughout the Empire gladly acknowledged their authority.

" What they paid serious attention to were food for the people, the duties of mourning and religious services.

" By their generosity, they won the heart of the people ; by sincerity they caused the people to have confidence in them ; by diligence in business, their achievements were great ; and by their justice, all were delighted."[3]

[1] *Analects*, bk. XIII, ch. ii.
[2] *Analects*, bk. xii, ch. xxii ; see also bk. II, ch. xix.
[3] *Analects*, bk. xx, ch. i.

Political Unity and Organization

The Minister of State

As already discussed, government is necessary because the people need intelligent leadership. Confucius, however, does not advance any ideal form of government; he merely says that here and there such and such principles of public administration should be observed and that such and such officials act in accordance with the existing laws or the existing rules of *li*. This is because no type of government is universally satisfactory. Conditions of life are different in different regions; and so the government should be organized and controlled according to the actual conditions of the territory. Thus says the *Book of Change*: "The ancient sage rulers examined into the traditions of the localities and temperament of the people in order to exercise their principles."[1]

Though Confucius has not advanced any ideal form of government he gives many rules as to what is an ideal public officer, in addition to those rules of ideal kingship which have been discussed in the previous section. The most important public officer is the minister of State who is the chief assistant of the king in government administration, and who is the example of all other public officers.

The first question in this connection is the question of selecting the minister of State: that is, how to select and who can be the minister of State. Anyone who is virtuous and wise, according to Confucius, is qualified to be a State minister. There is no special qualification such as ownership of property or blood relationship with the king. A commoner may rise to the prime ministership overnight.[2] The sovereign, however, should be very careful in appointing a State minister. There are two types

---

[1] *Book of Change, Hsiang Chuan*, pt. i, hex. xx.
[2] *Analects*, bk. xii, ch. xxii.

of reputable men. The first type is the "man of distinction" who is substantial and straightforward, who respects justice and is public-spirited, and lastly, who has the welfare of the nation at heart. The other type is "man of notoriety" who assumes the appearance of virtue, but is selfish and hypocritical.[1] Both may seem to be wise and good; both may have great fame in the nation; but there is a real difference in their ability and morals. They are easily confused, and so the sovereign must use great care in selection. Furthermore, one may be a great orator, and at the same time not a statesman[2]; and so the sovereign should not promote a man simply on account of his words.[3]

A great scholar who is prepared for State service should, in turn, be careful to select the sovereign who is to employ him. He must examine into the conditions of the nation, and the character of the sovereign before he enters into the service of the government. Should the sovereign be tyrannical and hate the virtuous, sooner or later the minister himself would suffer personal dangers: and a wise man should know how to protect himself. Confucius does not tolerate the theory that the end justifies the means. The political scholar must rise to power by the proper method. Illegal and corrupt means in securing power cannot be justified on the ground that his ultimate purpose is to secure political reform for the public good.[4]

As to the proper attitude of the minister of State towards the sovereign, the rule is that "he should serve his sovereign according to what is right: and when he finds himself unable to do so, he should

---

[1] *Analects*, bk. XII, ch. xx.   [2] *Analects*, bk. xv, ch. xxvi.
[3] *Analects*, bk. xv, ch. xxii.
[4] See *Analects*, bk. v, chs. i, xviii, xx; bk. VIII, ch. xiii; bk. xv, chs. vi, ix; bk. XVII, ch. i.

retire from power ".[1] This principle may be regarded as the Confucian principle of ministerial responsibility. To serve the sovereign is to serve the nation, for the sovereign represents the nation ; and so he should be responsible to the nation for what ought to be done. Confucius does not refer to personal loyalty. The minister should do what he believes to be right even though his policies may be contrary to the will of the king.[2]

When a minister is convinced that what the king or prince is doing or is going to do is wrong or against established customs, it is his duty to expostulate with the ruler with a view to preventing his proceeding. If the ruler persists in his own way, after having been questioned three times, the minister should resign.[3] When the minister has close blood relationship with the king or has great seniority of office, he may even put the king on probation for a temporary period as a means of effective expostulation. During such period of probation the minister may act as regent. This can be done upon unselfish and honest motives of the great minister.[4]

When the king is too old to attend the affairs of the State, the minister of State may also act as regent. When Yao the Great was too old, Shun was appointed by the king to act as regent. When Shun was " old and tired of work ", he appointed his minister, Yü, the regent.[5] When the old king is to abdicate, the regent minister may be nominated as the candidate to succeed him on the throne.[6] When the king passes

[1] *Analects*, bk. xi, ch. xxiii.
[2] *Analects*, bk. xiv, chs. xvii, xviii, xx, xxiii.
[3] *Analects*, bk. xvi, ch. i.
[4] *Shu Ching*, pt. iv, bk. v, sec. 2 ; *Li Chi*, bk. v.
[5] See *Shu Ching*, pt. i, bk. 1 ; pt. ii, bk. 1 ; also *Mencius*, pt. v, bk. 1, ch. iv.
[6] Yao said to Shun : " Hail to Thee, O Shun ! The God-ordained order of succession now rests upon thy person." *Analects*, bk. xx, ch. i.

away, the minister so nominated may be crowned as the new king, provided he has received his appointment by God and his nomination has been approved by the people.[1] Of course, the throne may be transmitted to the heir of the retiring sovereign if his son is worthy of the trust and if he has been favourably received by the people. In fact, Confucius remarks: "T'ang[2] and Yü[3] resigned the throne to their worthy ministers. The sovereign of the Hsia dynasty[4] and those of the Yin and Chou dynasties transmitted it to their sons. The principle of righteousness was the same in all these cases."[5]

Referring to the regular duties of the Minister of State, he assists the king in exercising the powers of government. He gives chief counsel to the king in the determination of political policies. He is the chief steward of the king in administrative work. The *Shu Ching* names eight aspects of administrative power: food, trade, religion, industry, education, justice, diplomacy, and war. These eight powers correspond to the eight functions of the government, and for each of these functions there should be provided proper subordinate officers.[6] The *Book of Record* and the *Spring and Autumn* explain in great detail the government system of feudal China and gives many constructive criticisms of value. It is from these criticisms that we ascertain the Confucian philosophy concerning political organization.[7]

---

[1] See *Shu Ching*, pt. i, bk. 1; pt. ii, bk. 1; also *Mencius*, pt. v, bk. i, chs. v, vi.
[2] Dynastic name of Yao the Great.
[3] Dynastic name of Shun.
[4] Yü the Great.
[5] Quoted by Mencius. See *Mencius*, pt. v, bk. ii, ch. vi.
[6] *Shu Ching*, pt. v, bk. iv.
[7] In fact, a book on Constitutional law of the Confucian School may be written from these materials.

Political Unity and Organization

Summary

In the time of Confucius political chaos prevailed due to the disintegration of the feudal system. The most noticeable trouble then, was the fact that the different classes of people no longer observed their own duties and rights. Thus, Confucius advocated political unity and strong political organization as solutions of existing problems.

The first principle of political organization of the Confucian School is that the government should be established and operated in accordance with natural laws. This is because, first, nature furnishes the examples of rectification; second, it furnishes the example of harmony; third, it has the quality of universal nourishment as a model of world salvation; and it has the quality of constancy. The government which endeavours to keep in harmony with nature will flourish. Otherwise, it will decay. The ways to conform to nature may be as these: (1) the realization of natural ideals; (2) the observation of the element of time and seasons; (3) the comprehension of the temperament of man; and (4) the study of things, animate and inanimate.

In the universe, heaven and earth are the bases; in the society, husband and wife are the bases. The family, therefore, is the foundation of social organization. Since State is a part of the society, and so the family should also be the foundation of the State. This is logical for five reasons: (1) The family is a social unit; (2) it is an educational unit; (3) it is an agency of rectification; (4) it is the primary school of training political capacity; (5) it is the smallest economic unit.

In the universe, heaven is the directing force; and in the family, father is the directing authority. In the State the position of the sovereign corresponds to that of heaven in the universe, and of father in the family. Confucius thus calls him the son of heaven and parent of the people. He is the directing authority of the State. In order to preserve the family virtues in political organization, Confucius became an ardent advocate of the doctrine of filial piety and of the institution of ancestor worship.

There must be political unity in the State. A unitary sovereign power is indispensable to preserving this political unity. The king is the personification of the State; and he is the source of all authority. Any law, order, or power which does not emanate from him is illegal.

The king, however, is not the ultimate foundation of political power ... this is in God. God created men, and selects one from among them to control them. The king, therefore, receives his authority from God; and he is called the " Son of Heaven " or rather the " First Son of Heaven ". Only the wise and virtuous man is qualified to receive this divine commission. A corrupt king is not a " Son of Heaven ", although he is in possession of the throne. Having no commission from God, he has no proper authority to govern the people. When the king has been duly chosen, he should have a centralized control of his government. If the subordinate officers of a government attempt to exercise the prerogatives of the sovereign, such government will inevitably fall.

Personal qualities of the sovereign are of vital importance to political unity for two reasons. First, being regarded as the model of the nation, his behaviour and character will be imitated by his people. Secondly, being the law-maker, the source of law would be corrupt if he personally cannot live up to it. Confucius gives many rules of ideal kingship such as love of people, respect for social justice, government economy, ability to use virtuous and wise ministers, generosity, sincerity, diligence in business, etc.

Confucius emphasizes the importance of intelligent leadership in the government; and so the selection of a virtuous minister of State is a matter of great significance. The minister of State, on one hand, is the assistant of the king in government administration and on the other hand the example of all other public officers. The minister of State should serve his sovereign according to what is right, and when he finds himself unable to do so he should resign from power. This is the Confucian principle of ministerial responsibility. When the king is too corrupt to stay on the top of the State or when the king is too old to attend public business, the minister of State may act as the regent of the government, provided his action is *bona fide* and has been approved by God and by the people. Under certain circumstances, when the king passes away, the regent minister of State may succeed him on the throne. The duties of the minister of State are heavy. He assists the king in exercising the powers of government. He is the chief counsel to the king in the determination of public policies. He is the chief steward of the king in administrative work.

CHAPTER V

THE PRINCIPLE OF LI

Confucius on *Li* : The functions of the *li*—History and authenticity of the *Li Chi*—The place of the *Li Chi* in the Classics—The place of *li* in the development of civilization.

Meaning and Programme of *Li* : *Li* and *Yüeh*—The necessity of *Li*—The practical programmes of *li*.

Constitutional Significance of the *Li* : As a principle of political organization—As the application of rectification —*Li* defines sphere of government authority and its limits as a principle of colonial administration.

The *Li* and *Yüeh* : Human nature and *li*—The ideal of *Yüeh*— The functions of *Yüeh*—The social nature of *Yüeh*—The ideal of social harmony.

Summary.

Confucius on *L*

In the mind of Confucius, *li* is a recognized code of behaviour. He remarks : " A wise man makes justice the substance of his being ; he carries it out with *li*, he speaks it with modesty ; and he attains it with sincerity." [1] According to Confucius, *li* has four important functions. In the first place, *li* furnished a kind of unwritten law in political control ; and should be observed by the sovereign, ministers, subordinate officers, and by the people themselves. By *li* loyalty of the officers and patriotism of the people are cultivated ; and without it the prestige of the ruler would be destroyed, thereby leaving the kingdom in chaos.[2]

[1] *Analects*, bk. xv, ch. xvii.
[2] *Analects*, bk. iii, chs. xviii, xix ; bk. iv, ch. xiii ; bk. xii, ch. xxv ; bk. xiii, ch. iv ; bk. xiv, ch. xliv.

The Principle of Li

Secondly, *li* is a socializing factor in moral discipline. A disciple of Confucius inquires about perfect virtue. Confucius answers: " Subdue one's self and conform to the ideal of *li*." He goes on to say that the regulation of one's faculties and actions in *li* is the initial step for the difficult task of cultivating the rule of love among mankind.[1]

Thirdly, *li* is a harmonizing factor in arts and literature. Confucius remarks: " A good man who studies extensively into the arts and literature, and directs his studies with *li*, is not likely to get into a wrong path."[2] Lastly, *li* is the builder of personality. Without *li* " politeness becomes pedantry," " caution becomes timidity," " courage becomes insubordination," and " righteousness makes men tyrannical."[3]

While *li* is the builder of personality and character, says Confucius, *yüeh* or "music" completes the process of formation; and so *li* and *yüeh* go together.[4] By reading the *Analects*, we will find many comments from Confucius on the existing music; and judging from these comments Confucius must be a great musician. On one occasion he, for the first time, heard played a piece of ancient music, since then he had studied it for three months " during which period he did not know the taste of his food ". He was then heard to say, " I should never have thought that music could be brought to such perfection."[5]

Since Confucius emphasized so much the importance of *li*, a group of his followers gave themselves up to the study of it. Up to the Western Han dynasty, there had been already several hundreds of volumes of records of ancient *li*, and most of these volumes were lost. The *Li Chi* is a short selection of the

[1] *Analects*, bk. xii, ch. i.   [2] *Analects*, bk. vi, ch. xxv.
[3] *Analects*, bk. viii, ch. viii; bk. xiv, ch. xiii; bk. viii, ch. ii.
[4] *Analects*, bk. viii, ch. viii.   [5] *Analects*, bk. vii, ch. xiii.

collection. The *Li Chi* or "The Record of Rites" is incorrectly known to the popular readers and publishers as one of the "Five Classics" of the Confucian School. The book was compiled by Tai Shêng, a scholar of the Western Han dynasty. This book is largely a selection of readings from an even more voluminous book of rites compiled by Tai Shêng's elder cousin, Tai Tê. Thus we call Tai Tê's *Li Chi* as *Ta Tai Li* (The Elder Tai's Record of Rites) and Tai Shêng's as *Hsiao Tai Li* (The Younger Tai's Record of Rites).

These two *Tai Li*, together with the *Chou Li* (The Official System of Chou) and the *I Li* (The Orthodox Canon of Rites) constitute the famous *San Li* (the Three *Li*) of the Confucian School. The *I Li* is accepted by the modern critical school as a reliable work of the Confucian era; but the authenticity of the *Chou Li* is totally rejected. It is the *I Li*, not the *Li Chi*, that should be one of the "Five Classics" or "Five Canons" of the Confucian Bible. Here you will please note that the *Li Chi* is a product of the fourth century after the death of Confucius; and that it is to be distinguished from the *I Li*.

Scholars of the "Higher Criticism" object to call the *Li Chi* even as a *Ching* or "Classic". We ought to understand, however, those reasons for which the *Li Chi* has taken a higher position than the *I Li* and the *Chou Li* and has ranked with the *Book of Poetry*, the *Book of Records*, the *Book of Change*, and the *Spring and Autumn*, forming one of the "Five Classics" for common reading. In the first place, the *Li Chi* is rich in information concerning currents of thinking of the Confucian school before the Han dynasty. It describes in great detail some of the social institutions of the Confucian era. Furthermore, the *Li Chi* does not, like the *Chou Li*, treat of mere matters peculiar to one dynasty, but of matters

The Principle of Li

important to all time ; nor like the *I Li*, of usages belonging to one or more of the official classes, but of those that concern all men. It is an excellent reference for the study of the Confucian principle of *Li* ; and according to the modern critical school, it is a quite reliable book.[1]

In the *Li Chi* the early Confucianists give utterance to their highest ideals of social and political order. The book describes in detail the rules governing the five social relationships, namely, the relation between husband and wife, between father and son, between elder and younger brothers, between friend and friend, and between sovereign and subject. The development of world civilization is divided into three stages : the age of disorder, the age of small tranquillity and the age of great similarity. The first age is a period of savagery. The second is the period in which we are living ; it is a period of nationalism, selfishness, politics, practical ideals, and obtainable order. The third age is a period of cosmopolitanism, humitarianism, and communism. The *li*, according to the *Li Chi* is to be used as a guide in establishing social and political order in the second age.[2] Appreciating the practical importance of this principle of *Li* and seeing how it lies at the basis of their civilization, the Chinese people have called their country " the country of *Li I* ".[3]

The Meaning and the Programme of Li

The word *Li* has no English equivalent. It has been erroneously translated as " rites " or

[1] Liang Ch'i-ch'ao : *Explanations of Important Books and the Method of Studying them* (1926, Ch'ing Hua Press), pp. 188, 189.

[2] See *Li Chi*, bk. vii.

[3] The words *Li I* are often used together. *I* is included, according to the orthodox commentators, in the conception of *li*. *Li I* thus forms a phrase describing perfect justice and refined culture.

"propriety". It has been suggested that the term "civilization" is its nearest English equivalent; but "civilization" is a broader term, without necessarily implying ethical values, while *li* is essentially a term suggesting such values.

The terms *li* and *yüeh*—which is commonly translated as "music", frequently go together. *Li Chi* says that "*li* means the prescription of reason, and *yüeh* means the definite limitation of harmony. The wise man makes no movement without reason, and does nothing without its definite limitation."[1] That is, *li* is a regulation of external behaviour based upon reason, while *yüeh* is a regulation of feelings based upon harmony. Both *li* and *yüeh* are means for achieving social harmony. In the light of this discussion, *Li Chi* may be interpreted as a Confucian social code of behaviour aiming at an ideal harmonious order, based upon reason and judgment.

Voicing the necessity of *li* as a means of social and political control, the *Li Chi* says: "There is the *li* that furnishes the means of determining the observance towards relatives, near and remote; of settling points which may cause suspicion or doubt; of distinguishing where there should be agreement and where difference; and of making clear what is right and what is wrong. . . . Duty, virtue, love, and righteousness cannot be fully carried out without *li*; nor can the means of education and rectification be perfected; nor can the quarrels and lawsuits be settled; nor can the duties between ruler and ruled, high and low, father and son, elder and younger brothers, be determined; nor can students for office and other learners in serving their masters have an attachment for them; nor can majesty and dignity be shown in assigning the different places at court, in the government of the armies, and in discharging the duties of office so as to secure the

[1] *Li Chi*, bk. xxv, 10.

The Principle of Li

operation of the laws. . . . The parrot can speak, and yet it is nothing more than a bird ; the ape can speak, and yet it is nothing more than a beast. Here now is a man who observes no *li*, is not his heart that of a beast ?[1] Therefore, when the wise ruler arose they framed the principles of *li* in order to teach men, and through their possession of those rules cause them to make a distinction between themselves and beasts."[2]

The practical programme of *li* in achieving the ideal of a harmonious moral order consists of three steps. In the first place, *li* provided principles for the establishment of a social fabric in which people are ranked in a consistent order of superiority and inferiority. In other words, *li* is an applied doctrine of rectification. In society the distinctions of priority must be clearly drawn. The individual must know definitely his own status and relations in society, and his proper rights and duties. The *li* aims to impress consciousness of status so strongly in men's minds that obedience to the general order will naturally ensue.[3]

In short, *li* means so to organize and relate the different parts of society as to leave no doubt or equivocation as to their mutual status.

In the second place, *li* provides a code of morality for social control. It defines clearly, the social and political duties of the individual. The code is to be enforced not by political compulsion but through individual conscience. *Li* assumes that there are good natural elements in the human mind, and that if these are only cultivated by systematic exercises, duties will be fulfilled spontaneously. *Li* does not create duties artificially, but assumes that it is natural,

---

[1] This statement gives rise to the idea that *li* means " civilization ".
[2] *Li Chi*, bk. I, sec. I, pt. i, ch. v.
[3] Compare Plato's concept of justice as described in *The Republic*.

for instance, for the father to be kind to his son and the son to be attached to his father. This is called "following human nature", which is the foundation of the *li*'s moral code. *Li* emphasizes the development of the naturally good sentiments and the observance of natural reason so that the greatest social harmony may be obtained.

In the third place *li* provides an ideal of social harmony emphasizing the individual's obligation to the society. *Li* is a principle of socialistic moral idealism and gives a new set of social values to be cultivated in the practical world in which we live. Accordingly, it establishes a faith of moral appreciation.[1]

Constitutional Significance of the *Li*

Li, as a principle of political control, describes in detail the organization of the feudal government. For instance, the Book of "Royal Regulation" (*Wang Chih*)[2] in the text of the *Li Chi* professes to give the regulation of the early kings in respect to the classes of the feudal nobles and officers and their emoluments, in respect to their sacrifices and their care for the aged, and in respect to the educational systems. Thus, *li* furnishes a background and a basis for those who attempt to bring about new political organization.

The fundamental idea is that the State should be organized according to natural laws. When the State is so organized, harmony and order will then be possible. However, natural laws are not definitely prescribed, and they can be comprehended only through social experience, that is, by the objective method. If experience has proved a certain

---

[1] See *Li Chi*, bk. vii.   [2] Bk. iii.

The Principle of Li

institution advantageous to social harmony, such an institution is in conformity with natural laws. That which has been proved to be detrimental to social harmony is contrary to nature. The book of *Li Chi* describes many governmental institutions in feudal China and the consequences of their operation; and thereby the individual is enabled to comprehend the operation of natural laws and is in a better position to adjust social phenomena to the natural order.

Confucius declares that rectification is the greatest function of government.[1] *Li* furnishes minute details for the application of the doctrine of rectification. It points out the relation between different States, the status of the new sovereign, of the officials and of the people, the regulation of the intercourse among them, and the rules of public ceremonies. In other words it is a cyclopædia of social etiquette for public servants.[2]

Furthermore, *li* defines the sphere of governmental authority and the functions of government. The book of *Yüeh Ling* or the "Proceedings of Government in the Different Months"[3] in the text of *Li Chi* is a detailed programme of what the government should do in the twelve months of the year, so that it may keep in harmony with natural forces. In this and in other books the *Li Chi* records the establishment of schools and charitable institutions, the regulation of industries, the distribution of land, the administration of justice, State provision for music and other recreative agencies, conservation, irrigation, the promotion of agriculture, the encouragement of immigration, the construction of canals, the opening of roads, military preparations, improvement of the civil service, diplomatic intercourse, and religious sacrifice.[4] It has been the practice in China, when

---
[1] *Analects*, bk. xiii, ch. iii. [2] See bks. i, iii–vi.
[3] *Li Chi*, bk. iv. [4] The theory is highly socialistic.

the government undertakes a new line of activity, to go to *li* for justification.[1]

At the same time *li* defines the limits of governmental authority. It deprives the sovereign of the assumption of absolute supremacy; since he is above his subjects, so God is above him. Because of *li* the sovereign dares not disregard this fact: as he wants others to obey him, he must obey the ordinances of God which are equivalent to right principles. If he should offend *li*, his right to govern is automatically forfeited. Like the Pope of Rome *li* can in a word instigate rebellion and threaten the throne of the ruler, be he king or emperor.[2]

Li may be used also as a principle of colonial administration. The difference between uncivilized nation and a civilized nation, says Confucius, is that the latter possesses *li* while the former does not. A nation possessing *li* is a civilized nation even though it be in a state of anarchy. On the other hand, a nation without *li* is a savage one, even though it possesses a government.[3] Therefore, the fundamental principle in governing and civilizing uncivilized peoples is to teach them the principle of *li*.

Li discriminates between right and wrong, and so it furnishes the foundation for legal adjudications.[4] In the *Analects* Confucius goes as far as to say that *Li* takes the place of crimes and lawsuits. He says: " If in government you depend upon laws, and maintain order by enforcing those laws by punishments, you will see that the people will try to avoid the punishment and that they will gradually lose the sense of shame. If, on the other hand, in government, you lead the people with virtue and regulate their

---

[1] *Li Chi*, bks. IV, VII, *et seq.*

[2] In fact, the classical literature of the Confucian School constitute a kind of unwritten constitution in China.

[3] *Analects*, bk. III, ch. V.   [4] *Li Chi*, bk. i.

actions with *li*, you will see that they will have a sense of shame for wrong-doing, and that they will emulate what is good." [1]

The *Li* and the *Yüeh*

So much for the uses of *li* in political control. Why is *li* so great ? The answer is that *li* approaches the problem of control in a more fundamental and more profound way than mere legislation or adjudication. It operates upon human nature, human feelings, and the operation of the human mind, while other systems operate upon the outward action of man. Since the inward feelings of man control his outward action, the mind should be the object of political control. Thus *li* has its field of operation in human nature.[2]

Moreover, customs are different in different regions ; temperaments are different in different races ; cultural backgrounds are different in different civilizations ; and " good " politics must recognize these factors. It is *li* which enables rulers and administrators to understand human nature, cultural background, racial temperament, and local traditions. In addition, as already stated, *li* makes it possible for one to comprehend natural laws, and consequently to conduct government more in harmony with nature.[3]

The ideal of *li* is social harmony. The greater the influence of *li*, the greater will be social harmony, until the ideal state is attained where no *li* is necessary —such is the state of great similarity. In the state of great similarity there will be only the best *yüeh* or " music ". The best *yüeh* is the expression of happiness

---

[1] *Analects*, bk. II, ch. iii. [2] *Li Chi*, bks. I, XVI, XVII.
[3] *Li Chi*, bk. III, sec. iii, 14, and bk. XVII, sec. i ; see also *Shu Ching*, pt. v, bks. IV, XXIV ; *Book of Poetry*, bk. I, pt. xiv, ode 3.

and satisfaction, being the result of harmony of feelings. All the modulations of the voice arise from the mind, and the various affections of the mind are produced by the stimulation of external things. "Music is the production of modulations of the voice, and its source is in the affections of the mind as it is influenced by external things."[1]

Thus, "when the mind is moved to sorrow, the sound is sharp and fading away; when it is moved to pleasure, the sound is slow and gentle; when it is moved to joy, the sound is exclamatory and soon disappears; when it is moved to reverence, the sound is straightforward, with an indication of humility; when it is moved to love, the sound is harmonious and soft. These six peculiarities of sound are not natural; they indicate the impressions produced by external things. On this account the ancient kings were watchful in regard to the things by which the mind was affected.

"And so the ancient kings," records *Li Chi*, "instituted *li* to direct man's aims correctly; *yüeh* to give harmony to their voice; laws to unify their product; and punishments to guard against their tendencies to evil. The end to which *li*, *yüeh*, justice, and law lead is one: they are the instruments by which the minds of the people are assimilated, and good order is made to appear."[2]

Yüeh has two essential uses. In the first place, by means of *yüeh* one ascertains the general sentiment of the people toward the government and the character of government itself. "All modulations of the voice", says the book of *Li Chi*, "spring from the minds of men." When the feelings are moved within, they are manifested in the sounds of the voice, and when these sounds are combined so as to form compositions,

[1] *Li Chi*, bk. VII, sec. 1, 2.
[2] *Li Chi*, bk. XVII, sec. 1, 3.

The Principle of Li

we have what is called *yin*.[1] Hence the *yin* of an age of good order indicates composure and enjoyment. The *yin* of an age of disorder indicates dissatisfaction and anger, and its government is perverse. The *yin* of a State going to ruin is expressive of sorrow and troubled thoughts. There is an interaction between the *yin* and the character of the government.[2] Therefore, by means of *yin* and *yüeh* the wise man knows the sentiments and wants of the people, and thereby he knows the methods of attaining good government.[3]

In the second place, *yüeh* has an harmonizing effect upon social forces ; through it the people will entertain good feelings towards their social environment and particularly toward their government. In explaining this point, *Li Chi* says that " the nature of man is static ". But when man acts upon the stimulation of external things, it is due to the exercises of his desires. Things come to him more and more, and his knowledge is increased. The manifestations of likes and dislikes then arise. When these are not regulated from within, and growing knowledge leads the mind astray from without, he cannot come back to himself, and his natural principle is extinguished.

" Now there is no end of things by which man is affected ; and when his likes and dislikes are not subject to regulation from within, he is changed into the nature of things that come before him. That is, he destroys the natural principle within, and gives the utmost indulgence to the desires by which man may be possessed. Thus we have the rebellious and deceitful heart, with licentious and violent disorder. The strong press upon the weak ; the many are cruel to the few ; the intelligent impose upon the ignorant ; the bold make it bitter for the timid ; the diseased are not nursed ; the care of the old, the young, the

---
[1] It may be translated as " musical air ".
[2] *Li Chi*, bk. XVII, sec. 1, 4.   [3] *Li Chi*, bk. XVII, sec. 1, 8.

orphans, and the childless are neglected; such is the great disorder which ensues.

"Therefore, when the ancient kings instituted their *li* and *yüeh*, they regulated them by consideration of the requirements of humanity.... *Li* afforded definite expression for the affections of the minds of the people; music secured the harmonious utterance of their voices; laws of government were designed to promote the performance of the *li* and *yüeh*; and punishments were designed to guard against the violation of them. When *li*, *yüeh*, laws and punishments, had everywhere full course, without irregularity or collision, the method of kingly rule was complete."[1]

In conclusion, the function of government is to cultivate rectification and virtue which lead to the greatest social harmony with the greatest happiness. Harmony being the maintenance of natural order, and happiness being the satisfaction of life, the words "the greatest social harmony with the greatest happiness," would mean "the greatest goodness", for, according to Confucius, goodness is advantageous to the development of life. In promoting this end, the government should recognize two things; internal nature and the external environment of man. Internal nature is originally and naturally good, while external environment is changeable and may be either good or bad. The development of this internal nature depends upon the influence of the environment. A perfectly good environment would develop the original good nature to its fullest extent. A bad environment would hinder the development of the original good nature and allow passions, desires, and feelings to have free play.

The function of *li*, then, is to cultivate an ideally good environment, while the function of *yüeh* is to regulate human desires and feelings. When both

[1] *Li Chi*, bk. xvii, sec. 1, 11–14.

are applied there will be a good environment to influence the individual, and a set of good feelings to react to the environment. The result will be a perfect development of human nature in perfect harmony with the heavenly nature, and there will be social harmony and social happiness. If such is the case, there is a naturally good order and as a result the laws, punishments, and other artificial instruments of political control will not be needed. The *Li* and *Yüeh*, therefore, are the fundamental essences of social and political control.[1]

Summary

The *Li Chi* is a book on the principles of social and political organization and control, and it should be used as a guide for rulers and administrators of a practical, civilized age such as our own. It aims at the establishment of an ideally harmonious social order based upon reason and judgment.

The importance of *li* as a system of political philosophy is in its six contributions : (1) it furnishes the principles of political organization ; (2) it furnishes details for the application of the doctrine of rectification ; (3) it discusses the functions of government ; (4) it prescribes the limitations of governmental authority ; (5) it advances principles of social administration ; and (6) it provides a foundation for crime and lawsuits.

The greatness of *li* as a principle of political control is the fact that it is founded on a recognition of human nature, human feelings, and the operation of the human mind. It penetrates the fundamentals of

---

[1] Bk. XVII, on *Yüeh Chi* (Records of Music) contains excellent discussions, not only on political philosophy, but also on social progress, behavioristic psychology and social processes.

political phenomena ; while other means of control, such as law and punishment, simply attempt to regulate only the external conduct of men.

While *li* aims to provide an ideal social and political environment, the *yüeh* or " music " aims to harmonize individual and group feelings. For rulers and administrators *yüeh* has two uses ; first, it enables them to ascertain the general sentiment of the people toward the government and political life ; and second, it cultivates a type of individual attitude that is most harmonious with the environment. The joint work of *li* and *yüeh* would produce social harmony and social happiness—which is the ultimate purpose of the State.

CHAPTER VI

THE PRINCIPLE OF BENEVOLENT GOVERNMENT

The five principles of benevolent government: Definitions and explanations.

The four evils of bad government: Definitions—The principles constitute the Confucian " Bill of Rights ".

The rule of virtue: The two requirements of benevolent government—Political ethics v. individual morality—The advantages of the rule of virtue.

The rule of love: The highest ideal of government—Confucius' negative rule and positive rule of love—Parental love v. political love—Romantic love v. political love.

Militarism, Nationalism, and Imperialism: Terms defined—The evils of Militarism—Necessity of military preparedness urged by Confucius—The nature of Confucian Nationalism—The interpretation of Mencius on benevolent imperialism.

Rules of public administration: The rules explained—The position of the prime minister—Military dictatorship and legalism.

Summary.

The principle of benevolent government may be briefly stated as follows : Government should be based upon virtue, and should operate for the benefit of the people just as parents affectionately care for their children. Good government is not the government which makes the nation powerful, wealthy, and supreme in arms, holding other peoples in subjugation. Nor is it the government which is efficient, feared, and obeyed by the people. On the contrary, the best government is one that loves the people and is loved by the people, and whose politics are based upon benevolence and righteousness.[1]

THE FIVE PRINCIPLES OF BENEVOLENT GOVERNMENT

A disciple of Confucius inquired of him the fundamental principles of government. In reply he gave five good principles of government and four bad principles of government. The five good principles of government, according to Confucius, were : " First, to benefit the people without wasting the resources of the country ; secondly, to encourage labour without cause for complaint ; thirdly, to desire for the enjoyments of life without being covetous ; fourthly, to be dignified without being supercilious ; fifthly, to inspire awe without being severe."[2] These five good principles, indeed, constitute the principles of benevolent government of Confucius. They may be discussed one by one.

The first principle of benevolent government, according to the sage, is that the government should work for the greatest welfare of the people at the greatest economy for the nation. In this principle Confucius would allow the State to undertake any sort of activity so long as such an activity increases the actual welfare of the people and so long as it does not impose upon the people too much financial burden. In telling how this principle can be carried out, Confucius suggested that " the government

[1] The Chinese term of " benevolent government " is *Jên Chêng* or *Wang Chêng*. *Jên* means " love " ; *Chêng* means " government ", and *Wang* means " glorious ". *Jên* and *I* often go together. They are sometimes translated as " benevolence and righteousness " or " humanity and justice " ; but these translations are not exact, for *Jên* and *I* have broader meanings, and have no English equivalents.

[2] *Analects*, bk. xx, ch. ii, sec. 1.

Principle of Benevolent Government

should promote such activities that are naturally beneficial to the people ".[1] The words " naturally beneficial " are very significant as they imply such conditions as natural resources, public opinion, government efficiency, etc. When Confucius lays down the principles of social welfare relative to government economy, the age-old controversy between socialism and individualism becomes practically meaningless.

The second principle of benevolent government is that the system of taxation should be so instituted that the people find no cause for complaint. In the time of Confucius the people were taxed in service. The autocratic government at that time often demanded the labour of the people during the busy seasons of farming, and so the people repined. Confucius says : " When the government demands labour from the people in proper manner and for their own good, who will repine ? "[2] American revolutionary fathers demanded taxation with representation because by having representation, taxes will be assessed and the funds from such taxes will be used according to the wish of the people. Inasmuch as Confucius regards the government as the parent and the teacher of the people rather than as a storekeeper of the people, he gives the responsibility for wise taxation to the government.

The third principle of benevolent government is that the government should devise ways and means to enrich the life of the people, material, spiritual and social, without being covetous. How can one avoid excessiveness or covetousness while he pursues for richer and better life ? Confucius replies : " Make it your aim to wish for moral well-being and you will never be liable to be covetous.[3] In other words, there is no limitation of love and goodness. There

---

[1] *Analects*, bk. xx, ch. ii, sec. 2.   [2] *Analects*, bk. xx, ch. ii, sec. 2.
[3] *Analects*, bk. xx, ch. ii, sec. 2.

is no limitation of the sphere of government activity as long as it is exercised in accordance with the principle of love. In this respect Confucius is extremely socialistic. To covet is to profiteer. Confucius, at the same time, definitely condemns governmental profiteering as it causes social unrest and political discontentment.[1]

In explaining the fourth principle of benevolent government, Confucius says : " Whether he has to do with many people or few, or with things great or small, he does not dare to indicate any disrespect ; that is what is meant by being dignified without being supercilious." [2] This may be called as the principle of equal respect. Be it majority or minority, the wish of the people must be attended with equal care and seriousness. Confucius urges the importance of respecting people. He says that the affairs of the people should be attended as if to partake in a great religious sacrifice.[3] At another occasion, Confucius remarks that when the rulers treat the people reverently the people will be loyal and respectful to the nation.[4]

The fifth principle of benevolent government is that the government should be revered, but not feared. In other words, its order should be respected and laws enforced due to the moral influence of the rulers, not to the severe punishment or drastic administration. In the previous chapter we have already discussed that personal example of goodness on the part of the ruler is essential to political unity. Here we find that the ruler's personal conduct is an essential part of the benevolent government. To show the way of " inspiring awe without being severe ", Confucius remarks that " the ruler has only to watch over every minute detail connected with his daily life, not only

[1] *Analects*, bk. IV, ch. xii. [2] *Analects*, bk. XX, ch. ii, sec. 2.
[3] *Analects*, bk. XII, ch. ii. [4] *Analects*, bk. II, ch. xx.

of conduct and bearing, but even in minor details of dress, so as to produce an effect upon the public mind which, without these influences, could only have been produced by fear ".[1] Government by fear is condemned by Confucius. He reproached one of his disciples who told a feudal prince that the political symbol of the great Chou dynasty was " fear ".[2]

The Four Evils of Bad Government

Confucius also gives four bad principles of government which should be avoided by the rulers. They are : the principle of cruelty, the principle of oppression, the principle of injury and the principle of meanness. Confucius explains : " The undue punishment of crimes committed through ignorance arising out of a neglected education is cruelty. The requirement of the people to do or not to do certain things suddenly without first clearly giving public notice is oppression. To leave orders at first in abeyance and uncertainty, and certainly to enforce their performance by severe punishment is injury. To treat subordinates as if bartering with them exactly and meanly, thus behaving like professional men, not like gentlemen, is meanness."[3] Any government that commits these four faults of political control may be called autocratic and unvirtuous government.

We may explain these four faults in modern terms. In the first place, cruelty is the punishment of the people for ignorance. The state, according to Confucius, is responsible for the education of its people. Confucius outlines three steps of political enlightenment : first, to get the nation populated ; secondly, to make the people economically well-to-do ; and lastly, to educate them.[4] Education is therefore

[1] *Analects*, bk. xx, ch. ii, sec. 2.   [2] *Analects*, bk. iii, ch. xxi.
[3] *Analects*, bk. xx, ch. ii, sec. 3.   [4] *Analects*, bk. xiii, ch. ix.

the highest function of the state. On the other hand, it is unwise for the state to require its people to do or not to do things without first instructing them. Take the case of battle. Confucius remarks : " To allow a people to go to battle without first instructing them is to betray them." [1] According to the common law, ignorance is not an excuse of the law. But Confucius would raise a very fundamental question in this connection : Have the people been given sufficient opportunity to be acquainted first with the provisions and significance of the law before it is put in force ?

The second fault is very close to the first fault. Oppression is to render the people liable to punishment for offences which have not been made clear to them due to insufficient notice. The spirit of the third fault resembles that of the *post facto* law which is made unconstitutional in practically all modern states. Confucius emphasizes generosity in government ; and so he condemns meanness.[2] He contends that a government without indulgent generosity is a sign of political degeneration.[3] At the same time he points out that government generosity should go with economy of highest degree.[4]

These five good principles and four bad principles of government as discussed above are of grave constitutional significance. Indeed, the four faults are essentially violations of individual rights, and the five rules of good government are constitutional guarantees and limitations which any democratic government ought to have. From the above discussion we may safely conclude that the principle of benevolent government rests upon the premise that government exists for the benefit of the people. Thus the end of government is not government itself but social

[1] *Analects*, bk. XIII, ch. xxx.   [2] The fourth fault.
[3] *Analects*, bk. III, ch. xxvi.
[4] See *Analects*, bk. VIII, ch. xxi ; *Analects*, bk. I, ch. iii.

harmony and social happiness. The latter, in turn, will create richer and better life for man. The people obey and support government because they believe that government can achieve good, that government is able to guarantee peace by preventing external aggression and internal disorder, and that government can do more to carry out the function of rectification than unorganized society. The Confucianists have long held the belief that benevolent government is the only type of government that is adequate to achieve these ends referred to above.[1] Now the question is: How can the benevolent government be realized? In this respect Confucius gives at least two requirements which every government must practice in order to realize a benevolent rule.

The Rule of Virtue and its Greatness

The first requirement of benevolent government is the rule of virtue. As a teacher of political morality, Confucius emphasizes the point that government is subject to the same ethical rules that apply to individuals. He does not separate ethics from politics, nor does he advocate the theory that the end justifies the means. Confucius declares that the rule of virtue is the safest means of achieving the good social life, saying: " The people need virtue more than either fire or water. I have seen men die for treading on water and fire, but I have never seen a man die from pursuing the course of virtue.[2] The philosopher Chu Hsi comments on this in these words: " The want of fire and water is hurtful only to man's body, but to be without virtue is to lose one's mind

---

[1] See *Mencius*, bk. I, pt. i, chs. vi, vii; bk. II, pt. i, ch. v; bk. IV, pt. i, ch. ii; *Li Chi*, bk. VI, sec. I; bk. XXVI, 1–5.
[2] *Analects*, bk. XV, ch. xxxiv.

(the higher nature), and so it is more necessary to man than water and fire."

Furthermore the rule of virtue is the easiest means of achieving the proper end of the state, because virtue is closest to man.[1] Confucius says, " Is virtue a thing remote? I wish to be virtuous, and lo! Virtue is at hand."[2] That is, a government of virtue is one that approaches perfect harmony with human nature, and there is nothing easier than to develop the natural faculties of man. " The path of virtue," says the *Great Learning*, " is not far from man. When men try to pursue a course, which is far from the common indications of consciousness, this course can not be considered the path of virtue. When a wise man has control of the government, he governs according to nature."[3]

Since the rule of virtue is most natural, it is the most universal, for human nature is the same in all peoples, although they may possess different traditions, cultures, and temperament.[4] It is also the most fundamental, since it rectifies or governs not only external actions, but also the mind and the feelings which control all motives and actions.[5]

---

[1] See *Analects*, bk. IV, ch. xiii. [2] *Analects*, bk. VII, ch. xxix.
[3] The *Great Learning*, Commentary, ch. ix, sec. 1; *Chung Yung*, ch. xiii.
[4] A disciple of Confucius inquired what one should do in order to keep harmonious relationships with fellow men. Confucius answered: " If your words are sincere and truthful and your actions are earnest and serious, you will get along well with men even in barbarous countries. But if your words are not sincere and truthful, and your actions are not earnest and serious, even in your own country or in your own home, how can you get along well with men?" In this statement Confucius stressed the universality of truthfulness, earnestness and faithfulness. See *Analects*, bk. xv, ch. v. On another occasion Confucius remarks that if the rule of virtue is practised, peoples of all lands will acknowledge their allegiance to such a government. *Analects*, bk. xiii, ch. iv.
[5] See *Li Chi*, bk. VII, sec. 11, also the *Great Learning*, the Confucian Text, sec. 1-5; Commentary, chs. iv, vii.

PRINCIPLE OF BENEVOLENT GOVERNMENT

The *Great Learning* maintains that the rule of virtue is dynamic. It always achieves and still remains. It undergoes no degeneration or corruption. In a state where the rule of virtue prevails the people are always happy and eager to work, and they are optimistic and active. In other words they are progressive. This is possible because the people enjoy their life. They see the brilliant results of their work, and consequently they have renewed spirit and achieve.[1]

At the same time, government of virtue prevents restlessness on the part of the people. Under the rule of virtue, there is a realization of rectification and the application of *li*, whereby the people know definitely what their individual status is in the state and what they should do in their daily life. This definiteness prevents, on the one hand, individual and social disorganization and uncertainty of public opinion, and, on the other hand, it promotes unity and order.[2]

Finally, a government of virtue is the happiest rule. It is the only form of government that can develop the greatest possible social harmony. There would be profound affection between the governor and the governed. The people would always be grateful for the achievements of the government, and the government would always appreciate the good will of the people. All persons would incline toward a virtuous, harmonious life. Man would have proper work and woman would have a proper home. The child would receive a proper education and the aged would command the proper respect and be properly provided for. Everyone would devote more time to the cultivation of art, learning, music, and religion.

---

[1] Commentary, ch. xi.
[2] See *Analects*, bk. I, ch. xii; bk. VIII, ch. xvi; bk. xv, ch. iv.

Thus government of virtue is a government of *li, yüeh*, virtue, and religion.¹

The Rule of Love and its Greatness

The second requirement of the benevolent government is love of the people. "In conducting the government of a great nation," Confucius says, "there must be reverent attention to business and the cultivation of honest rule ; economy in expenditure and love for men ; and taxing the people at proper seasons."² In this statement love of the people is emphasized. A disciple once said to Confucius. "If there is a man who carries out extensively good works for the welfare of the people and is really able to benefit the multitude, what would you say of such a man : could he be called a virtuous man?" "Why call him only a virtuous man," answered Confucius; "if one must call such a man by a name, call him a holy or sainted man. For, judged by the works of which you speak, even the ancient Emperors Yao and Shun felt their shortcomings.³ Thus love of the people is the highest ideal of government.

Confucius gives two rules as to how this love should be carried out, a negative rule and a positive rule. The negative rule is : "Whatsoever things you do not wish that others should do unto you, do not do unto them."⁴ The positive rule is : "A virtuous man wishing to be established himself, seeks also to establish others ; and wishing to enlighten himself, seeks also to enlighten others."⁵ To establish means to rectify ; and to enlighten means to possess a rich, spiritual and material life. The ideal of love in government is by far more fundamental than such modern political

---
[1] *Li Chi*, bks. VII and XVII. [2] *Analects*, bk. I, ch. iii.
[3] *Analects*, bk. VI, ch. xxviii. [4] *Analects*, bk. XII, ch. ii.
[5] *Analects*, bk. VI, ch. xxviii.

Principle of Benevolent Government

ideals as liberty, equality, fraternity, and democracy. When these rules are practised, there will be no class conflict in the nation, no exploitation, no inequality, no autocracy, no social injustice. On the contrary, there will be great harmony and social happiness. As Confucius puts it : " The old people will be contented ; friends will possess confidence ; and young people will be inspired." [1]

In the Classics, rulers are called the fathers and mothers of the people. Thus, the sovereign is the father and mother of the nation ; likewise the magistrate is the father and mother of his own district. This term implies the duty of loving the people as the parent loves his child.[2]

The *Great Learning* regards the love of the people just as natural as the mother's love of the child. The mother does not have to learn how to ascertain the wants of her child, she knows these wants instinctively when she is possessed of profound parental devotion. She does not need to learn how to rear children before she marries. Likewise, when the ruler has the welfare of the people at heart, he does not have to take great pains to learn what the people want, his benevolent politics will naturally fulfil the needs and desires of the people.[3]

The love between ruler and ruled is reciprocal. When the ruler loves the people, the people will love the ruler. In the *Book of Poetry* this governmental love is frequently compared with romantic love. A benevolent, virtuous and wise ruler will be loved just as a beautiful, pure, and loyal sweetheart is loved. A selfish, licentious and foolish ruler will be deserted by the people, just as a maiden who is unkind, untrue and ugly is deserted by her lover. When a man and

---

[1] *Analects*, bk. v, ch. xxv.
[2] *Vide supra*, ch. iv, also *Li Chi*, bk. xxvi, 1–3.
[3] The *Great Learning*, Commentary, ch. ix.

a woman fall in love with each other, they are devoted to each other. Likewise when the ruler and the ruled love each other, the government and the people will be in perfect harmony, and each will be sympathetic with and helpful to the other.[1]

MILITARISM, NATIONALISM, AND BENEVOLENT IMPERIALISM

Having discussed the two requirements of benevolent government, it is now possible to discuss the attitude of Confucius and his disciples toward militarism and imperialism.

According to the Confucian teachings, militarism is contrary to the principle of benevolent government. The *Spring and Autumn* records some four hundred wars within a period of two hundred and forty-two years; and the author condemns all of them, since war is contrary to humanity. Mencius says that in *Spring and Autumn* there are no righteous wars. He holds that there is no absolute justification for any war.[2] The *Book of Poetry* contains a number of poems picturing the calamity of broken homes, the sorrow of widows, and the crying of mothers to show the human waste of war.

The Confucianists, however, are not advocates of peace at any price. The *Book of Change* declares that wise rulers provide strong forts in order to protect the country from foreign aggression.[3] Confucius himself was asked what was essential in the government of a country. He replied that there must be sufficient food for the people, sufficient military equipment, and the confidence of the people in their government.[4] Thus military equipment, along with

[1] The *Book of Poetry*, contains a great number of odes expressing this idea.
[2] *Mencius*, bk. VII, pt. ii, ch. ii.
[3] *Book of Change*, T'uan Chuan, pt. i, hex. xxix.
[4] *Analects*, bk. VII, ch. vii.

economic sufficiency and popular trust, are regarded by Confucius as the three essentials of political security. The *Book of Change* declares that the function of military forces and military expeditions is that of rectification. When military force is used for the purpose of rectification, it will not only bring no harm to the people, but deliver them from tyranny and lead them to goodness.[1]

A nation not only should have sufficient military equipment, but also should train its men well. Confucius declares that " to lead an uninstructed people to war is to throw them away ".[2] Again " let a good man teach the people seven years, and they may then be led to war ".[3] According to the *Li Chi*, in a certain time of the year the government should teach the people military tactics by means of hunting trips.[4]

The *Book of Change* says : " There is water in the ground. *Army*, the wise man trains the mass of people in military art." [5] This refers to the system of training the farmers for war. There is army in the farm just as the phenomena of having water in the ground, and in times of peace they are civilians or farmers, and in times of war all people are regular soldiers. By means of this system there will be no need of heavy expenditure for maintaining a standing army, and the people will not be imposed upon by long service. The rank and file of the people will be soldiers, and the soldiers will all come from the class of ordinary respectable citizens. This is the safest, most adequate, military equipment.[6]

Having had sufficient military strength, Confucius

[1] *Book of Change, Hsiang Chuan*, pt. i, hex. vii.
[2] *Analects*, bk. VIII, ch. xxx.   [3] *Analects*, bk. XIII, ch. xxix.
[4] Bk. IV, sec. 3, pt. iii, 13–15.   [5] *Hsiang Chuan*, pt. i, hex. vii.
[6] Hsieh Wei-yu, *The Analysis of I Phenomena*, bk. II, under the *Hsiang Chuan*, pt. i, hex. vii.

warns his people against the reckless use of war. Mencius says that Confucius " would never commit an act of unrighteousness or put to death one innocent person in order to gain the control of an Empire ".[1] In other words, Confucius would justify no military expedition even though it may bring the liberation of a great fallen empire if an act of injustice or a murder has to be committed in order to achieve such an end. Since war is a very delicate matter, the selection of the commander-in-chief is essential. He must be a man, according to Confucius, " who proceeds to action full of solicitude, and who is fond of adjusting his plans and then carries them into execution." A man who is brave but thoughtless—such as the type " who would unarmed attack a tiger, or cross a river without a boat, dying without any regret "—cannot be used as military general.[2]

Confucius as well as his disciples are ardent nationalists. When he found it useless for him to stay at the kingdom of Ch'i, he left the state without hesitation. But when he resigned from his office in the state of Lu he left the country slowly because it was his native state.[3] He was very sensitive in defence of the honour of his nation and the head of the nation, his king. Lamenting the people of his time who did not respect their king, he remarked : " The heathen hordes of the North and East, even, acknowledge the authority of their chiefs, whereas now in China respect for authority no longer exists anywhere." [4] Mr. Ku Hung-ming, a noted Confucian scholar, wrote the following comment on this statement of Confucius :

" The watchword of Chinese chivalry is *tsun wang yang i* (Honour the king and break the heathen). These four words, taken in their true sense and not

[1] *Mencius*, bk. II, pt. i, ch. ii. [2] *Analects*, bk. VII, ch. x.
[3] *Mencius*, bk. V, pt. ii, ch. i. [4] *Analects*, bk. III, ch. v.

in their common vulgar sense, have created the Modern Japan of to-day. Tennyson, interpreting the chivalry of Europe in the dialect of Europe, makes his knights of chivalry swear :—' To reverence the king as if he were their conscience, and their conscience as their king. To break the heathen and uphold the Christ.' "[1]

Confucius is also an imperialist in the sense he believes in the extension of the influence of the benevolent government to all backward peoples in order to make them enlightened and progressive. Confucius says : " If remoter people are not submissive, all the influences of civil culture and virtue are to be cultivated to attract them to be so ; and when they have been so attracted they must be made contented and tranquil."[2]

Mencius, the greatest follower of Confucius, interprets very effectively the Confucian idea of imperialism in these words : " If a ruler honours the virtuous and employs the able, so that the offices shall all be filled by individuals of distinction and mark, then all the scholars of the Empire will be pleased, and wish to stand in his court. If, in the market-place of his capital, he levy a ground rent on the shops, but do not tax the goods, or enforce the proper regulations without levying a ground rent, then all the traders of the Empire will be pleased, and wish to store their goods in his market-place.

" If, at his frontiers there be an inspection of persons, but no tax charged on goods or other articles, then all the travellers of the Empire will be pleased, and wish to make their tours on his roads. If he requires that the husbandmen give their mutual aid to cultivate the public field and exact no other tax from them, then all the husbandmen of the Empire will be pleased and wish to plough in his fields.

[1] Ku Hung-ming, tr.: *The Discourses and Sayings of Confucius* (1898), p. 15, note. [2] *Analects*, Book XVI, ch. i.

"If from the occupiers of the shops in his market-place he does not exact the fine of the individual idler, or of the hamlet's quota of cloth, then all the people of the Empire will be pleased, and wish to come and be his people. If a ruler can truly practise these five things, then the people in the neighbouring kingdoms will look up to him as a parent. From the first birth of mankind till now, never has any one led children to attack their parents and succeeded in his design. Thus, such a ruler will not have an enemy in all the Empire, and he who has no enemy in the Empire is the minister of heaven. Never has there been a ruler in such a case who did not attain to the imperial supremacy."[1]

To prevent tyranny and absolutism is also a ground for imperialism by force. When a people are suffering from tyranny, naturally they will hate their own government and they will be inclined toward some other benevolent government, should there be any. When their wish for the other benevolent government is well crystallized, the will of Heaven is for the latter as against their own government. Then this benevolent government is in duty bound to overthrow the tyrannical government. In such a case force may be used if necessary.

When the tyrannical government is overthrown, the conquering State may annex the conquered State if the people of the conquered State are willing to be annexed. Otherwise, the annexation is not justified. Moreover, if both the people and the government together are bad and immoral, the benevolent government is in duty bound to conquer that nation, overthrow the government, and proceed to rectify the people. In such cases, consent of the conquered people is not necessary.[2]

---

[1] *Mencius*, bk. II, pt. i, ch. v.
[2] This theory is uniformly expressed in the *Shu Ching*, the *Book of Change*, the *Book of Poetry*, and the *Spring and Autumn*. It is most effectively interpreted by Mencius.

Principle of Benevolent Government

Rules of Public Administration

So much for the theory of benevolent government. We may now discuss the practical suggestions of Confucius in the way of public administration in order to bring about a benevolent rule. In the first place, the rulers and conductors of government should know thoroughly the conditions of the country, including seasonal changes, customs, traditions, geographical positions, social problems, and the wishes of the people. Knowing these conditions, the conductors of government should take careful note of natural and social calamities, such as floods, drought, war, and revolution. After observing carefully natural and social phenomena, they should undertake to remove the causes of all trouble.[1]

Natural calamities such as floods, drought, and bad years, according to the Classics, are due to the maladministration of social and political organization; and hence they are evidences of future calamities. Whenever a natural difficulty arises the conductor of government should immediately examine into the social and political conditions of the nation. On the other hand, a favourable natural phenomena such as a good year is an indication of social prosperity and good order.[2]

In the second place, the conductor of government should "hold the mean". Confucius says: "There was Shun. He, indeed, was very wise. Shun loved to question others, and to study their words, though they might be shallow. He concealed what was bad in them, and displayed what was good. He took hold of their extremes, determined the mean, then

[1] See *Book of Change, Hsiang Chuan*, pt. ii, hex. lxiii; *Analects*, bk. VII, ch. x, xii.
[2] See *Book of Change, T'uan Chuan*, pt. i, hexs. ii, xxii; pt. ii, hex. li; *Shu Ching*, pt. ii, bk. III.

employed it in his government of the people."[1] The *Book of Change* declares that to be firm in holding to the principle, to be rectified, and to hold the mean are the qualities of *Ch'ien*, which term designates the greatest and purest of the ideals of virtue.[2] What Confucius meant by holding a " mean " is to approach a problem by seeking the widest differences of opinions and by making the most careful study of the facts in the spirit of absolute impartiality and unselfishness, and then to solve it moderately, practicably, and logically in accordance with the best ethical rules, so that by means of its solution the problem is in perfect harmony with other social and natural phenomena.[3]

In the third place, public spirit is essential in the proper conduct of government affairs. Chi K'ang was distressed about the increasing number of robberies in the State, and inquired of Confucius a way to remedy the situation. Confucius replied : " If you, as a ruler, were not covetous, sir, although you encourage your people to be so, they would not steal."[4] In this conversation Confucius emphasizes the point that in a well-ordered State unselfishness is a necessity on the part of the government.

Confucius condemns favouritism and partisanship.[5] Accordingly, Confucius would oppose the existence of political factions and the practice of political campaigning. On the other hand, he does recognize the principle that underlies modern party government, since he says that " those whose courses are different cannot lay plans for one another ".[6] That is, an agreement of fundamental principles is necessary to concord in the execution of political policies and in running the government.

[1] *Chung Yung*, ch. vi.   [2] *T'uan Chuan* pt. i, hex. i.
[3] See Chu Hsi's Commentary on *Chung Yung*, ch. ix.
[4] *Analects*, bk. xii, ch. xviii.   [5] *Analects*, bk. ii, ch. xiv.
[6] *Analects*, bk. xv, ch. xxxix.

Principle of Benevolent Government

Fourthly, the government should promote the economic welfare of the people. Tzŭ-kung asked what is fundamental in governing the people. Confucius replied: " Enrich them. Having enriched them, educate them." [1] Confucius and his disciples point out a great many rules for promoting the economic life of the people. First, the government should be economical. Extravagance is a sign of tyranny and political degeneration.[2] Moreover, the government itself should not monopolize wealth. Let the people be rich. If the people are rich, the government also will be rich; but if the government centralize the wealth in its own hands, the people will be left in poverty.[3] The government should not hamper private production. For instance, during the busy days of the year the government should not require the farmer to contribute any personal service, so that he might not lose any time in the cultivation of the land.[4] What is more, the government should use positive means to encourage production and increase social wealth, such as irrigation, conservation, promotion of industry, commerce, and agriculture, the encouragement of immigration, and the business regulations.[5]

The fifth principle in the proper conduct of public administration is " to keep busy ". Confucius says that " the art of government is to keep the affairs of government before the mind without weariness, and to practise them with undeviating consistency ".[6] The institution of benevolent government based upon virtue and *li* means a thoroughgoing political reorganization. From watching the smallest phenomena in the State to observing the operation

---

[1] *Analects*, bk. XIII, ch. ix.
[2] *Analects*, bk. I, ch. v; bk. VII, ch. xxv.
[3] *Analects*, bk. XII, ch. ix. [4] *Analects*, bk. I, ch. v.
[5] *Vide infra*, ch. vii. [6] *Analects*, bk. XII, ch. xiv.

of the fundamental policies of government, administrators should occupy themselves busily with affairs at every moment.

The sixth and last principle in the proper conduct of public administration is to choose honest, unselfish, and capable public officers. The golden rule of civil service is "to employ the upright and put aside all the corrupt".[1] In this way there will result two immediate effects. First, the corrupt will be made to be virtuous and honest.[2] Second, more upright men will be willing to serve the government. Confucius says: "Employ first the services of your various officers, pardon small faults, and raise to office men of virtue and talents." He was asked how one could know the men of virtue and talents so that they might be promoted to high office. Confucius replied: "Raise to office those you know. As to those whom you do not know, will others neglect to recommend them?"[3]

The head of the civil service is the prime minister. Accordingly the sovereign should first select a virtuous, wise minister. Tzŭ-hsia, a disciple of Confucius, explaining the Confucian golden rule of civil service, says: "Truly rich is his saying! Shun, being in possession of the kingdom, selected Kao Yao, and all who were devoid of virtue disappeared."[4] So a wise choice of the prime minister may possibly establish a benevolent government even though the king personally lacks wisdom and virtue.[5]

MILITARY DICTATORSHIP AND LEGALISM

The contrasts of the benevolent government are first, military dictatorship, and second, the purely

[1] *Analects*, bk. II, ch. xix; bk. XII, ch. xxii.
[2] *Analects*, bk. XII, ch. xxii.   [3] *Analects*, bk. XIII, ch. ii.
[4] *Analects*, bk. XII, ch. xxii.   [5] *Analects*, bk. XIV, ch. xx.

Principle of Benevolent Government

legalistic government. Confucius is opposed to both these forms of government. Military dictatorship can be maintained by means of "killing" only. Confucius says: "In carrying on your government, why should you use killing at all? Let your evinced desires be for what is good, and the people will be good. The moral power of the rulers is as the wind, and that of the people is as the grass. Whithersoever the wind blows, the grass is sure to bend."[1]

There is no indication that Confucius opposes use of law and the enforcement of law by the punishment. But Confucius is opposed to the government that depends purely upon strict law and severe punishment without making an effort to use reformatory measures and intelligent education. He points out the inherent weakness of the purely legalistic government, saying: "If in government you depend upon laws, and maintain order by enforcing those laws by punishment, the people will try to avoid punishment and will gradually lose the sense of shame for wrong-doing. If, on the other hand, in government you depend upon the rule of virtue, and maintain order by encouraging the practice of *li*, the people will have a sense of shame for wrong-doing and, moreover, will emulate what is good."[2] This is probably the strongest argument Confucius has ever given for the benevolent government as against the government of drastic laws and severe punishment.

Summary

The principle of benevolent government may be briefly stated as follows: Government should be based upon virtue and parental love, and operate for the benefit of the governed. Confucius gives

[1] *Analects*, bk. XII, ch. xix.
[2] *Analects*, bk. II, ch. iii.

five principles of benevolent government. First, the government should work for the greatest welfare of the people at the greatest economy for the nation. Secondly, the system of taxation should be so instituted that the people find no cause for complaint. Thirdly, the government should devise ways and means to produce better and richer life for the people without being covetous on the part of the government. Fourthly, the government should respect equally all classes of people and avoid any pride or prejudice. Lastly, the government should be loved and reverenced, but not feared. Confucius also points out four evils of bad government, namely, cruelty, oppression, injury, and meanness.

Benevolent government contains two integral elements : the rule of virtue and the parental love of the ruler for the ruled. Confucius declares that the rule of virtue is the easiest, the happiest, the most natural, the most universal, and the most progressive form of government. The rule of love is the highest ideal of government. Confucius shows two ways of carrying out this rule of love. Positively, the rulers should establish others in virtue and enlightenment as they would do to themselves. Negatively, the rulers should not do to the people as they would not wish done to themselves.

Confucius is opposed to militarism, but he is not a pacifist at any price. He urges that a nation must have sufficient military equipment and give proper military training to the people for self-defence. He also urges the development of patriotism in the wisest sense of the word. He and his disciples are advocates of benevolent imperialism, that is, the influence of the benevolent government should be extended throughout the world with unselfish motives either for the civilization of undeveloped peoples or for the overthrow of tyranny.

Principle of Benevolent Government

The proper conduct of public administration is essential to the realization of the benevolent rule, and this can be attained by : (1) an intelligent understanding of the conditions of the nation by the government ; (2) by the institution of an administration of " moderation " ; (3) by the public spirit of rulers ; (4) by the promotion of economic welfare ; (5) by the industry of rulers ; and (6) by an honest and efficient civil service.

Military dictatorship and pure legalism are contrary to the spirit of benevolent government ; and so they are opposed by Confucius. What is needed in getting a strong government is neither brutal military force nor strict law and severe punishment, but rectification through education and moral influence.

CHAPTER VII

FUNCTIONS OF THE STATE AND GOVERNMENT REGULATION

Government as the greatest of social institutions: The positive and negative functions of government.

Requisites of government: The importance of public confidence in government—Economic life in political organization—Social justice.

The sphere of government activity: The eight functions of government—The system of tithe—The militia and the police—Government regulation of social wealth: The golden rule on the province of government.

Agriculture: The *ching t'ien* system—The ideal system of local government—The place of the *ching* in the State.

Industrial and commercial regulations: Government operation of industries—Labour and immigration—Public utilities—Monopoly.

Relief, recreation, and education: Principles of philanthropy—Respect to the old—The value of poetry—The four types of recreation—The functions of music—Political significance of district drinking and of the game of archery—The meaning of worship—The *Li Chi's* system of public education.

Summary.

Confucius was asked by the Duke of Ai as to what was the greatest of human relationships. Confucius replied: " The political ! " In other words, government is the greatest of human institutions. The Duke of Ai asked what was the meaning of government. Confucius answered: " Government is rectification ! "[1]

[1] *Li Chi*, bk. xxiv, 8.

Functions of the State

When we speak of the functions of government and government regulation, we mean the specific activities or things that the government should do to bring about a realization of the important function of rectification. Activities of the government may be directed in two ways, positive and negative. Positively it promotes five blessings, namely, long life, abundance of wealth, happiness, enjoyment of virtue, and the following of the will of God. Negatively it avoids six calamities, namely, early death, sickness, misery, poverty, vice, and weakness.[1] The theory of five blessings and six calamities would give a wide range of powers to the State. For instance, a long life is the result of good health, and so the State may take necessary measures to protect the health of its citizens. According to Confucius, abundance of wealth is necessary before the people have the time and energy necessary to the cultivation of learning and virtue. Then, Confucius would permit the State to do all it can to bring about equitable distribution of wealth and the increase of wealth. Moreover, happiness results from soundness of body, restfulness of mind, and satisfaction of desires. Enjoyment of virtue is more than the possession of virtue; it attains to the stage of *li* and *yüeh* where the people are able to enjoy naturally the rule of virtue. The following of the will of God is a state of perfect social and natural harmony: it is the final result of rectification. In order to achieve these ends, the State necessarily takes positive measures of promoting education and of establishing codes of worship, plus the entire set of functions known as social and economic regulation. The latter functions are specially necessary to prevent the six calamities, namely, early death, sickness, misery, poverty, vice, and weakness.

[1] *Shu Ching*, pt. v, bk. iv.

Requisites of Government

Before surveying the functions of government, it is logical to discuss what are the requisites for the existence of government. Confucius pointed out that certain factors are required in every government. When Tzŭ-kung inquired about government, Confucius replied that the requisites of government are that there be a sufficiency of food, a sufficiency of military equipment, and the faith of the people in their government. Tzŭ-kung asked, "If it cannot be helped and one of these must be parted with, which of the three should be foregone first?" "The military equipment," replied Confucius. Tzŭ-kung again asked, "If it cannot be helped and one of the remaining two must be parted with, which of them should be foregone?" Confucius replied, "Part with the food. From ancient times death has been the lot of all men; but if the people have no faith in their rulers, there can be no State."[1]

In this conversation Confucius emphasized the point that the faith of the people in government is the most important element in the political organization. Confucius further declares that if the government possess the confidence of the people, they would believe that whatever the government does is for their benefit and not for selfish ends. Under these circumstances, the government could advance and achieve things; and the acts of the government would be deemed benevolent. On the other hand, if the government does not possess the confidence of the people, its acts would be deemed oppressive.[2] Thus the *Li Chi* says that the initial work of rectification is to cultivate that situation where husband and wife have their separate functions; between father and

---

[1] *Analects*, bk. XII, ch. vii. [2] *Analects*, bk. XIX, ch. x.

son there is affection; and between sovereign and ruler there is faith.[1]

The *Great Learning* goes further to explain that confidence of the people is necessary in raising revenue for supporting the government: " By gaining the people, the kingdom is gained, and by losing the people, the kingdom is lost. On this account the ruler should first concern himself with his own virtue. Possessing virtue, he will win the people. Possessing the people, he will win the realm. Possessing the realm, he will command revenue. Possessing revenue he will have resources for all demand."[2] In other words, revenue is necessary for the maintenance and development of governmental activities, and the support of the people is essential in raising revenue. This support can be gained only by instilling confidence in the hearts of the people.

In discussing the functions of government, Confucius and his disciples emphasize the importance of the economic well-being of the people. They believe that the origin of civilization is chiefly due to economic conditions, and that government came into existence for the purpose of maintaining a peaceful society wherein economic life might be promoted.[3] Throughout the Confucian Classics that economic well-being is of primary importance to the people, and that the rectification or cultivation of virtue can be brought about only after the satisfaction of the fundamental necessities of life—such as food, clothing, and shelter—are uniformly stressed.

On the surface such a theory seems to be in contradiction to the theory that the faith of the people is the most important element in the State; but in fact there is no lack of harmony. In the first place, man has to live; and to do this he must have food,

---

[1] *Li Chi*, bk. xxiv, 8.   [2] Commentary, ch. x.
[3] *Vide supra*, ch. ii.

clothing, and shelter. Therefore, "food," which implies all aspects of fundamental economic life, must come before other things. It was in hunting "food" that man first had to organize; but in all organizations, faith has been the strongest social tie.

Death, indeed, is an important matter; and so the State should provide sufficient military equipment for self-protection. But if the people in a society are without faith and if the getting of food were their sole aim of escaping from death and their highest ideal, they would do anything in any way for the sake of their physical betterment. In such a society, no one would trust his fellow men, and each person would be an enemy to every other. Society could not exist and civilization would perish. The individual would have to face a difficult struggle for life, in which the strongest, not the best, survive. So Confucius says, " I do not know how a man without faith is to get on. How can a large carriage be made to go without the cross-bar for yoking the oxen, or a small carriage without the arrangement for yoking the horses?"[1] Just as the carriage without a yoke could not be made to go, society without faith could not continue to live. If society cannot exist, the existence of the State would be impossible.

Confucius, therefore, wisely put faith above food and military equipment. Food is the primary mean of building up society; military equipment protects society from external and internal disturbances; and faith is the highest working force to maintain and develop social and political organization. " When a ruler attaches importance to the State, he loves the people. When he loves the people, punishments and penalties are just. When punishments and penalties are just, the people are peaceful. When people are peaceful, wealth is sufficient. Where

[1] *Analects*, bk. II, ch. xxii.

wealth is sufficient, all purposes can be realized. When all purposes can be realized, the society of *li* will flourish. From the flourishment of the society of *li* came all enjoyment of *yüeh*."¹ The ideal is the State of *li yüeh*,² a state of perfect social harmony and the highest moral excellence.

Equitable distribution of wealth, according to Confucius, is essential in cultivating the faith of the people in their government. He says: "I have heard that the rulers should not be concerned that they have not enough possessions and territories, but should be concerned that possessions are not equally distributed: they should not be concerned that they are poor, but should be concerned that the people are not contented. For with equal distribution, there will be no poverty; with mutual good will, there will be no want; and with contentment among the people, there can be no downfall and dissolution."³

The Great Learning says: "In a State, pecuniary gain is not to be considered as prosperity, but its prosperity will be found in righteousness."⁴ If a government has wealth and power as its chief object, it will fall under the control of some "mean man". The term "mean man" is used to designate one who does not experience the higher inspirations of life, such as love and justice, but aims only at immediate pleasure, such as wealth and vanity. When such men are employed in the government, calamities and injuries together will befall it. In such a situation, although good men come to the rescue of the State, it would be difficult to remedy the evil. On the other hand, if the government aims at benevolent politics, the people will trust the government, material

---

[1] *Li Chi*, bk. xiv, 19.
[2] This term may be translated as the "state of propriety and music".
[3] *Analects*, bk. xvi, ch. i. [4] Commentary, ch. x.

prosperity will naturally grow, and the government will be stable. It is stable because it is built upon the foundation of faith and democracy. The *Great Learning* declares: " Never has there been a case of a sovereign who loved benevolence, without the result that his people loved righteousness. Never has there been a case where the people have loved righteousness and the affairs of the sovereign have not been carried to completion. And never has there been a case where the wealth in such a State, collected in the treasuries and arsenals, did not continue in the sovereign's possession." [1]

THE SPHERE OF GOVERNMENT AUTHORITY

Viewing the fact that government is the greatest of human institutions, and that it exists for the benefit of the people, Confucius and his disciples would allow a wide sphere of power to the government. Furthermore, the government may be viewed as a large family. The primary purpose of the family is the perpetuation of the human race. The rearing of children, the promotion of economic well-being, the training of individual character, and teaching of virtue and knowledge are its essential functions. Likewise, the State has three important functions, namely, the increase of population, the development of the economic life of the people, and the promotion of education.[2] Just as the father can do to the son or for the son that which he sincerely believes to be for the good of his son, so the sovereign can do whatever he sincerely and honestly believes to be for the good of his people. This idea is present in all the Confucian writings, and on the basis of this idea Confucius advances much socialistic philosophy.

[1] *Commentaries*, ch. x.   [2] *Analects*, bk. XIII, ch. ix.

Functions of the State

The book of "Great Model" in the *Shu Ching* is very valuable for the light it throws on the principles of social and political control. It classifies the functions of government into eight different groups : (1) Those concerning food, such as agriculture, irrigation, the regulation of the seasons, and the utilization of the natural elements of substances [1] ; (2) those concerning commodities, such as industry, commerce, labour, and the use of money ; (3) those concerning religion such as sacrifices and ancestor worship ; (4) those concerning public works such as public buildings and national parks ; (5) those concerning education such as the establishment of schools and the teaching of virtue, science, and military tactics ; (6) those concerning justice, such as the enactment and enforcement of Law, and the imposition of punishments ; (7) those concerning the entertainment of guests, such as diplomacy, the reception of foreign representatives, international conferences, and the entertainment of other public guests ; and (8) those concerning the army, such as military equipment, the training of soldiers, and police protection.[2]

The order of the classification is of considerable significance. First of all, food is of primary importance in order to satisfy hunger. Next in order is commodity, which includes all industry, commerce, the regulation of competition, the use of money, the establishment of prices, and all aspects of commercial and industrial life. The first two groups of functions represent practically the entire range of economic activities. After the material wants are satisfied, religious worship follows in importance. The idea of religious worship is thankfulness to the

---

[1] They are the five elements or *wu hsing*, namely, water, fire, metal, wood, and earth.
[2] *Shu Ching*, pt. v, bk. iv.

Origin [1] for the creation of material welfare. The fourth group is concerned with public works with a view of improving the physical environment. The fifth group is concerned with education in the development of intellectual and moral powers; and the sixth group is concerned with justice in the enforcement of law. Thus the state of *li* will be developed; rectification will prevail; and the people will be happy. Hence the seventh group which includes pleasant gatherings between the governors and the governed, between higher and lower officials, and between representatives of different nations, is developed to promote intranational as well as international harmony. Finally, the army is maintained to keep peace in society, to extend benevolent imperialism, and to insure an orderly development of life.

Confucius, himself, however, is not a Utopianist. He does not have any ideal classification relating to the sphere of governmental authority. He meets the problems as they come, and tells here and there in the volume of ancient writings what should be done and what should not be done. These ideas are further elaborated by his disciples. We shall now treat a group of fundamental principles concerning the functions of government and indicate the range of activities which are especially stressed by Confucius and his disciples as being necessary for the establishment and maintenance of benevolent government.

According to modern political science there are certain powers that are *essential* to the existence of the State. They are the financial power, the power of defence against both internal and external dangers, and the power of administering justice. In the

[1] In Chinese, *Pên*. It means fundamental or origin. In theological terminology, it means God.

Confucian classics these powers are definitely recognized.

The financial power includes the power to tax and the power to spend. Confucius and his disciples advocate moderate taxes, saying: "Employ them only at the proper time, and make the imposts light, for this is the way to encourage the people."[1] In ancient China there were two principal forms of contributions: personal service and the payment of money or commodities. Personal service, according to Confucius, should be required only at the "proper" time; that is, when the people have leisure and when personal service is required; it should not interfere with the work of the people. To impose a light tax means to impose a tax of only 10 per cent—the ideal scale of Confucian taxation. That is to say, 10 per cent of the total income should go to the State, and taxation should be no heavier and no lighter. This is the system of tithe.[2]

One of the ancient princes disliked the Confucian idea of tithe. He complained to Yu Jo, a disciple of Confucius, that he did not get enough revenue for the State, even though he taxed the people 20 per cent of their income. He inquired of Yu Jo what was to be done. Yu Jo advised the prince to adopt the Confucian system of tithe. Voicing the opinion of his master, he said: "If the people have plenty, their prince will not be left to want alone. If the people are in want, their prince cannot enjoy plenty alone!"[3] In other words, no government can be benefited by excessively taxing the people. The government will have to rise or fall with the people.

---

[1] *Chung Yung*, ch. xx, sec. 14. The *Analects* quotes practically the same thing in bk. I, ch. v.

[2] This idea is discussed at length in the *Spring and Autumn*, the *Shu Ching*, and the *Mencius*.

[3] *Analects*, bk. XII, ch. ix.

Mencius defends the system of tithe vigorously. If the rate of taxation is more than 10 per cent, the people would suffer from excessive burden. If the rate is below 10 per cent, say, the rate being one-twentieth, the revenue would be insufficient to maintain even the ordinary functions of government. In the case of the former, there would be riot and unrest among the people. In the case of the latter, the government would become weak and inactive. So, according to Mencius, the system of tithe is the ideal system of taxation. In the country districts, he urges the adoption of the "nine-squares' division" with one square cultivated on the system of mutual aid; and in the more central parts of the State, he advises to levy a tenth, to be paid by cultivators themselves.[1]

As one of the eight groups of the functions of the State, the State must have military and police forces to protect itself from external and internal disturbances. Thus Confucius considers military equipment as the third essential of the State. According to the *Li Chi*, all men of the State—except those who are too old, too young, or otherwise disabled—should be required to render military service. A police system should also be established; policemen and detectives should be employed to watch the markets, shops, and city thoroughfares. They should take charge of fighters, noise-makers, peace-disturbers, offenders, transgressors, peculiar strangers, and thieves. If the offence is heavy and comes within the realm of criminal law, it should go to the court of justice.[2]

The judicial powers of the State include the codification of criminal law, the establishment of judicial tribunals, the exercise of punishments, and the pardoning of convicts.[3] The relation of law and

---

[1] *Mencius*, bk. III, pt. i, ch. iv; bk. VI, pt. ii, ch. x.
[2] *Li Chi*, bks. III and IV.
[3] See *Analects*, bk. XII, chs. xii, xiii; bk. XIII, ch. iii; bk. XX, ch. i; *Li Chi*, bk. III.

morality to the administration of justice will be discussed in a later section.

Government Regulation of Social Wealth

Throughout the Classics government is considered the proper institution to regulate the distribution of social profits. As already stated, the positive functions of the government consist of five blessings, namely, long life, abundance of wealth, pleasant society, the enjoyment of virtue, and the following of the will of God. These five blessings are closely interrelated. For instance, when a man has pleasant society he is likely to live longer than he who is in constant misery and distress; and a man who has an abundance of wealth usually lives more pleasantly than do the poor people. The *Book of Records* urges that the sovereign " concentrate in his own hands the sources of these five blessings in order to distribute them equitably among the people ". That is, the sources of the five blessings should be in the control of the government through which they should be equitably distributed, so that the weak may be helped and the strong curbed.[1]

How far would Confucius have the government go in the matter of social regulation? The answer is found in this golden rule: " Follow what is of profit to the people, and profit them.[2] That is, the government should make those regulations that are of actual profit to the people under the peculiar conditions of the time and place.

In his philosophy, his daily life, and in his practical politics, Confucius always recognizes the importance of the peculiar situation with which he is dealing.[3] Often times he states that the same principle is good

---

[1] *Shu Ching*, pt. v, bk. iv. [2] *Analects*, bk. xx, ch. ii.
[3] *Mencius*, bk. v, pt. ii, ch. i.

for one situation and bad for another, and that the same situation can be rightly dealt with in many ways. Likewise in the matter of the government regulation no one policy is universally profitable. In the determination of the policies of government regulation the body of natural law must be recognized. Otherwise there would be wanting natural and social harmony, and governmental regulation would bring about calamity rather than good.

Agriculture

The promotion of agriculture is considered by Confucius and his school to be the basic element of all of the economic functions of government. In the famous *ching t'ien* system of the Confucian School, it is hoped that two purposes may be achieved : the nationalization of land and the equitable distribution of land, according to the size and the needs of individual families. The system of *ching t'ien* actually operated in an imperfect manner before the time of Confucius, but the system recorded in the Classics of Confucius is largely a theory. According to this scheme, a square *li* forms a *ching*,[1] and contains nine hundred *mu*. The central square of *ching* is called the public field ; and the surrounding eight squares are called private fields to be assigned to eight families. Thus each family receives one hundred *mu* of the private field from the government, and gives its labour to the public for the cultivation of ten *mu* in the public field. This is the system of tithe—the ideal system of taxation. A standard family, in addition to the one hundred *mu* in private field, receives two and half *mu* in public field for

---

[1] In ancient China the land was divided up in the form of *ching* or 井. Since the shape of the field was like the word 井, it was called *ching t'ien*. One *ching* contains nine squares of land.

cottage, five *mu* for house in town, and ten *mu* of public land.¹ The *Book of Poetry* says : " All under Heaven is the land of the king ! "² This poem indicates that the land should belong to the State and that individuals should have only the right to use the land. Thus land should not be handed to descendants nor be sold.

Based upon the *ching t'ien* system, the Confucianists in Han dynasty have worked out an ideal local government which is very interesting. The system is this : during spring, summer, and autumn, all of the people should work in the field ; and in winter when there is no work on the farm the people should stay in town. The people should be given houses in the town, which should not be located far from the field. A town covers several villages. A village is made up of eighty families coming from ten *ching*. Eight families occupy one block, and eight blocks make up a village. Each family occupies five *mu* of land. Around the house they should plant mulberry trees, with which the women should cultivate silkworms. After the harvest when the people live in town, the men and women should keep themselves busy with spinning, weaving, studying, singing, or engaging in some special trade or occupation. There should be a school in each village, the school house serving also as a place of religious sacrifice and a meeting place for social and political activities. As stated elsewhere, the ideal military system of the Confucian School is to " keep soldiers on the farm ", namely, the farmers are at the same time soldiers. The village is a military unit, and ten *ching*

¹ The *ching t'ien* system has had a very important place in Chinese economic history. Its original resources are found in *Li Chi*, bk. III, *Mencius*, bk. I, pt. i, chs. iii, vii ; bk. III, pt. i, ch. iii ; bk. v, pt. ii, ch. ii ; bk. VII, pt. i, ch. xxii ; *Kung-yang's Commentary*, 15th year of Duke Hsuan.
² *Book of Poetry*, bk. II (*Hsiao Ya*), ode 50 (*Pei Shan*).

together supply one chariot. In time of peace they are co-workers at home, and in time of war they are co-fighters in the battlefield.[1]

It should be noted that the *ching t'ien* system is as individualistic as it is socialistic. Although the land belongs to the State and is non-transferable, each man has his own land, his own cottage, his own home, his own mulberry trees, vegetables, fruits and animals, and other properties enjoyed by him. He reaps what he has produced in the field and he has also to pay taxes to the government.

It should be noticed also that the *ching t'ien* system is a group system based on territory, regardless of any blood-relationship. It is not an ethnic unit. In the field one *ching* is the unit of division, and consists of eight families ; in the town, one village is the unit, and consists of eighty families. The *ching t'ien* is an economic unit of the State, in point of size next to the family. It is a taxpaying unit, for the public field of each *ching* must be cultivated by the co-operative efforts of the eight families. It is also a political, educational, social, ethical, and religious unit.

The *ching t'ien* system is the foundation of the entire Confucian governmental system. It includes local self-government, since officials are elected by the people themselves ; and it is the germ of the Confucian idea of democracy for each village has a school, and the school house is the place of public worship, of social gathering, and of political caucuses. The people of the *ching* because of their acquaintance, tend to develop close friendship and deep affection. Their relationship is almost as close as that of the family. They assist each other in sickness and in work. Thus the institution of *ching t'ien* is the foundation of political reorganization.

[1] *Kung-yang's Commentary*, 1st year of Duke Hsuan.

Functions of the State

Industrial and Commercial Regulations

In the eight-fold classification of governmental functions, "commodity" is grouped next to "food". The word "commodity" includes all governmental functions concerning industry and commerce. That government should do everything possible to encourage industry and commerce, and negatively it should regulate them properly to protect the welfare of the people, is urged throughout the Classics. "Markets opened at midday," says the *Book of Change*, "thus bringing together all the people, and assembling in one place all their goods. They made their exchange and retired, every one having got what he wanted."[1] In this passage the author described how the sage rulers of the ancient were diligent in promoting commerce and how they had made their people happy.

Although Confucius did not advocate government participation in industries, a system of government operations of industries was recorded at the time of Confucius—which was during the true handicraft stage of industry. According to this system taxes were paid in commodities more than in money. Therefore the government received all kinds of raw materials and unfinished goods, which required manufacture. On this account, government factories were established. Every important industry had a factory, and all the factories were under the direction of a government department. The artisans of high grade were government officers, while the common artisans were government employees. They received salaries and wages from the government, and the government supplied all the materials and tools and took the finished products. These products were not to be sold in ordinary markets, but were to be consumed by the government itself, for it was the accepted philosophy

---

[1] *Book of Change*, the Great Appendix, pt. ii, ch. ii.

that government must not compete with the common people.¹

Accumulation of capital by the State for public activities is also considered as a factor in successful administration. According to *Li Chi*, a State as a whole should have an accumulation of capital sufficient for at least nine years.² Such an accumulation may be brought about by saving. Confucius speaks of saving, not only for the private family, but also for the State. In the *Book of Change* there is a chapter called " chieh ", which means " abstinence " or saving. The chief point of this book is that " the making of regulations should be based upon the principle of saving, so that they will not injure the wealth or hurt the people ".³ The idea being that as soon as wealth is injured, the people are hurt. If one wishes to avoid injuring wealth, there must be some sort of regulations—such as financial or business legislation according to the principle of " chieh ". Hence, saving is the basic principle in the preservation of wealth for the benefit of the people.

As between capital and labour, Confucius and his disciples would champion the rights of labour. The *Great Learning* declares that the population of a nation is more important than its wealth, and that the ruler should pay attention rather to the welfare of the people than to the gathering of wealth.⁴ The *Analects* tells that Confucius bowed forward to the crossbar of his carriage to anyone bearing tables of population. This shows that he realizes the importance of the number of

---

¹ *Li Chi*, bks. I, II, III, IV.
² According to the *Li Chi* the accumulation should be made in grain. In ancient China grain was the chief commodity. Its importance as a medium of exchange was almost equal to money. Grain was a form of capital. See *Li Chi*, bk. III, sec. 3.
³ *Book of Change*, *T'uan Chuan*, pt. ii, hex. lx.
⁴ *Great Learning*, Commentaries, ch. x, sec. 12–13.

people.¹ Thus Confucius advocates government encouragement of immigration. Indeed, he regards immigration as a sign of good government. He says that there is good government when those who are near are made happy and those who are far off are attracted to immigrate to the country.² He says further : " If a ruler loves propriety, the people will be reverent to him. If he loves righteousness, the people will follow his example. If he loves good faith, the people will be sincere. Now when these things take place, the people from all quarters will come to him, bearing their children on their backs." ³ We may say this is the immigration policy of Confucius.

In the *Chung Yung*, the immigration of skilled artisans is advocated in order to promote industry. It says : " By encouraging all classes of artisans to come in, wealth is made sufficient. By indulgent treatment of foreigners, the people of all quarters will come. . . By daily and monthly examinations of their working conditions, and by making their income adequate to the cost of living—this is the way to encourage different classes of artisans. To escort them respectfully on their departure and welcome them on their coming, to commend the good among them, and show compassion to the incompetent—this is the way to treat foreigners indulgently." ⁴

It should be noted that Confucius advocated the encouragement of immigration not simply on economic grounds but also for political, ethical, and social reasons. Confucius approves of the establishment of a universal empire, based on the principle of benevolent government, so that the whole world might become a single society of *li* and *yüeh*, with great social harmony and social pleasure. The encouragement

---

[1] *Analects*, bk. x, ch. xvi. [2] *Analects*, bk. III, ch. xvi.
[3] *Analects*, bk. XIII, ch. iv. [4] ch. xx, sec. 12–14.

of immigration would bring about international comity, benevolent politics, and the advancement of culture and civilization. It is, therefore, a stepping stone in the direction of the establishment of universal benevolent government.[1]

Government operation, government ownership, and government regulation of public utilities are mentioned in the Confucian Classics. The building of public roads, the improvement of water transportation, and the opening of canals are considered public functions.[2] The government is even charged with the construction of carriages and boats. There should be uniformity and standardization in the system of transportation throughout the world.[3]

Confucius is opposed to monopoly. Social profits should be open to all as an important factor in maintaining justice and equity among the people.[4] According to the principles of the *Spring and Autumn*, the famous mountains and great meres are not transferred to any private or semi-public interest. "Since they are the natural resources of heaven and earth, and are not produced by human power, they ought to be shared in common with all the people."[5]

As a method of preventing monopoly, the Confucian School sets up the principle that the emperor, the feudal princes, and all salaried officials should be excluded from the economic field and not permitted to compete with the common people. The idea is to leave profits to the people, and to prevent those who

---

[1] This point is expressed in his theory of *Ta T'ung*. See *Chung Yung*, ch. xx.

[2] In this connection Confucius praises the good work of Emperor Yü as a model work. See *Analects*, bk. VIII, ch. xxi.

[3] *Li Chi*, bk. IV, *Chung Yung*, ch. xxviii.

[4] See *Analects*, bk. VI, ch. iii; bk. XI, ch. xvi; bk. VI, ch. xxviii.

[5] *Kung-yang's Commentary*, 16th year of Duke Huan.

have political influence from monopolizing social wealth. For this reason, any one who enters into public life should give up his private business.[1]

Another method of preventing monopoly is government control of prices by adjusting demand and supply. In the *Book of Change* it is said, " the superior man diminishes where there is an excess, and increases where there is any deficit, in order to bring about a level according to the nature of things."[2] Excess and deficit here have to do with relations between supply and demand. Adjustment by the superior man means government regulation.

According to the " Royal Regulation " there should be no duties on imported and exported goods, although rent may be charged for leasing a market-place.[3] The idea here is to develop national industry and international commerce in order that the benevolent politics may be extended to foreign traders, and thus internationalism be promoted. In order to carry out this idea, Confucius and his disciples advocate free international trade. Meanwhile, government measures to regulate intra-State and inter-State commerce are urged by the Confucian School. The " Royal Regulation " records that certain things which are dangerous to social order, such as munitions, are prohibited in the market; commodities which do not come up to legal standards in measures or quality or kind are also excluded. Inspectors should be provided in the market, and travellers should be examined.[4] Since weights and measures are the most important instruments of commerce, they also must

---

[1] *Spring and Autumn*, ch. i; the *Great Learning*, Commentaries, ch. x; *Li Chi*, bk. IX, secs. 11, 12; bk. XXVII, 32.
[2] *Book of Change*, Hsiang Chuan, pt. i, hex. xv.
[3] *Li Chi*, bk. III, 11.
[4] *Li Chi*, bk. III, sec. 4, 17.

be regulated carefully and uniformally by the government.[1] Careful examination does not mean exclusion of foreign trade ; rather it encourages honest trading. In this way, the whole world will be benefited by honest business and honest government.

Relief, Recreation and Education.

Philanthropy is considered by Confucius as one of the most important of the functions of benevolent government. On one occasion Confucius signed that " even Yao and Shun felt their shortcomings " in " carrying out extensively good works for the welfare of the people and delivering the multitude from misery ".[2] In *Li Chi* it is said that "competent provision should be secured for the aged until their death, employment for the able-bodied, and ample sustenance for the young. The government should show kindness and compassion to widows, orphans, childless men, and those who are disabled by disease, so that they may all be sufficiently maintained. All men should have their proper work, and women their proper homes."[3] The " Royal Regulations " declares that " One who while quite young loses his father is called an orphan ; an old man who has no son is called a solitary person ; an old man who has no wife is called a widower ; and an old woman who has no husband is called a widow. These four classes are the poorest of Heaven's people, having none to whom to tell their wants. They should all receive regular allowances. The dumb, the deaf, the lame, those who have lost a member, the pigmies, and the artisans are all fed according to the work which they are able to do."[4]

[1] *Analects*, bk. xx, ch. i. [2] *Analects*, bk. vi, ch. xxviii.
[3] Bk. vii, sec. 1, 2. [4] *Li Chi*, bk. iii, sec. v, 13–14.

Functions of the State

These statements contain the Confucian principles of public relief which may be stated as follows: (1) the government should take care of those who are either too young or too old to work; (2) the government should provide work for able-bodied persons who are out of employment; (3) the government should take care of those who are physically disabled and who find it very difficult to make their own living; and (4) the dependents upon public relief should work as much as they are able. In the latter case, the unemployed artisans who have their handicrafts are not given regular allowances, but simply supported by their own labour at tasks which are provided by the State.

The old should not only be supported by the government, but should also be respected by the authorities. *Li Chi* suggests that there are five things by means of which a good government may be secured: the honour of the virtuous, the honour to the nobles, the honour to the old, the reverence to the aged, and the kindness shown to the young.[1] Among these five things, two refer to the treatment to the old: the old should not only be respected, but also honoured. The idea of the respect for the old is political and ethical. That is, the aged are the older generation or the fathers of society. If they are respected by the government, the people will be filial to their own parents; when they are thus filial, they will be good and loyal people.[2] Therefore, to respect the old is directly to teach filial piety and indirectly to develop patriotism and respect for law.

Confucius points out in many places the political importance of recreation which, including poetry, archery, hunting and music. "Poetry," says Confucius, "calls out the sentiment. It stimulates observation. It enlarges the sympathies and moderates

[1] *Li Chi*, bk. xxi, sec. i, 13.   [2] *Li Chi*, bk. xxvii, 24.

the resentment felt against injustice. Poetry, in fact, teaches us lessons for the duties of social and political life. At the same time it makes us acquainted with the names of birds, beasts and plants."[1] On another occasion, Confucius contends that the knowledge of poetry with practical ability enables one to conduct wisely government and diplomatic affairs.[2] *Li* and *Yüeh*, according to Confucius, are essential factors in rectification.[3] They include all such forms of recreation as poetry, music, archery, etc.

In the *Li Chi*, elaborate system of State regulation of recreation is recorded. There are found four different types of recreation, namely, music, district drinking, the game of archery, and hunting. The component parts of music are four, namely, musical instruments, poetry, singing, and dancing—the latter being of two kinds, civil and military. *Li Chi* declares that "Poetry gives expression to the thoughts; singing belongs to the notes of the voice; and dancing puts the body into action in harmony with the sentiments. These three things originate in the mind, and musical instruments accompany them."[4] As already stated, music has two political values: (1) it harmonizes social forces as a substitute for political control; and (2) it enables the government to ascertain the feelings and sentiments of the people and better understand the people.[5] On this account, government should promote music on the one hand, and regulate it on the other.

First, vulgar music should be prohibited. Music, indeed, is an object of pleasure and is beneficial to

---

[1] *Analects*, bk. XVII, ch. ix.
[2] *Analects*, bk. XIII, ch. v. See also *Analects*, bk. III, chs. vii, xx, xxiii; bk. VII, ch. xxxi.
[3] *Analects*, bk. XIII, ch. iii.
[4] *Li Chi*, bk. XVII, sec. ii, 21.
[5] *Vide supra*, ch. v.

society ; but it should not be allowed to be licentious and conducive to immorality. Music, therefore, should be not only beautiful, but also good.[1] All music must be performed according to the rules of *li*.[2] Since music is the product of the human mind, and anything arising from the mind of man is natural. The ideal music is in perfect harmony with nature.[3] Social dancing between man and woman, however, is condemned in the *Li Chi*, for it violates the principle that men and women should be properly segregated.[4]

The second form of public recreation according to the *Li Chi*, is "district drinking", a popular custom in ancient China. District drinking takes place on four occasions : (1) when best students are elected and sent to the ruler ; (2) when the ministers and great officials give entertainments to the best men of that State ; (3) when the head of the district assembles the people to practice archery ; and (4) when the president of the town observes the post-harvest sacrifice. After harvest the people, having no more work in the fields, should be given a rest. Generally district-drinking is a social gathering of the people in the school house, and the president of the town is the host. A feast with wines, music, dances, and other social entertainments are the principal features of district drinking. Good fellowship and merriment are emphasized. When this takes place at the election of the best students, the ruler or his delegate is the host. When it takes place in honour of the best men in the State, the minister is the host. Likewise the head of the district is the host on the occasion of the assembling of the people to practice archery.

[1] *Analects*, bk. III, ch. xxv ; bk. VIII, ch. xv ; bk. xv, ch. x ; bk. XVII, chs. i, viii.
[2] *Analects*, bk. III, ch. viii ; bk. VII, ch. 6 ; bk. VIII, ch. viii.
[3] *Li Chi*, bk. XVII, sec. i, 1–2, 28.
[4] *Li Chi*, bk. XVII, sec. iii, 7–8.

"District drinking" is a powerful agency of social and political control. First, it promotes good fellowship and recreation. After a long period of hard labour the people need rest and enjoyment.[1] Secondly, it trains the people in good manners for, in the rites of "district drinking", honour, humanity, purity, and respect are emphasized. All of the proceedings of the occasion follow strictly the regulations of *li*. During the occasion the old are respected and the young receive good treatment. By drinking wine their labour during the year comes to a happy end, and its results are well celebrated. Thus the people come to know the enjoyment of work and the importance of national goods; and they also learn the principle of saving.[2]

Finally, district drinking is an influential agency in rectification, and hence is of tremendous political significance. The *Li Chi* says that during the occasion he sees "the distinction between the high and low, the discrimination in the multitude or paucity of the observances to different parties, the harmony and joy without disorder, the brotherly deference to elders without omitting any, and the happy feasting without turbulence or confusion. The observation of these five things is sufficient to secure the rectification of the people and the tranquillity of the State. When the State is tranquil, all under heaven will be the same. Therefore, I say that when I look on at the festivity in the country districts I understand how easily benevolent imperialism may obtain a free course."[3]

Like district drinking, the game of archery was an ancient custom, and in fact it was the national game of ancient China. It was practiced by every man from the Emperor down. Should a man be unable to take part in this game, it was a very shameful thing. There

---

[1] *Li Chi*, bk. XLII, i.   [2] *Li Chi*, bk. XLII, vii, 10–12.
[3] *Li Chi*, bk. XLII, xv.

were three principal kinds of archery ; the great archery, under the eyes of the sovereign ; the guests' archery, which might be held at the royal court or during the visits of the princes among themselves ; and the festive archery for amusement. With only slight differences regulations for archery were substantially the same in all three types. Ordinary district-archery or festive archery was practiced twice a year, in the spring and autumn ; and it was held at the school-house of a district. However, it might be practiced at any time. If it was at a social gathering, it was called social archery.[1]

It is unnecessary to discuss the details of the game, but a few general remarks are in place. The game is coupled with music and a feast, and is presided over by a master of archery and has many curators. The game of archery consists of shooting arrows. The arrows of the winner must pierce the target which is made of cloth. While shooting, music is played and the arrow must be in harmony with the music ; otherwise it is not counted as a point, even though it pierces the target. After the game is over the ceremonies are like those of district drinking—consisting of drinking, feasting, dancing, and the playing of music strictly in accordance with etiquette.

According to *Li Chi*, the government should take active steps to encourage the practice of the game of archery, which should be taught in government schools. This game is regarded as of tremendous social and political value. It teaches propriety, rites, and military tactics. In ancient times archery was the chief art of war, hence it was necessary for national defence. Archery promotes physical development, since it requires great vigour and strength. District archery includes the procedure of district drinking, combining the benefits of both. It fixes the regulation

[1] *Li Chi*, bk. XLIII, 5–7 ; *Analects*, bk. III, ch. vii.

between seniors and juniors, and tends to make society harmonious. As an agent for recreation, the game calls forth a certain social pleasure in the gathering of different classes and of men of different ages for the purposes of enjoying themselves in drinking, archery, music and feasting. There is also the physical pleasure in the exercise of the whole body for a whole day, and the pleasure in winning the game by showing personal qualities.[1]

In addition, archery was used in ancient China by the emperor as a test in selecting feudal princes, ministers, great officials and students. In the same way the princes, ministers, and great officials selected students for their employments. Archery thus was a kind of civil service examination, and it was necessary qualification for election. It is interesting to note that when a boy was born a bow was placed on the left of the door; and when he was only three days old he began to be carried for the shooting arrows. This indicates that archery was a necessary profession for all boys.[2]

The *Li Chi* declares that the maintenance of public parks and the encouragement of hunting are government functions. The people should be allowed to enjoy the public parks just as much as the sovereign, the princes, or the high officials. The public park should be large, be located outside the city, and should have forests and wild animals; hence it was used as a hunting ground. The government, according to the Classics, should encourage hunting since it increases physical vigour and teaches military tactics; but it should be well regulated so that it may not be carried too far and destroy nature.[3]

Religion and education are important agencies for social and political control. Confucius believes in

[1] *Li Chi*, bks. IV, xliii. [2] *Li Chi*, bk. XLIII, 5; bk. XXXVII.
[3] *Li Chi*, bks. III and IV.

one God. At the same time he says that the people should offer sacrifices to all forms of natural phenomena which do good to human life, especially agricultural life, with the idea of thanksgiving. For instance, the earth produces grain and contributes to man's welfare. In return man should offer sacrifices at a certain time of year. Likewise man should offer sacrifices to mountains, rivers, oceans, cats, dogs, cows, rain, thunder, snow, and to all other kinds of natural phenomena. In offering such sacrifices, there is no such superstitious implication that spirits may render blessings to worshippers. The sacrifices rest purely on ethical grounds, that is, a return of good will for a good deed.[1]

In speaking of the origin of religion the *Li Chi* says that "the first development of religion began with food and drink. Primitive people roasted millet and pieces of pork on heated stoves. They excavated the gourd in the form of a jar, and scooped the wine from it with their two hands; and they fashioned a handle of clay, and struck with it an earthen drum. Simple as these arrangements were, the people seemed to be able to express by them their reverence for spiritual beings."[2] So elemental is the religious life, that the State, which should be governed by the recognition of the principles of human nature, must regulate the religious activities of the people. The chief activities of State in connection with religious life take the form of prayer for the people by rulers and officials, of providing ceremonial gatherings for sacrifices, of regulating ancestral worship, of teaching the principles of thanksgiving to nature for its good to man, of teaching the relation of public and private virtue to the service of Heaven, of providing and regulating

[1] See *Analects*, bk. xx, ch. i; bk. iii, chs. xiv, xv, xvii; bk. vi, ch. xx; bk. viii, ch. xxi.
[2] Bk. vii, sec. i, 6.

cemetery grounds, and of providing school houses for religious activities.[1]

Confucius advocates public education, particularly free universal education with no distinction of class, sex, or race.[2] In the *Li Chi*, an elaborate system of education was recorded. In the centre of a village which contains eighty families, there should be a school house. This is part of the *ching t'ien* system. The aged and virtuous men should be elected teachers of the school ; usually they are recruited from the retired officials of the government. Such a school of a village is called a local school. It should open in the tenth month when the agricultural work has been finished, and should close in the first month when the agricultural work begins again. At eight years of age the child should begin to go to school and should study reading, writing, mathematics, geography, and the ethical rules of the family and society.

Next in succession to the local schools should come the district school, the provincial college, the national academy, and the imperial university. A local school should be in every village ; a district school in every district ; a provincial college in every province ; a national academy in every capital city of every feudal State ; and an imperial university in the imperial capital. All these schools should be supported by the government. In schools both knowledge and character should be emphasized ; and there must be a balance of mental and moral training. In addition, the teaching of citizenship, such as the duties of public service, the organization of the government, and the spheres of political authority, should be emphasized. Military tactics should also be taught.[3]

---

[1] *Li Chi*, bk. IV.
[2] *Analects*, bk. XV, ch. xxxviii.
[3] *Li Chi*, bk. XVI, 4–22 ; see also *Analects*, bk. XIII, chs. xxix–xxx.

Functions of the State

Summary

The government is the most important of human institutions. Its purpose is both positive and negative. Positively it promotes five blessings, namely, long life, abundance of wealth, a pleasant society, the enjoyment of virtue, and the following of the will of God. Negatively it avoids six calamities, namely, early death, sickness, misery, poverty, vice, and weakness.

There are three requisites of government, namely, food, military equipment, and faith of the people in government. Faith is the most important of all. Confucius gives a wide sphere to governmental authority in saying that the sovereign may do whatever he sincerely and honestly believes to be for the good of the people—just as the father would do for his son. These functions may be classified under eight main headings, namely, food, commodity, religion, public works, education, justice, entertainment of guests, and the army. Confucius, however, does not strictly follow this classification in discussing the activities of government : he simply takes up the problems as they come and discusses what should be or should not be done by the government.

The State has financial powers, including the power to tax and power to spend. Confucius advocates direct taxes only. A light tax or tithe from land production is the ideal standard. Economy in public expenditure is urged by Confucius. The State has also military powers and judicial powers. The former includes the power of military preparation, the power to declare war, and the power to establish police ; while the latter includes the power to provide criminal codes, to establish courts, and to inflict punishments.

Confucius condemns a *laissez-faire* policy, and advocates governmental regulation. He says that "we are not troubled with fears of poverty, but are troubled with fears of a lack of equality of wealth", for inequality of wealth is the cause of poverty and social chaos. Thus Confucius urges that the regulation of wealth is a fundamental function of the State. He lays down the golden rule as to how far government regulation should go: "Find what is profitable to the people and profit them." There is no one policy of government regulation that is universally applicable. Policies must be established in accordance with the conditions of place, of time, and of people, together with an appreciation of the fundamental principles of human nature.

Confucius and his disciples advocate the nationalization of land and the equitable distribution of land in accordance with needs. In recognizing these two principles the Confucian School proposes the *ching t'ien* system, whereby the land belongs to the government, and the people are given shares of land in accordance with their family conditions. In addition to the *ching t'ien* system, many measures are presented for the promotion of agriculture—which should be regarded as basic in government activities. These include the study of seasonal changes, the examination of physical environment, the development of agricultural education, the control of grain trade, and the issuance of grain loans. The conservation of living creatures, forests, and mines is also urged by the Confucian School. The control of drainage and the building of public roads should be regarded as public functions.

Government participation in industries and the accumulation of capitals by the State are considered factors in successful administration. Confucius and his disciples have always held human or labour interests above capital or property interests. They propose State control of population, State distribution of population and State encouragement of immigration.

Government control of public utilities should be encouraged, and monopoly should be abolished. As a way to prevent monopoly, all government officials should be prohibited from engaging in business which competes with the industries of the common people. Measures and weights should be examined and standardized by the government ; and free trade should be established.

Referring to social legislation, the aged, widows, orphans, unemployed, and other unfortunates should be taken care of by the State. Old men should be honoured and respected. Moreover, social recreation should be provided by the government. Such recreation may take the form of music, district drinking, the game of archery, and hunting.

Finally, religion and education are the most fundamental of all the functions of the State. Education includes both the teaching of knowledge and the training of virtuous character.

CHAPTER VIII
LAW AND JUSTICE

Functions of legal justice and its limitations : Importance of the sense of shame—Law is needed in the age of practical politics—Confucius on human nature—The different classes of people.

The development of justice : Criminal justice the last step of rectification—Justice should begin with government—Education before punishment.

The administration of justice : The rule in the *Li Chi*—Ultimate source of justice is in God, not in the sovereign—Impartiality necessary—The " Punishment of Lu "—Punishment is to profit life rather than destroying life—Rules of judicial administration in the " Royal Regulations "—Public trial, democratic references, and the use of precedents—Intention is not liable to punishment—Full benefits be given to the defendant.

Reform and Nihilism : The highest ideal of criminal justice is that of reform ; hence the ultimate unnecessity of law—The rule of virtue is above the rule of law.

Summary.

Rule of virtue, according to Confucius, is above the rule of law. There are at least two reasons for his opposition to pure legalism : the first is the limitation of law in performing the function of rectification ; and the second is the unnecessity of criminal justice under a perfect rule of virtue.

LIMITATIONS TO LEGALISM

Law can only regulate the external behaviour of man, but man's behaviour depends upon his mind. If the mind is rectified, his behaviour will be rectified.

Law and Justice

If the mind is not rectified, he is liable to commit anti-social acts. The innate force that prevents a man from committing crimes is his sense of shame which can be developed only by means of education and moral discipline. When the sense of shame of the people is not developed, law and punishment, however strict and severe, will not satisfactorily prevent them from wrong-doing. What is worse, the people will try to evade the law and to escape from being punished. At length the people will lose the sense of shame altogether.[1]

On the other hand, when the people have been intelligently educated and trained for moral goodness under the rule of virtue, there will be no criminal deeds or violations of law because the people will have a sense of shame. In this case, law will become practically useless. When a noble was worried at the frequency of robberies, and asked Confucius what should be done to prevent them, Confucius replied that if the government was not covetous, the people would not attempt to steal even though they might be rewarded by the government for doing it.[2] At another time Confucius was asked whether or not it was wise to use capital punishment against corruption and dishonesty. In similar spirit Confucius told his enquirer that if the ruler was virtuous the people would be virtuous and that capital punishment would be useless.[3] In the *Analects*, Confucius says that under a virtuous rule the orders of the government will be effective even though they are not followed by law and punishment; and that under a corrupt rule the people will not obey the orders of the government even though they are liable to severe punishment.[4]

Now the questions are: Is law needed at all under the Confucian system of government? If so, what

[1] *Analects*, bk. II, ch. iii. [2] *Analects*, bk. XII, ch. xviii.
[3] *Analects*, bk. XII, ch. xix. [4] *Analects*, bk. XIII, ch. vi.

are the functions of law and justice? The system of legal justice, according to the Confucian School, is needed in this present age of practical politics as long as there are people whose moral nature is too low to be regulated voluntarily by the teaching of virtue and *li*.[1] This is a question of the relation between human nature and legal justice.

Human Nature and Legal Justice

We may discuss first the Confucian concept of human nature. Confucius says: " Man was born upright."[2] Again he says, "By nature all men are nearly alike; and by habit they get to be wide apart ".[3] In other words, all men were born with the faculties to be good, but through environmental influences and habits men become very different from one another. Furthermore, some were born with superior intelligence and others with average or inferior intelligence.[4] Though education should be given to all people without discrimination of classes,[5] the effect of education to individuals' ability of self control varies according to the differences in intelligence. Persons of superior intelligence can be led naturally to virtue and cannot be readily affected by evil environment. On the other hand, persons of inferior intelligence are always very easily affected by bad environment; and they cannot be rectified by mere voluntary method such as education, *li*, or moral discipline. Thus Confucius says: " You may speak of high things to those whose intelligence is above the

---

[1] The Confucian School outlines political evolution into three stages, namely the stage of savagery, the stage of small tranquillity, and the stage of great similarity. We belong to the second stage, which is an age of practical politics. *Vide infra*, ch. xii.
[2] *Analects*, bk. vi, ch. xvii.   [3] *Analects*, bk. xvii, ch. ii.
[4] *Analects*, bk. vi, ch. xix.   [5] *Analects*, bk. xv, ch. xxxviii.

average ; but you may not speak the same to those whose intelligence is below the average."¹ Again : " There are only the wise of the highest class and the stupid of the lowest class who cannot be changed ".²

It is this " stupid of the lowest class " that constitutes a problem to the society and the State. " The highest class of men," Confucius says, " are those who are born with a natural understanding. The next class are those who acquire understanding by study and application. There are others again who are born naturally dull, but who yet by strenuous efforts try to acquire understanding ; such men may be considered the next class. Those who are born naturally dull and yet will not take the trouble to acquire understanding ; such men are the lowest class of the people."³ Since this lowest class of the people cannot be changed by learning or the teaching of virtue, such forceful methods as law and punishment must be used to rectify them, or, using the Confucian terminology, to " bring them up to the level " of the good people.⁴ In other words, law and the system of justice are to supplement political education, *li*, and moral discipline, in completing the function of rectification.

The scientific concept of positive law was not developed in ancient China until the period of Warring States. Under the feudal system, social and political uniformity was sought through tradition, custom, social propriety, and government orders. There was no " government of law " in the modern sense of the term. During these days what was called law was criminal law. There was no civil law. What was

---

[1] *Analects*, bk. VI, ch. xix. [2] *Analects*, bk. XVII, ch. iii.
[3] *Analects*, bk. XVI, ch. ix.
[4] *Ch'i Hsing* means to seek uniformity through punishment. See *Analects*, bk. II, ch. iii.

called justice was criminal justice, not civil justice. Thus, the *Book of Change* says : " Punishments are applied in order to enforce law ".[1] The *Shu Ching* records the address of Shun to Kao Yao, the chief justice of his government in these words : " You become the Judge. Let five punishments be justly applied."[2]

The Development of Justice

So much for the concept of law and justice. We may now consider the place of justice in political order. Confucius says : " If names be not correct, language cannot be in accordance with the truths of things. When language be not in accordance with the truths of things affairs cannot be carried on to success. When affairs cannot be carried on to success, *li* and music will not flourish. When *li* and music do not flourish, punishments will not be properly awarded. When punishments are not properly awarded, the people will be at a loss to know what to do."[3] When the people know exactly what to do, it means that there is political tranquillity, namely, the execution of rectification, the standardization of orders, the improvement of public administration, the development of *li* and music, and the attainment of criminal justice. Rectification is the first and criminal justice is the last step in securing political tranquillity.

The development of justice, therefore, begins with the government itself. Government must be rectified and founded upon proper authority. When the government is rectified, and politics are conducted in the proper way, law and justice may attain their ends. While Confucius was a judge in the State of Lu, a man sued his son in the criminal court

[1] *Hsiang Chuan*, pt. i, hex. iv.   [2] Bk. i. Pt. i.
[3] *Analects*, bk. xiii, ch. iii.

and Confucius ordered the arrest of the son. The case was tried for three months, but the son could not be found guilty. The father petitioned Confucius to withdraw the case, and the son was pardoned. Confucius was accused of inconsistency, since having declared that filial piety is the basis of government, he now pardoned an unfilial son. Confucius remarked with a sorrowful air :

"Alas, how can one punish the people for committing crimes when the government itself is lawless ? It is to torture the innocent when the people are not educated ; yet they are liable to be punished when they violate the law. When an army has been defeated, one must not punish the soldiers, but those who have neglected to train the soldiers. When the laws are not obeyed one should not first blame the people, but should blame the government that has neglected to educate the people. Without having educated the people first, if the laws are violated the people are not guilty.

"To write the laws carelessly and elaborately, and then enforce them vigorously and punish heavily the the people for violations of laws is tyranny. To tax the people without regular procedure is despotism. To ask the people to do things without training them first is cruelty. Not until all three are absent—tyranny, despotism, and cruelty—may one apply criminal punishments. . . . Thus the ancients first rectified themselves and then rectified the people by moral education. Not being sufficient, they used wise men to lead them in practice. Being still not sufficient, they issued orders, wrote laws, and provided police to intimidate or reform them by force. Within three years the people were morally enlightened. Until then, when the wicked people disobeyed the law, the ancient rulers exercised punishments. In this case the people knew what was guilty and what was not guilty."[1] In short, "punishment without education is tyranny."[2]

Administration of Justice

Since punishment, according to Confucius, is the last resort for rectification, and is usually used towards the lowest class of people, the high and middle classes can be taught and rectified by *li* and so they need not be governed by penal justice. This gives to the famous rule of the Confucian School that the ordinary code of punishments should not be used by government officials above the rank of *ta fu* or the "Great Official".[3] This rule is peculiar and is based upon expediency. Great officials above the rank of *ta fu* are supposed to have self-control, to possess a sense of shame, and to violate no law. Therefore, they are not governed by the same criminal code as ordinary people.

Authority in the administration of criminal justice has its ultimate source in God. *Shu Ching* declares that the different forms of punishment are instruments of God for the purpose of punishing the sinful and guilty people. Thus the power of imposing a penalty is not an inherent or absolute right of the sovereign. The sovereign exercises the power for God and in accordance with the will of God. Since the will of God is expressed by the general attitude of the mass of people, the sovereign and his subordinate officials should administer criminal justice in accordance with the will of the people.[4]

Moreover, the administration of criminal justice must be conducted with great care. The body and the life of the people are sacred and should not be violated except in accordance with proper authority

[1] *Hsün Tzŭ*, bk. xxviii. [2] *Analects*, bk. xx, ch. ii.
[3] *Li Chi*, bk. i, sec. i, pt. iv, 10. [4] *Shu Ching*, pt. v, bk. ix.

and the will of God. When a man is executed, he will never revive; when a body is injured by punishment, it can never be redeemed. Therefore great kindness and a sympathetic attitude must be preserved in the exercise of criminal punishments.[1]

To be impartial is the sacred duty of judicial officers. The "Punishment of Lu"[2] records the words of King Mu: "I think with reverence of the subject of punishment, for the end of it is to promote virtue. How God, wishing to help the people, has made us His representatives here below. Be intelligent and honest in hearing each side of a case. The right ordering of the people depends on the impartial hearing of the pleas on both sides. Do not seek for personal advantage by means of these pleas. Gains obtained by corruption are not precious acquisitions; they are rather an accumulation of guilt, and will be punished by God."[3]

Punishment of Lu

According to the "Punishment of Lu", criminal punishment should be made a source of blessing, for it is due to its use that the people obtain repose and tranquillity. With this in view, the "Punishment of Lu" gives a number of rules of judicial practice. When both parties are present, and the documents in the case and the witnesses are all complete, the judge should listen carefully to the statements that

---

[1] *Shu Ching*, pt. v, bk. ix.
[2] The "Royal Regulation" in the *Li Chi* and the "Punishment of Lu" in the *Shu Ching* are valuable documents in the study of ancient criminal jurisprudence. From these two books, many rules concerning legal procedure may be deduced.
[3] *Shu Ching*, bk. xxvii, pt. v.

may be made with the evidence on both sides, whether incriminating or exculpating. When the judge has examined these statements thoroughly, and fully understands the points of law involved, he should adjust the case by meting out one of the " five punishments ". If none of the five punishments cover the case, he should adjust it in accordance with one of the next lower series of punishments, namely, the " five redemption-fines." If these, again, do not meet the case, the judge should reckon it among the five " cases of errors ".

The five cases of errors are offences of inadvertence. They should be very leniently dealt with, and perhaps be pardoned. In settling the five cases of error there are evils to be guarded against—such as being warped by the influence of power, or by private grudge, or by female solicitation, or by bribes, or by applications for special favour. Any one of these should be held equal to the crime before the judge. The judge should examine these evils carefully, so that the establishment of the five cases of error will not cause corruption, but help the innocent.

In rendering the decision, when there are doubts as to inflicting any of the five punishments, the inflictions of punishment should be forborne. Likewise when there are doubts as to the infliction of any of the five fines, it should also be forborne. The judge should carefully examine the case in order that he may overcome every difficulty in the case before sentence is pronounced. Every phase of the case should be clear and every consideration should be admitted, and obsolete laws should not be applied. In short, the judge should examine the case with kindness and benevolence, decide the case lawfully, and judge carefully and intelligently. In everything the judge should stand in awe of the dread majesty of God.

Where the crime calls for one of the higher punishments but "there are mitigating circumstances", the judge should apply the next lower series of punishments, Where the case calls for one of the lower punishments but "there are aggravating circumstances", the next higher series of punishments should be applied. The light and heavy fines are to be apportioned in the same way by the balance of circumstances. The age of the defendant should also be considered in fixing punishments.[1]

THE "ROYAL REGULATION".

The "Royal Regulation" records an ideal system of judicial administration. In fact, the system is partly a practice drawn from the Chou dynasty and partly a theory of the Confucian School. According to the "Royal Regulation" the judge should make the laws clear to the people so that the people may be warned of criminal charges and litigations. In order to obtain the true merits of a case and to secure justice, he may unofficially refer the facts of the case to his colleagues, associates, subordinates, and the people for their opinion in the matter. When the evidences in a criminal case have thus been all taken into consideration and judgment has been given, the clerk reports the entire case to the magistrate of the district, who in turn reports it to the minister of justice of the central government. After having carefully examined the case and found it lawfully and justly conducted, the minister reports it to the king, who upon receiving the report deputes his councillors to make a review of it. It is only after the approval of the report by the councillors that the punishment is decided upon. In reviewing the case the councillors should make

[1] *Shu Ching*, pt. v, bk. xxvii.

three searches for extenuating circumstances. Once decided upon, the punishment, however light it may be, can never be remitted.

In case, according to the "Royal Regulation", that the defendant has only a criminal intent without committing an act, the case should be dismissed. On the other hand, where the criminal act is not prompted by a criminal intent or only an intent whose degree of criminality falls below that of the criminality of the act, distinctions should be made accordingly.

In trying a criminal case where the natural affection as that subsisting between parent and child or the legal relation as that subsisting between sovereign and subject influences the criminal act of the defendant, due considerations should be given. To determine the exact character of his guilt, the judge should consider the gravity or lightness of the offence and carefully try to fathom the mental and moral capacity of the offender; the judge should exert his intelligence to the utmost, and give the fullest play to his generous and loving feeling in rendering final judgment. If the criminal charge appears doubtful to him, he should take the people into counsel; and if they also doubt, the defendant should be pardoned. At the same time the judge should examine analogous cases, great and small, and then give his decision.

Punishments should be natural, reasonable, and proportionate to the crimes. When a doubtful case permits a choice between two grades of punishment, the lighter one is to be preferred; when it allows a choice between two forms of remission, the higher one is to be granted. Inadvertent offences should be determined by the circumstances in each particular case. Before inflicting a capital punishment, the judge must have the approval of the subordinate officers and the approval of the people.[1]

[1] *Li Chi*, bk. III, sec. iv.

LAW AND JUSTICE

REFORM AND NIHILISM

So much for the rules of judicial administration. They are not only important principles of legal ethics, but are also of great constitutional significance. Before the advent of the written constitution in 1911, they had served as a sort of bill of rights for over two thousand years.

Apart from the political interpretation of the theory of punishment, Confucius points out the sociological significance of punishment. He says: " If you speak to a man in the strict words of the law, he will probably agree with you; but the important point is that he should reform his conduct."[1] Confucius points out the very modern idea of reform in punishment. In this way, the lowest class of people can be reformed, and in the end institutions for penal justice can be entirely abolished. Confucius on one occasion after he had been appointed to a judicial office in his native State, remarked: " While sitting in court, in deciding upon the suits that come before me, I am like any other body. What is important, however, is to cause the people to have no litigations."[2] To cause the people to have no litigations is the highest ideal of Confucius. There are two ways to cause the complete absence of litigations and disuse of penal institutions. The *Book of Changes* gives a negative way, that is, " Do not encourage litigations ",[3] and " the wise man makes punishments clear and laws affective ".[4] The positive way is to promote education and *li*. Confucius says: " By extensively studying the arts and literature, and keeping himself controlled by *li*, one may thus not err from what is right ".[5]

[1] *Analects*, bk. IX, ch. xxiii. [2] *Analects*, bk. XII, ch. xiii.
[3] *Book of Change*, Hsiang Chuan, pt. i, hex. vi.
[4] *Book of Change*, Hsiang Chuan, pt. i, hex. xxi.
[5] *Analects*, bk. XII, ch. xv.

Political Philosophy of Confucianism

Summary

Confucius maintains that the rule of virtue is above the rule of law. The latter is passive and negative, preventing the people from doing wrong; while the former is active and positive, encouraging people to do good. Furthermore, moral rule influences conscience and hence its influence is universal and unlimited. Legal rule governs only outward activities. People may attempt to evade law and to escape from punishment. At length they lose self respect completely. On the other hand, when the people are virtuous and enlightened law and punishment will become useless.

The system of legal justice, however, is necessary to preserve social order in the present age of practical politics as long as there are people whose moral nature is too low to be regulated voluntarily by the teaching of virtue and *li*. While all men are born with faculties to be good, they are not all equal in intelligence. Men of lowest intelligence possess very limited power of self-control; and so they cannot be made upright by voluntary method alone. Law and justice are to supplement education and *li* to rectify this lowest class of people. Confucius points out five steps of political tranquillity; the last of which is penal justice. In other words, penal justice should not be used unless it is absolutely necessary.

Since Confucius expounded his theory of legal justice, the following principles of judicial administration of the Confucian School have been developed: (1) the ordinary code of criminal law should be applied only to the lowest class in the society; and so high officials who are supposed to be the models of virtue for the people should be governed under a different code; (2) the ultimate source of judicial power is in God, not in the sovereign; (3) adjudication must be conducted with great care and with the idea of profiting life rather than destroying life and happiness ; and (4) adjudications must be carried out with absolute impartiality.

The " Royal Regulation " and the " Punishment of Lu " contain a rather complete code of criminal procedure of the Confucian School. In these rules, the life, liberty, and personal happiness of the people are carefully regarded. The idea that full benefits must be given to the defendant is emphasized. Attention should be given to the peculiar conditions of each particular case. Public trial, democratic references and the use of precedents are required in deciding important cases.

Confucius declares that the fundamental purpose of punishment is reform. The highest ideal of adjudications is " to cause the people to have no litigations ", by making the law to be understood by the people, by discouraging litigations, and by the development of education and *li*.

CHAPTER IX

DEMOCRACY AND REPRESENTATION

The theory of political stewardship : Origin of the theory—The theory briefly stated.
Public opinion : The people as the ultimate interpreters of sovereignty—The power of public opinion—Ways of ascertaining public sentiment.
Government by the consent of the governed : Bases of this theory—The doctrine of the *Great Learning*—The interpretation of Mencius. Importance of popular confidence.
The theory of revolution : When justifiable ?—The principle of revolution in the *Book of Change*.
Liberty, equality, and equity : Equality of mankind and world brotherhood—Evils of partisanship—Inequality is a social menace—Constitutional monarchism—Democratization of public pleasure—The equity of nature—No slavery—Political status of women.
Local self-government : The *ching t'ien* system—The ideal system described—Local self-government and the theory of unitary sovereignty.
The theory of educational representation : Good men essential to good government—The system described—Representative features of the system.
Summary.

THE THEORY OF POLITICAL STEWARDSHIP

The entire Confucian philosophy of democracy is founded on the theory of political stewardship.[1]

[1] The Chinese word *Mu* means shepherd or steward. The ruler is called *Jên Mu* or "shepherd of man". In other words, he is the steward of God entrusted with the duty of political control of the masses.

This theory had a very ancient origin. Democratic concepts of theocratic-political nature were very popular long before the days of Confucius, but they were scattered and unsystematic. When Confucius and his disciples edited the *Book of Records*, the *Book of Rites*, and the *Book of Poetry*, they re-interpreted and reduced these scattered ideas into a systematic theory of political sovereignty. In fact, this theory of political stewardship constituted an integral part of the political teaching of the Confucian School.

In the twentieth book of the *Analects*, the words of ancient sage rulers and of Confucius were recorded in order to illustrate in most practical manner the development of the royal doctrines from the ancient sage rulers to Confucius and to show how Confucius was the proper successor of these sages and emperors. The principles set forth in the twentieth book were concerned with government; and indeed this book itself presented a comprehensive system of political philosophy. The Book began with the words of Yao the Great as follows:

"Oh! you, Shun, the Heaven-determined order of succession now rests in your person. Sincerely hold fast the due Mean. If there shall be distress and want within the Four Seas, the Heavenly revenue will come to a perpetual end."

From the standpoint of political philosophy, this statement was significant as it pronounced the theory of political stewardship. In the first place, the " order of succession " was determined by " Heaven ". In other words, God had the ultimate political authority. Secondly, Yao's selecting Shun on the throne was to carry out the order of God; and Shun's authority was delegated, not from Yao, but from God. He was the steward of God. In the third place, Shun had the authority only so long as he had been dutiful and worked for the welfare of the people. This authority would be taken away from him as soon as the people suffered from his misgovernment.

The theory of political stewardship may be briefly stated as follows : God, being the creator of all people, is the ultimate source of political authority. God selects from the masses a man to be king and as such to control, teach, and nourish the people. The king, therefore, theoretically receives his appointment from God as His steward on earth. The appointment is made upon the recognition of his wisdom and virtue, as well as upon his moral and political leadership among the masses of people. A man who possesses such wisdom and virtue, and is recognized as a moral and political leader among the people, is called a " Minister of Heaven "—who alone is legally qualified to serve as king.

Several important rules of political democracy are deduced from this theory of stewardship. They are : (1) in the conduct of state affairs, public opinion must be respected ; (2) government should exist by the consent of the governed ; (3) the king may be deposed on the ground of tyranny, and revolution for such a purpose is justifiable ; (4) government should operate for the welfare of the people ; and (5) liberty, equality, and impartiality should be maintained. These five principles will be discussed in subsequent pages.

Public Opinion

The theoretical ground for obeying public opinion may be briefly stated. God is the ultimate sovereign; and the king, being his representative on earth, is an immediate interpreter of the will of God. Who should judge the truth of his interpretation ? Confucius holds that the people should judge. Although the king is the legislator, the people should be the ultimate judges in deciding what is the will of God, and whether the laws and actions of the king have truthfully interpreted the will of God. The will of the people, according to the teachings of the Confucian Classics, is the will of God, based on the ground that God always wishes to benefit the people and considers what the people want. The *Shu Ching* says : " God loves the people. Whatever the people desires, God gives them."[1]

God does not confer any special favour upon anyone in making him king. One is made king because he has won the love and support of the people through his virtue and ability.[2] The will of God is to make the people tranquil and happy. The people know best how to make themselves tranquil and happy. Thus the king should " like what the people like, and hate what the people hate ". The king must devote his attention to ascertaining the needs of his people and their desires in order to make them tranquil and happy. In short, " in conducting government the hearts of the people must be won ".[3]

The *Shu Ching* warns those who disrespect public opinion, saying :

It was the lesson of our great forefathers :
The people should be cherished and not looked down upon.
The people are the root of a country ;
When the root is firm, the country is tranquil.
When I look at all under heaven,
Even the little man and woman
May surpass me in wisdom and virtue.
If the king makes mistakes repeatedly in conducting government,
Dissatisfaction will prevail and dangers will appear.
Before they appear, they should be guarded against.
In my dealing with the millions of the people
I should feel as if I were driving six horses with a rotten rein.
The ruler of men should have reverence for his duties.[4]

[1] Pt. v, bk. i, sec. i.   [2] Pt. iv, bk. vi.
[3] Pt. ii, bk. iii ; pt. ii, bk. iv ; pt. iv, bk. vi ; pt. v, bk. iv ; see also the *Great Learning*. Commentaries, ch. x.   [4] Pt. iii, bk. iii.

Likewise, the *Shu Ching* declares that a little cause of political dissatisfaction may grow and spread like a forest fire.[1] So powerful is the force of public opinion and so dangerous is the anger of the people, that rulers should give their utmost respect and attention to popular wishes.

Inasmuch as public opinion is so powerful, Confucius and his early disciples suggest several practical ways of finding out the exact wishes of the people. The first way is to listen to the advice of State ministers. As already pointed out, the State ministers should sometimes be chosen from among the common people; those who are selected from rank and file would know thoroughly the actual conditions and desires of the people.[2] Since they are the "models and representatives of the people", they should not only assist the sovereign in conducting public affairs, but also should correct the thoughts, ideas, and actions of the sovereign. They should remonstrate with the sovereign whenever he is wrong.[3]

The second way of ascertaining public opinion is to study folk songs, poems, and lyrics written by ordinary people. In these songs, poems, and lyrics the people voice their opinions and feelings toward the Government. According to the *Ching T'ien* system of the Confucian School, the people live in town from the tenth month of the year to the first month of the next year. During this time the people devote their time to art, literature, and culture. If they have any cause of dissatisfaction, men and women sing together expressing their feelings in the form of poetry. They have absolute freedom of choosing any subject,

---

[1] Pt. iv, bk. vii, sec. 1.
[2] See *Analects*, bk. xii, ch. xxii.
[3] Confucius once scored one of his disciples in government service for failure to remonstrate with his ruler who was doing wrong. See *Analects*, bk. xvi, ch. i.

referring either to themselves or to the court and government.

Then, in the first month of the year, when the people are about to leave town for the field, the government should send out old men and old women who are supported by the State as commissioners to collect these poems. They ring the wooden-tongued bell along the roads to gather poetry from the people. Thus, these poems are collected and transferred from the villages to a State officer who in turn transfers them to the imperial government. After the grand music master arranges the poetry according to its styles and time, it is presented to the emperor. Therefore, "even if the emperor does not go out of the palace he hears all opinions and all grievances of the people."[1]

The third way is for the king to send out delegates to all parts of the country at a certain time of the year to examine into the conduct of public officers, study the opinions of the people, and investigating the needs of the nation. The king himself may make visiting tours through the country. These visits should be personal and unofficial. On such tours he should get interviews with all kinds of people—scholars, farmers, artisans, and merchants. He may examine the work of officials, and in this way discover political corruption, popular grievances, and cases of social injustice. He may also find some great scholar who may be placed in an important government position.[2]

Government by the Consent of the Governed

The second principle of political democracy derived from the Confucian doctrine of stewardship is the theory that government should exist by the consent of

[1] *Shu Ching*, pt. iii, bk. iv ; *Li Chi*, bks. iii, iv.
[2] *Li Chi*, bk. III, sec. ii, 13–18.

the governed. This theory is based upon several logical grounds. First, the government should exist by the consent of the governed because God creates government solely for the benefit of the governed, and their wish is the wish of God. They know better than others how to take care of themselves, to ascertain their own needs, and to fulfil their own desires. Thus, their consent to the government is the consent of God, and by the consent of God the government is made lawful or constitutional. Any government which does not possess the consent of the governed is illegal, and contrary to the standards of rectification. Therefore, the *Great Learning* declares that : " By winning the support of the people, the kingdom is won ; by losing the support of the people, the kingdom is lost.[1] That is, the length of the existence of a particular government depends upon the consent and the support of the people.

The second logical ground of maintaining that government should be by the consent of the governed is based upon the moral attainment and common consciousness of the people. Ch'êng T'ang, of the Yin dynasty (1766–1122 B.C.), the first successful revolutionist in China, declared that the "Great God has conferred on the common people a moral sense, compliance with which would show their nature invariably right ".[2] In the *Book of Poetry* the same view is expressed : " Heaven, in giving birth to the multitude of the people, annexed its law to every faculty and relationship. The people possess this normal nature and they love normal virtue." [3]

Referring to the fact that the common consciousness of the people is the making or unmaking of their

---

[1] Commentaries, ch. x, sec. 5.
[2] Pt. iv, bk. iii, sec. 2.
[3] Bk. iii (*Ta Ya*), Decade III, ode 6 (*Chêng Min*).

leadership or their modelship, *Shu Ching* observes that: "There is no absolute model of virtue; a supreme regard for what is good makes a model for it. There is no absolute characteristic as to what is good which is to be supremely regarded; it is found where there is conformity with the common consciousness as to what is good".[1] The "model of virtue" is the essence of being a minister of heaven and of becoming a king, and it is judged solely by the people themselves. If the common consciousness is in favour of a man becoming the leader of the people, he is made king, and if it is against him, he is helpless.

Mencius interprets this in a very concrete way. When the king of the State of Ch'i asked Mencius whether he should annex the State of Yen, Mencius replied: "If the people of Yen will be pleased at your taking possession of their country, you may do so. . . . If the people of Yen will not be pleased at your taking possession of their country, you should not do so."[2] In other words, the annexation of a conquered State should require the consent of the people of that State. Similar principle is, of course, applied to all governments.

On another occasion King Hsiang of Liang asked Mencius how the nation could be settled. He replied that it would be settled by uniting all feudal States under a centralized rule. The king asked how the empire could be united. Mencius answered that when a ruler practices benevolent politics, all the people of the empire will unitedly and unanimously give the empire to him.[3] The essence of this conversation is that the people are the bestowers of the empire; it interprets very clearly the Confucian doctrine of government by the consent of the governed.

---

[1] Pt. iv, bk. vi. [2] *Mencius*, bk. i, pt. i, ch. x.
[3] *Mencius*, bk. I, pt. i, ch. vi.

How can one win the consent of the people ? Confucius replied, by winning the confidence of the people. Confucius pointed out sufficiency of food, sufficiency of military equipment, and the confidence of the people in their ruler as the requisites of government. Confucius further remarked that if it could not be helped, the military equipment and food might be dispensed with, but that no nation could enjoy peace and prosperity without the confidence of the people in their government.[1] On another occasion Confucius pointed out the respect for people's business, sincerity, economy in government, love of the people, and proper taxation as essentials of running a successful government.[2] In other words, these five factors—respect, sincerity, economy, love of the people, and proper taxation, are the means of securing the confidence of the people, and are the ways to *jên chêng* or " benevolent politics ".

The *Great Learning* explains further : " When one loves what the people love, and hates what the people hate ", the hearts of the people will be won. On the other hand, " When a ruler likes those whom the mass dislikes, and dislikes those whom the mass likes, he naturally outrages the feelings of the mass. Calamities will prevail."[3] In saying this, it does not mean that the government should follow whatever the people desire, whether good or bad. The statement refers only to desires and wishes flowing from the original nature of man, which is perfectly good. This, again, goes back to the Confucian principle that government must be based upon natural laws. In fact, if the people are bad and devoid of the goodness of nature, it is the duty of the government to rectify them and develop their original nature to the fullest extent.

[1] *Analects*, bk. xii, ch. vii.   [2] *Analects*, bk. i, ch. v.
[3] Ch. x, sec. iii, xvii.

On the other hand, Confucius pointed out the fact that public opinion is not always right in saying: "When the multitude hate a man, it is necessary to examine into the case. When the multitude like a man, it is necessary to examine into the case." [1]

The Theory of Revolution

The third principle of political democracy derived from the doctrine of stewardship is the theory of revolution. God creates government for the welfare of the people. If the government is selfish and tyrannical, causing distress and suffering among the people, it is against the will of God and is guilty before Him. If a ruler is repeatedly bad, his appointment from God to govern will be forfeited, and he will be liable to punishment from God. Thus *Shu Ching* declares that "By accumulating hatred among the people, he banishes himself from God".[2]

There is a question as to when a revolution by force is justifiable. The Classics clearly suggest that a revolution by force should take place only as a last resort to improve political conditions and after all peaceful means have been tried out. The peaceful methods of making improvements consist of various forms of remonstrations with the ruler. *Li Chi* says that the "Ministers and officers should remonstrate with their ruler, but not speak ill of him. If the ruler were idle and inefficient, they should energise him. If the government is going to wreck, they should reorganize it.[3] The people have equal right with the ministers and other officers to remonstrate with the government by means of folksongs, poems, and lyrics, to which the government should pay the utmost attention.

[1] *Analects*, bk. xv, ch. xxvii.   [2] Pt. v, bk. i, sec. iii.
[3] Bk. xv, 21.

When all peaceful methods have failed to rectify the wrongdoing of the government, one who has the qualifications of a "minister of heaven" may undertake to reorganize the government by arms. According to the *Shu Ching* and the *Spring and Autumn*, a revolution would be justified in the face of these five conditions : (1) the existence at the head of the government of a tyrant whom peaceful methods have failed to reform or remove ; (2) a demand by all the people in the empire for a political change as a means of their salvation ; (3) the possession of superior virtue and wisdom on the part of the revolutionary leader, with all the people regarding him as their moral and political leader ; (4) the evident existence of unselfish motives on the part of the revolutionists ; (5) a promise that the new government will carry out benevolent politics.[1]

The Classics repeatedly declare that to take up arms against a tyrannical rule is not a rebellion but a deed carrying out the will of God ; that to kill a tyrant is not murder, but a blessing to the people ; and that to instigate revolution against a tyrant is not the right of some privileged class, but the duty of the virtuous and wise leaders of the masses.[2] Five hundred and seventy-one years before Confucius, Chou Wu Wang executed the emperor Chou and put his head on the top of a flag. Confucius did not regard the action of Wu Wang as a rebellion, but praised Wu Wang as a sage. Mencius interprets this instance of Chou as follows : having lost the commission of God by his misdeeds, Chou was not a sovereign but an outcast ; his death was a penalty of God inflicted through the anger of the people and at the hands of the revolutionists.[3] To emphasize the advantages of political

---

[1] See *Shu Ching*, pt. iv, bks. i, ii ; pt. v, bks. i, ii, xiii.
[2] *Shu Ching*, pt. iv, bks. i, ii ; pt. v, bks. i. ii.
[3] *Mencius*, bk. i, pt. ii, ch. viii.

Democracy and Representation

revolution, a chapter in the *Book of Change* is devoted to "Revolution". Here it says that "Heaven and earth are revolutionary, so that the four seasons complete their functions. The revolutions of T'ang and of Wu were in accordance with the will of God, and in response to the wishes of men. Great, indeed is that which takes place in a time of revolution."[1] In other words, revolution is in complete harmony with the laws of nature. It prevents tyranny on the one hand, and stimulates the vitality of the people on the other. Revolution, therefore, is a social blessing.

Liberty, Equality, and Equity

The fourth rule of political democracy, namely, that government should operate for the benefit of the governed, has been discussed in detail in the chapters dealing with the "Principles of Benevolent Government" and the "Government of *Li*". The fifth rule is concerned with liberty, equality, and equity. Here the theory is that all men are children of God, and are equal in the eyes of God. Thus, the *Analects* says, "Within Four Seas all are brethren".[2] Since partisanship and favouritism are contrary to the spirit of equity and equality, they are condemned by Confucius. He declares: "The virtuous man is impartial, not partisan; the unvirtuous is partisan, not impartial."[3] Again: "The virtuous man is proud but not quarrelsome; he is sociable, but belongs to no party."[4] Here Confucius condemns party politics in the sense it introduces the "class" spirit or "gang" spirit. On the other hand, he does not ignore the necessity of modern party government

---

[1] *T'uan Chuan*, pt. ii, hex. xlix. [2] *Analects*, bk. xii, ch. v.
[3] *Analects*, bk. ii, ch. xiv. [4] *Analects*, bk. xv, ch. xxi.

where a group of people having similar principles work together for the interest of the nation. He says: " Men of totally different principles can never act together." [1]

Confucius warns that the danger of a nation lies not in want of wealth and man, but in inequality of distributing wealth and rights of men.[2] The *Li Chi* upholds that the State is a public property and belongs to all men.[3] In other words, all members of the State should have equal political rights in the ideal State.[4] Thus Confucius maintains that in education there should be no recognition of class because education builds the road to political progress, the first step toward democracy.[5] For similar reasons Confucius and his disciples deplore hereditary monarchy and hereditary nobility. *Li Chi* declares that the existence of hereditary monarchy is a sign of political degeneration, and that hereditary nobility did not exist during the ancient ideal days.[6]

Confucius and his disciples are undoubtedly favourably disposed toward democracy, although the benevolent government of Confucius is monarchical in form. Each of the four parts of the *Book of Poetry* begins with King Wên who represents the type of constitutional monarchy. The *Shu Ching* begins with Yao and Shun, who represents the type of elective monarchy. The *Spring and Autumn* begins with King Wên and ends with Yao and Shun. This would seem to indicate that the ideal government should be a democracy in fact, irrespective of its monarchical or republican form.

Public pleasure should be democratized. That the people should be allowed to participate in the

---

[1] *Analects*, bk. xv, ch. xxxix.   [2] *Analects*, bk. xvi, ch. i.
[3] See *Li Chi*, bk. vii.   [4] *Vide infra*, ch. xii.
[5] *Analects*, bk. xv, ch. xxxviii.
[6] Bk. vii, sec. 1, 3; bk. ix. sec. 3, 5.

pleasures of a ruler, and that a ruler must not seek enjoyment alone run through the *Book of Poetry*. Mencius interprets the latter as this : " The ancient kings shared their pleasure with the people, and so they could have pleasure." Furthermore, Mencius points out that, even though a ruler has parks and luxuries, he will not be able to enjoy them if he is at variance with the people.[1]

Equality and equity go together. As already said, public administration should be conducted upon the idea that the State belongs to everybody, and that no one has special claim to a favoured object. One should follow the example of heaven and earth, which are equally good to all. One should possess the virtue of the large mountain which treats all hunters and miners equally without special favour. Thus the State should endeavour to add to those who are deficient and to deplete those who have over-abundance. One should maintain the " level balance " of things. For instance, in a society, the wealthy people should be heavily taxed and the poor should be liberally aided.[2]

It is also in the idea of equity that one should respect even the poorest and the meanest in the society, and should stand unyielding and graceful even before the highest and noblest man of the nation. " Unyielding " refers to holding firm to one's principles ; " graceful " refers to the maintenance of a respectful manner and the absence of flattery and self-laudation ; and the " noblest and highest " refers to the sovereign or prince, or to a powerful master.[3]

The Confucian School does not advocate slavery. In enumerating the six classes of people in the State— namely, kings and princes, scholars and great officials,

[1] *Mencius*, bk. i, pt. i, ch. ii.
[2] *Book of Change, Hsiang Chuan*, pt. i, hex. xv ; pt. ii, hex. li.
[3] *Shu Ching*, pt. v, bk. iv.

artisans, farmers, merchants, and working women—no mention is made of a slave class. According to the Confucian system of social organization, all the manual work should be done in the family by the children; in society, by young men; in the government, by the government employees. There is no need for slaves. Confucius himself, for example, had no slave. The drivers of his carriage were his pupils; and he said that for himself he would "take up driving as a profession". The idea is that everyone should learn the duties of a servant and thus serve himself.[1]

Confucian ideas concerning the political status of woman are not always consistent. Throughout the Classics, there is expressed the general attitude that women should be submissive to man and that the dominance of woman is an abnormal social phenomena. In the *Spring and Autumn*, political control by woman and the attendance of international conferences by woman are condemned.[2] At the same time, women may become government officials. Under the *ching t'ien* system, those women who have no children at the age of fifty should be supported by the government; and they may be appointed commissioners for the gathering of poetry from the people during the spring.[3]

Personal liberty is emphasized by Confucius. Since man is the noblest of the creations of God, his body and his property should not be violated without proper authority. For this reason judicial administration, which concerns the life and property of the people, should be conducted upon a "three references" system and with extraordinary care.[4]

---

[1] *Analects*, bk. x, ch. ii.   [2] Chs. iii, v, vii, viii.
[3] *Spring and Autumn*, ch. vii (fifteenth year).
[4] *Vide supra*, ch. viii.

Democracy and Representation

In the *Li Chi*, freedom of speech, freedom of movement, and freedom of occupation are mentioned.[1]

Local Self-Government

Local self-government is the foundation of democracy. "When I study the rural government," Confucius remarks, "I see the easiest road to benevolent politics."[2] To this point, Mencius interprets that local self-government is to be found in the *ching t'ien* system of Confucius, saying :—" The first thing towards a benevolent government is to lay down the boundaries in order to divide land into equal squares. ... In country districts observe the nine-square division and reserve one division to be cultivated on the system of mutual aid. In the central parts of the State, make the people pay for themselves a tenth part of their produce. From the highest officers down to the lowest, each one must have his holy field, consisting of fifty *mu*. Let the supernumerary males have their twenty-five *mu*. There will be no desertion of fields even on occasions of death or removal. People of the same neighbourhood (*ching*) render friendly assistance to one another in watching the field and in sickness. Thus the people are brought to live in affection and harmony."[3]

The Confucianists of the Han dynasty goes further to interpret the Confucian system of local government as follows :

" If there is want of food and clothing, even Yao and Shun will not be able to stop theft. If there is the inequality between rich and poor, even Chief

---

[1] *Li Chi*, bks. iii, iv.
[2] *Li Chi*, bk. xlii. Confucius personally was very fond of rural life, and was very attentive to the etiquette in rural communities. See *Analects*, bk. x, chs. i, x.
[3] *Mencius*, bk. iii, pt. i, ch. iii, sec. 13–18.

Justice Kao Yao will not be able to end the oppression of the weak by the more powerful. Thus the ancient sages invented the *Ching t'ien* system by means of which every individual is given an equal amount of property.

"According to this system, every married couple receives from the government one hundred *mu* of land. Each family is composed of five individuals. The unit of local government in the country is *lü* or " village ", and in town the *li* or " neighbourhood ". Each village or neighbourhood consists of eighty families. In the village, the people elect an old and virtuous man called *fu lao* or " patriarch " ; and an eloquent, energetic man called *li cheng* or " justice ". They are entitled to double amount of land and to ride on horseback. They receive a certain official rank from the central government.

"During spring and summer all of the people work in the field. During autumn and winter they come to town. While they work in the field in the morning and evening the patriarch and the justice, as overseers, sit in the houses which are on the two sides of the gate of the village. Those who go out too late are not allowed to go out ; and those who do not bring fuel back are not allowed to come in.

"When farming is finished, people live in town. They do weaving, handicrafts of all kinds, or engage in literary labour. . . . Men and women sing together to express their discontentment. Those who are hungry sing for food ; and those who are tired sing for rest.

"When men have reached sixty or women reached fifty without child, they are supported by the central government ; and are sent to the villages to gather poems from common people. These poems will be handed to the village officials, then to the town officials, to the officials of the central government ; and finally to the Emperor. Thus the Emperor understands the sentiment of the people throughout the nation without going out of his door.

"After the tenth month, the patriarch takes up instructional duties in the village school. Children reaching eight years of age are sent to the grammar schools and fifteen years of age to the high schools. The most intelligent students are transferred to colleges from these village schools.

"According to this system, there is one year's saving out of three years of work; and three years of saving out of nine years of work. After thirty years of work there will be ten years of saving. When they have ten years of savings, the people will be freed from any possible danger of flood, drought or famine. Everybody in the Empire will be happy and prosperous. In this way the *ching t'ien* system brings joy to the land."[1]

The idea that the patriarch and the justice must receive an official rank from the central government although they come to office by popular election has political significance; as this is an illustration of the concept of sovereignty of the Confucian School. According to Confucian political philosophy, although the people should have ultimate control of State affairs, there must be a unit, a system, and an organization in the State. The State in which everybody is his own master, managing his own affairs, judging his own own actions, doing whatever he wishes, and owing obedience to no law and authority, would soon fall into a hopeless anarchy.

In order to compromise individual liberty and political integration, Confucius and his disciples advocate a unitary source of sovereign power on the one hand, and the theories of political democracy on the other hand. While the people should obey

[1] *Kung-yang's Commentary*, fifteenth year of Duke Hsuan. Ho's Commentary.

the government, the government should obey public opinion. At one time Confucius declares that the duty of the government is to teach, to rectify, and to nourish the mass of people; at another time he indicates that the people possess perfect moral faculties, knowing what is best for them. In the matter of village government, the people should elect their local officers, conduct their local affairs, be the masters of their own business. At the same time, these local officers—the patriarch and the justice . . . should receive an official rank from the central government. By such official rank, the central government gives its approval to the people's action.

In this case the theory of local self-government as suggested above is in complete harmony with the Confucian theory of unitary sovereignty or monarchism, namely, the king should be the sole source of political authority. Otherwise, if the people may elect anybody without being subject to the approval of the central government, and if anybody other than the king can legally confer upon another person certain political power, the result will be anything but order, unity, and organization in the State. The entire procedure may be a matter of form or of name; but it is nevertheless important. The doctrine of rectification holds that "if the name is not correct, the language will be confused. If the language be confused, the business of the people cannot be carried on successfully. If the business of the people cannot be carried on successfully, *li* and *yüeh* will not flourish. If *li* and *yüeh* do not flourish, law and justice will not conform to the mean. If law and justice do not conform to the mean, the people will suffer from confusion and anarchy."

Therefore, these elective local officers should be subject to the approval of the central government. They should receive no salary from the government, but they should be entitled to a double share of land and to ride on horseback. The patriarch should be the head of the village; his political status should be that of the king or the father of the village, that is, the parent of the people in the village. Therefore, he should be old, virtuous, and respected. The justice should take care of the administrative duties in the village; and he should literally be the prime minister of the patriarch. Thus, he should be eloquent, wise, and energetic.

The Theory of Educational Representation

The system of local government referred to above is closely connected with the system of education. As already pointed out, Confucius believes that good men are essential to a good government; and that the way to train good men is by a system of universal free education.[1] According to Confucius, there should be no distinction of classes in education; nor should there be any preaching of dogmas.[2] Confucius urges repeatedly that in government virtuous and trained men should be employed; but he never mentions nobles or rich people in connection with public service. In other words, he recognizes no property qualifications, nor special privileged class, nor racial or social discriminations in office. Besides the test of education which includes both conduct and knowledge, equal opportunities in political work should be provided for all. He advises the rulers of his time that good men be elected and their good work be rewarded and that bad people be dismissed.[3]

The *Li Chi* records the Confucian system of education and election as this: There are five grades of

---

[1] See *Analects*, bk. xix, ch. xxii; *Chung Yung*, ch. xx.
[2] *Analects*, bk. xv, ch. xxx; bk. xviii, ch. viii.
[3] *Analects*, bk. ii, ch. xix.

schools; the local school, the district school, the provincial college, the national academy, and the imperial university. The best students of the local school are elected and transferred to the district school; the best of the district school, receiving the degree of " select scholar ", are elected and transferred to the provincial college; and the best of the provincial college, receiving the degree of " eminent scholar " are elected and transferred to the national academy. Every three years the feudal princes send the best students from their national academies to the emperor and allow them to study at the imperial university. The best students of the imperial university are called " complete scholars ". If in their conduct and capacity they are equally well qualified, they are distinguished by " archery ". On that occasion the successful students receive the official title " advance scholar " or " scholar ready for employment ". In this way the students will promote themselves by their capacities; and the emperor will appoint the officials by an examination of their merits.

After the officials have come into office, there is also an examination of their merits every three years. The examination is based entirely on the service of the officials and the success of such service in improving the moral, intellectual, economic, and social conditions of the people. After three examinations, officials are either degraded or promoted. The examinations are based not merely upon popular sentiment, but more upon an investigation of facts.[1] This system of educational election has representative features. In the first place, the students are elected without regard to class, sex, or racial distinctions. They come from every locality and every class of the people. Being the best in their respective locality or class these

[1] *Li Chi*, bk. III, sec. iv, 3–7; bk. XLIII; *Kung-yang's Commentary*, third year of Duke Yin.

students best represent the interests of their class or family, but upon recognition of his virtue and ability, he may be employed in the position of prime minister. Upon entering the government service, he has ample opportunities to practise his policies.

There was no aristocracy in education. The *Li Chi* declares that " even the oldest son of the emperor by his legitimate queen is only an ordinary student ".[1] According to " Royal Regulation ", the sons of the emperor, the princes, and the officials should study at the same university with the students chosen from among the common people ; and they should be divided into classes not by ranks but by ages.[2] This system is extremely sane and democratic. When the government institutions are filled with students so elected, they would be really administered by the direct representatives of the common people. In the elections held in schools the common people should be allowed to participate in the choice of the best scholars. Although there is no popular vote, the selection would not be far from an expression of popular sentiment. Moreover, the students come from different political divisions, and although there is no legal responsibility to their native localities, there would be moral and social responsibility, which is really stronger than legal responsibility. In fact, in Chinese society, until recently, scholars were generally regarded by the people of their locality as their representatives in the public affairs. This was a practical illustration of the influence of Confucian teachings.

Summary

From the Confucian doctrine of stewardship, namely, that the king is an ordinary person selected

---

[1] Bk. ix, sec. iii, 5. [2] *Li Chi*, bk. iii, sec. iv, 4–5.

by God upon his merit to serve as a steward of God in the control of the affairs of the people for the welfare of the people, there are deduced five theories of political democracy. In the first place, the government must respect public opinion. The will of the people is the will of God, and thus the king should obey both the will of the people and the will of God. Confucius declares that public opinion is powerful and dangerous : it could make and unmake a dynasty. There are four ways of ascertaining public opinion : by listening to the advice of ministers, by collecting popular poetry and folksongs, by sending out official inspectors to different places, and by the personal tours of the king throughout the country.

In the second place, government should be based upon the consent of the governed. This is because people know better than the government how to take care of themselves, and the judgment of common consciousness is usually better than the idea of a single man. The way to get the consent of the people is to win their hearts ; and the way to win their hearts is to practise the principles of benevolent government.

In the third place, the people have a duty as well as a right to carry on revolution as the last resort in stopping tyranny. Peaceful methods and remonstrations with the rulers should precede political change by force. Revolution is regarded as a social blessing ; it guards against tyranny and promotes the vitality of the people. It is in complete harmony with the natural law.

In the fourth place, the government exists for the welfare of the people.

In the fifth place, liberty, equality, and equity should be preserved. The State belongs equally to all ; and so hereditary nobility, hereditary monarchy, and despotism are deplored. Confucius and his disciples seem to advocate a democracy under the form of an elective monarchy or constitutional monarchy. The people should share the pleasures of a ruler. The State should maintain a division of labour ; and all classes of working people, including the king himself, should be equal.

Equity, in Confucian philosophy, condemns favouritism, partisanship, and selfishness in administration. The government should help the insufficient and deplete the abundant in order to maintain the " level of balance ". The poorest people in the State should be respected, and the noblest people should not be flattered. Slavery has no place in the Confucian system. Women are denied social privileges on the one hand and granted political rights on the other, according to the existing conditions.

Local self-government is recognized in the Confucian system of government. In the village the people may elect their own officers, who should be approved by the central government. The Confucian theory of educational election suggests the distinctly new idea of representation. Under this system, students from all localities and all classes should be promoted from a lower educational institution to a higher educational institution, then to a government post, and finally controlling government affairs and exercising legislative and administrative power.

CHAPTER X

THE DOCTRINE OF CHUNG YUNG

The Definition of *Chung Yung* : The psychological aspect of political control—The essential qualities of *Chung Yung*—Contribution of the book to political philosophy—The *hsing*, the *tao*, and the *chiao*—*Ch'êng* as the object of education.

The nature of *Chung Yung* : As the ideal of human actions—Its potential influence—The three virtues of *Chung Yung*.

The practical principles of *Chung Yung* in government : (1) Control of men over men ; (2) Reciprocal sympathy and mutual faith ; (3) Concord of word and action ; (4) Observation of surrounding conditions ; (5) Religion and filial piety to supplement political control ; (6) A Methodology in the art of government—The nine standard rules of successful administration—Six principles of international ethics.

Ch'êng as the fundamental of good government: The vast importance of natural sincerity—*Ch'êng* as a factor of socialization—The three principles of social happiness—The outcome of perfect man's rule.

Summary.

The Definition of Chung Yung

The Book of *Chung Yung*, one of the " Four Books," is a volume on social psychology and human nature produced by the early school of Confucian thought. " This work," says Ch'êng I (1033–1108), in his *Commentaries to the Chung Yung*, contains the law of the mind, which was handed down by Confucius from one to another, in the Confucian School, till Tzŭ Ssŭ, fearing that in the course of time errors should arise about it, committed it to writing, and delivered it to Mencius. The first book speaks of one principle, it next spreads this out and embraces all things; finally it returns and gathers them all up under the one principle." That the book was written by the grandson of the sage has no basis; and scholars of the " Higher Criticism " disagree as to the time the book was written. Some contend that this book was written before the time of Mencius; others are of the opinion that it was written after Mencius.

There is, too, no agreement among Orientalists as to the definition of the words *Chung Yung*. Dr. James Legge translated the title of the book, *Chung Yung*, into English as the " Doctrine of the Mean ". But this does not express exactly the meaning of the Chinese term. *Chung* means something more than the " mean " in English language. Indeed, ordinarily *chung* signifies " middle ". But in the book of *Chung Yung* it means a condition in which " all the feelings and emotions such as pleasure, anger, sorrow, or joy are not stirred ", but are hidden in the individual as his innateness or nature. This suggests the idea, advocated by many modern sociologists and social psychologists, that man as an organism was born with a bundle of tendencies. Modern scholars maintain that these tendencies are not organized but exist at random. As soon as the child was born, he was ready to respond or to react at random to external stimuli or environment. The book of *Chung Yung* seems to have advanced a different theory on this point. It seems to maintain that these innate tendencies in man are organized in a naturally perfect order without any conflict. Such a state of innate order may be termed as the *chung*. The *chung* is "the great root from which all human actions spring forth".[1]

As soon as the individual comes into contact with external things, his feelings such as pleasure, anger, sorrow, or joy are aroused, and the innate order is consequently disturbed. "When these feelings have been stirred and they act in their due degree," a state of harmony exists between the individual and society. Such a condition of social harmony may be called the *Yung*. The *yung* is "the universal path which all people should pursue".[2] *Chung* is a static term, while *yung* is a dynamic one.

Chung Yung has certain essential qualities. In the state of innate order the quality of equilibrium or balance is essential. It signifies the centre of gravity of individual feelings. For example, here is a stick. One should "determine its mean by measuring the two ends". When held at either end the stick is not in a state of balance; hence it is liable to drop down. In the language of the *Chung Yung* the innateness of the stick is not at balance. The mean of the stick is its centre of gravity; and to hold its mean puts the stick in the firmest situation, in which it will not fall. Feelings of an individual unacted upon are in a state of equilibrium or mutual balance. This state of mutual balance presents the undisturbed order, the innate order.

In the state of social harmony the quality of concord or of organization is important. Feelings when disturbed must act in due degree, so that one feeling will not be in conflict with another. This concord of outward actions is a result of holding the mutual balance of individual feelings, or concretely the mean of all circumstances.

Finally, "let the state of equilibrium and concord exist in perfection and a happy order will prevail

[1] *Chung Yung*, ch. i, sec. 4.   [2] *Chung Yung*, ch. i, sec. 4.

in the universe and all things will be nourished and will flourish." In other words, when the feelings are duly utilized, the state of equilibrium and concord exists. Hence, world peace and cosmic order will result. Men in particular and things, animate and inanimate, in general will act within the right path of development according to their proper positions. Out of such peace and order, social progress results.[1]

The fundamental contribution of the book of *Chung Yung* to social and political philosophy may be briefly stated. Society is composed of the interrelated outward feelings of associated individuals. Political rulers and social administrators, whose ultimate aim is to render social goodness or service, should recognize the factor of individual feeling and social harmony. Thus, they should understand the relation of the innate feelings of the individual and his actions growing out of these feelings. They should comprehend the doctrine of innate order and social harmony which is the guiding principle in public administration. They should endeavour to regulate the feelings of the people. That is, they should cultivate the psychology of the people. This doctrine is elaborated in detail into thirty-two chapters in the book of *Chung Yung*.

These thirty-two chapters begin with the statement, " What God has endowed is called the nature or *hsing* ; accordance with nature is called the path of reason or *tao* ; and the cultivation of the path of reason is called education or *chiao*.[2] In other words, cosmically God has created the universe in which things, animate or inanimate, such as sun, moon, stars, clouds, lightnings, minerals, plants, animals, human beings, mountains, rivers, and all other natural things are arranged in order and work together

[1] *Chung Yung*, ch. i, sec. 1–4 ; ch. vi.
[2] *Chung Yung*, ch. i, sec. 1.

harmoniously. This orderly arrangement of cosmic things is called nature; and harmonious working together in accordance with natural order is said to have pursued the right path, the path of reason. It is through education that we try to comprehend nature and to cultivate the path of reason.[1]

Each human being is a small cosmos. He is endowed by God with a moral nature, in which the state of innate order or of *chung* exists. When he comes into contact with society, he must act in such a way as to insure social harmony; that is, he must act naturally. If he acts in such a way, he pursues the path of reason. The aim of education is to interpret the state of nature so that the individual can look upon it as the guide or the ideal of his actions; consequently he will discover the right way to act, which is called the path of reason.

The state of nature is the truth. The interpretation of truth is called *ch'êng*, which may be translated into English as "sincerity". The understanding of the state of nature and the path of reason is called *ming*, which may be translated as "intelligence". God possesses the quality of sincerity in Himself, while man has to acquire it through education.[2] "When we have intelligence resulting from sincerity," quoted the *Chung Yung*, "this condition is to be ascribed to nature; when we have sincerity resulting from intelligence, this condition is to be ascribed to education."[3]

Thus the entire book of *Chung Yung* may be said to be devoted to three things: first, the nature of *chung yung*; second, the practical principles of *chung yung*; and third, *ch'êng*, or interpretation of truth as the fundamental of good government and universal happiness.

[1] *Chung Yung*, ch. xxvi.   [2] *Chung Yung*, ch. xx, sec. 18.
[3] *Chung Yung*, ch. xxi.

Doctrine of Chung Yung

The Nature of *Chung Yung*

Chung Yung is the ideal of human actions. The course leading to this ideal is the path of reason. One who acts toward this *chung yung* is a virtuous man. One who acts contrary to it is a mean man. The virtuous man knows the principle of evolution and the path of reason. He is always careful to be on the path of reason, and he dares not leave this path for an instant. He is cautious about what is unseen and unheard. The thing unseen and unheard is the will of God. The will of God is that the good and virtuous men should be honoured and profited and the bad and evil ones should be punished and destroyed. The mean or unworthy man does not understand nature, nor the path of reason, nor the general course of social development. He does not understand God, and has nothing to fear. He is without caution. Thus he acts contrary to *chung yung*.[1]

The course toward *chung yung* seems to be a difficult one. The *Chung Yung* declares that "it is possible to govern a state with perfect justice. It is possible for a poor officer to give up voluntarily his position and emolument. It is possible for a cowardly person to risk for a cause the blade of a sharpened sword. But it seems to be almost impossible to attain the course toward *chung yung*".[2] Again it says: "Perfect is the virtue which is according to *chung yung*! Rarely have they long been among the people, who could practise it!"[3]

According to the *Chung Yung*, the path of reason which leads to *chung yung* is not far from man.[4] It is a common course for everybody, for poor as well

---

[1] *Chung Yung*, chs. i and ii. [2] *Chung Yung*, ch. ix.
[3] *Chung Yung*, ch. iii; *Analects*, bk. vi, ch. xxvii.
[4] *Chung Yung*, ch. xiii.

as for rich, for common people as well as for nobles, for unintelligent as well as for intelligent.[1] It is but common sense.

Why then is the path of reason not understood by the people? Why do the people not walk in the path of reason? It is simply because the man of talent goes beyond the proper degree; and the inferior man does not come up to it. Thus, the virtue of *chung yung* is not practised. Again, the intelligent man knows more than common sense, hence he does not care to study it; while the stupid one does not know enough about it, and is therefore lacking in knowledge. And so the path of reason is not properly understood. For example, every man possesses feelings. Pleasure, anger, sorrow, and joy are common to all people; but very few people experience them in a proper degree. Everybody eats and drinks; yet very few people could eat and drink to the proper amount. Some eat or drink too much, and others not enough.[2] So easy is it to eat and drink, that one scarcely achieves the mean.

The influence of *Chung Yung* reaches far and wide. " Common men and women, however ignored in human affairs, may intermeddle with the knowledge of it; yet in its utmost reaches, there is that which even the sage does not know. Common men and women, however mean in character, can carry it into practice; yet in its utmost reaches, there is that which even the sage is not able to carry into practice. Great as heaven and earth are, men still find some things in them with which to be dissatisfied. Thus, on the one hand, the doctrine is so great that nothing would be found able to embrace it; and on the other hand, it is so minute that nothing would be able to split it . . . The path of reason may be found, in its simple elements, in the intercourse of common

---

[1] *Chung Yung*, chs xii.   [2] *Chung Yung*, chs. i and iv.

men and women; but in its utmost reaches, it shines brightly through the great universe."[1]

Chung Yung may be achieved through three virtues, namely, wisdom, love, and courage.[2] If one of these virtues be absent, there is no way of advancing to the path of reason and perfecting the work of *chung yung*. Three concrete examples illustrating the three virtues were given in the persons of Shun, Yen Hui, and Chi-lu.[3] The *Chung Yung* says: "There was Shun. He indeed was greatly wise! Shun loved to interrogate others, and to study their words, though they might be shallow. He concealed what was bad in others' conduct, and displayed what was good. He examined the two extremes in matters and opinions, and determined the mean and employed it in his government of the people. It was by this that he was Shun."[4]

Speaking of Yen Hui: "This was the virtue of Hui. He was in the course of *chung yung*! Whenever he found what was good, he was constantly cautious not to deviate from it."[5]

Lastly, the *Chung Yung* quotes a conversation between Confucius and Tzŭ-lu, illustrating the best quality of courage.

Tzŭ-lu asked about courage. Confucius replied: "Do you mean the courage of the south, the courage of the north, or the courage of which you should cultivate yourself?

"To show forbearance and gentleness in teaching others, and not to avenge unreasonable insults—this is the courage of the southern regions, and the gentleman cultivating such a character. To lie under arms and die without regret—this is the courage of

---

[1] *Chung Yung*, ch. xii.   [2] *Chih, Jên*, and *Yung*.
[3] Shun was a sage ruler of ancient China; Yen Hui and Chi-lu were disciples of Confucius.
[4] *Chung Yung*, ch. vi.   [5] *Chung Yung*, ch. viii.

the northern regions, and the rude man cultivating such a character.

"But the virtuous man pursues a different way in cultivating courage. He cultivates a friendly harmony with others, without being weak in mind. How courageous he is! He uses the mean of two extremes, without inclining to either side. How courageous he is! When good government exists, he carries out his fundamental principles without leaning to others. How courageous he is! When bad government dominates, he pursues on the path of reason until death without changing. How courageous he is!"[1]

The Practical Principles of *Chung Yung* in Government

Confucius and his disciples, in fact, all Confucianists regarded government as the greatest institution to cultivate the virtue of the people and to promote universal happiness. Thus, the government is the principal place where the practical principles of *chung yung* are applied. The first principle, according to the *Chung Yung*, is that government is the control of man over man. Through it better men should help the inferior by means of authoritative control, universal education, and material nourishment. Thus the governing man should possess superior virtues as he is the leader, the shepherd, the guide, or the example of the masses. On the other hand the masses should be governed according to their nature and what is proper for them.[2]

In order to attain *chung yung* in government, reciprocal sympathy and mutual faith must exist between ruler and ruled. This is the second practical

[1] *Chung Yung*, ch. x. [2] *Chung Yung*, chs. xiii, xx.

principle of *chung yung*. It may be stated briefly in its two interpretations—negative and positive. Negatively, what you do not like to do to yourself, do not do to others. This principle may serve the rulers as a guide to their actions. " I must not do anything to the people that I do not like to do to myself as a commoner." Positively, you must do to others, as you would require others to do to you. Thus, you should serve your father as you would require your son to serve you ; you should serve your monarch as you would require your subordinate to serve you ; you should serve your older brother as you would require your younger brother to serve you : and so on through all social and political relationships.[1]

The third practical principle of *chung yung* in government is that there should be concord of word and action. A ruler carries out what he has said, and say only what he has done. Thus he must be particularly careful to maintain the truth in action and conversation. If in his action there is anything defective, he should exert himself. If in his words there is any excess, he should not allow himself license.[2]

The fourth principle of *chung yung* in government is that the ruler should act properly according to the conditions of the situation in which he finds himself : he should not change the condition of his situation to suit his own principles. The latter would never work well. Point out an example of the virtuous man, it was said : " In a position of wealth and honour, the virtuous man does what is proper to a position of wealth and honour. In a poor and low position, he does what is proper to a poor and low position. Situated among barbarous tribes, he does what is proper to a situation among barbarous tribes. In

[1] *Chung Yung*, ch. xiii.   [2] *Chung Yung*, ch. xiii.

a position of sorrow and difficulty, he does what is proper to a situation of sorrow and difficulty. The virtuous man can find himself in no situation in which he is not himself.

"In a high position, he should not treat his subordinates contemptuously. In a low situation, he should not court the favour of his superiors. He should keep himself in his proper place, and seek nothing from others. Thus, he has no complaints against the environment. He does not murmur against God, nor grumble against man.

"Therefore he is quiet and calm, waiting for the appointments of God; while the mean man walks in the dangerous paths, looking for lucky occurrences." [1]

The fifth principle of *chung yung* in government is that a proper knowledge and practice of the duties of religion and filial piety would amply equip a ruler for all the duties of his government. In this connection, many concrete instances, such as the work of Shun, King Wên, King Wu, and that of the Duke of Chou were pointed out.[2] Speaking of King Wu and of the Duke of Chou, the *Chung Yung* says: "How far-extending was the filial piety of King Wu and the Duke of Chou? Filial piety is seen in the skilful carrying out of the wishes of their forefathers, and the skilful carrying forward of their undertakings ... By means of the ceremonies of the ancestral temple, they distinguished the royal kindred according to their order of descent. By ordering the parties present according to their rank, they distinguished the more noble and the less. By the arrangement of the services, they made a distinction of talents and worth. In the ceremony of general pledging, the inferiors presented the cup to their superiors, and something was given the lowest to

[1] *Chung Yung*, ch. xiv.
[2] They all were sage rulers in ancient China.

do. At the concluding feast the distinction of age was made.

"They inherited the official places of their forefathers, practised their ceremonies, and performed their music. They reverenced those whom they honoured, and loved those whom they regarded with affection. Thus they served the dead as they would have served the living; they served the departed as they would have served them had they continued among them.

"By the ceremonies of the sacrifices in churches, they served God; and by the ceremonies of the ancestral hall, they memorized their ancestors. He who understands these religious ceremonies and principles of filial piety, would find the government of a kingdom as easy as to look into his palm!"[1]

The sixth principle of *chung yung* in government is that there is a methodology in the art of government. It advances orderly from step to step. Such an order is compared with travelling. When one goes a distance, he must first traverse the space that is near. When one ascends a high mountain, he must begin at the lowest step.[2] Likewise the administration of government consists of getting proper men. Such men are to be obtained by means of the ruler's own character.[3] With the right men the growth of government is rapid, just as vegetation grows rapidly in the earth.[4] The character of the ruler can be cultivated by following the path of reason. The path of reason can be found through the practice of the virtue of love, which is a fundamental in humanity.[5] In other words, love is the foundation of human civilization, and through it man is man.

Cultivation of personality is, therefore, essential to social well-being and good government. The

---

[1] *Chung Yung*, ch. xix.
[2] *Chung Yung*, ch. xv.
[3] *Chung Yung*, ch. xx, sec. 4.
[4] *Chung Yung*, ch. xx, sec. 3.
[5] *Chung Yung*, ch. xx, sec. 4–5.

Sovereign, who is the shepherd of the masses and their personal example of good conduct, should possess perfect virtue.[1]

The cultivation of personality consists of three virtues, namely, wisdom, love, and courage. To be fond of study and investigation is the way to acquire wisdom and knowledge ; to practise with vigour the rules of virtue is the way to obtain love ; and to possess the sense of shame that one may not deviate from the path of reason and that he may not do unrighteous things, is the way to obtain courage.[2] These three virtues should be practised. Men may not have equal innate ability ; and so some practise them with native enjoyment ; some from a desire for their advantages ; and some by strenuous effort.[3]

Cultivation of personality has three requirements, namely, love of family, love of men, and love of God. Out of love of family and love of man evolve duties of human relationships, namely, duties between the soveriegn and his people, between father and son, between husband and wife, between elder and younger brothers, and between friends.[4] The five universal duties should be well understood. Some may be born with a knowledge of these duties ; some may learn them through study, and some may acquire them after painful experiences.[5]

All rulers or administrators should have nine standard rules to follow, namely, cultivation of personality, honouring of men of virtue and talents, affection toward relatives, respect toward great ministers, kindness toward subordinate government officers and employees, love of the people, promotion of industries, hospitality toward foreigners, and benevolence toward foreign states.[6]

[1] *Chung Yung*, ch. xx, sec. 19.   [2] *Chung Yung*, ch. xx, sec. 10.
[3] *Chung Yung*, ch. xx, sec. 9.   [4] *Chung Yung*, ch. xx, sec. 7–8.
[5] *Chung Yung*, ch. xx, sec. 9.   [6] *Chung Yung*, ch. xx, sec. 12.

Doctrine of Chung Yung

The meaning of these terms is described in great detail in the book of *Chung Yung*. There are two ways for a ruler to cultivate his personality, namely, to be devoted to public ceremonies and to confine his action within the limits of *li*.

To honour men of virtue and talents implies four rules: first, the ruler should keep away from the slandering and gluttonous officials; secondly, he should keep himself from the seduction of feminine beauty and other evils; thirdly, he should keep away from the influence of the wealthy; and fourthly, he should honour the virtuous and talented and employ them in the government.

How may a sovereign show affection for his royal relatives? It is suggested by the *Chung Yung*: " Honour them according to their proper rank of nobility, give them due amount of emolument, and be sympathetic with their fortunes and misfortunes. By this way, his royal relatives will be encouraged to be loyal to him. The way to respect the great ministers is to give them a sufficient number of assistants to discharge efficiently their orders and commissions. The way to be kind to government officials and employees is to trust them with faith, to supervise them with efficiency, and to give them generous pay."

The love of the people implies two things: first, the government should tax the labour or services of the people only at the proper time and on the proper occasion; and secondly, the tax rate should be low. When the common people are lightly taxed and are required to contribute their services to the government only at the proper time they will have ample time to take good care of themselves and practise the rules of virtue.

Industries have two essentials, machinery and labour. There are two ways of encouraging industries: first, through frequent examinations and inventions, improvement and more perfect equipment are obtained; and secondly, through proper wages and provisions the efficiency of labour is preserved. Should these two rules be practiced, labour will be abundant and industry prosperous.

How may a ruler be hospitable to foreigners? The answer is found in the practice of four rules: first, welcome those who come; second, be kind to those who leave; third, honour and use the good people among them; and fourth, educate or reform the bad and incompetent among them.

Finally, the book of *Chung Yung* points out six principles of international ethics by which benevolence toward foreign states may be cultivated and world peace secured. They are: first, to give support to the restoration of certain legitimate government whose existence has been interrupted by an illegal government; second, to fight for a foreign nation in gaining its independence or revival after it has been conquered by a despotic power; third, to help in restoring order in those states that are in chaos; fourth, to support the states that are in danger or peril; fifth, to send envoys to foreign states or receive envoys from them at the proper time, on the proper occasion, and with the proper rituals; and sixth, to give liberal support to foreign governments and welcome those that reciprocate.[1]

What will be the effect of putting these nine standard rules of governmental administration into practise? The *Chung Yung* says: "By the ruler's cultivation of his own personality, the path of reason will be set forth. By his honouring men of virtue and talents there will result an efficient and honest civil service. By his affection for royal relatives, harmony and good will will prevail among the families. By his

---

[1] *Chung Yung*, ch. xx, sec. 14.

respecting the great ministers, the ruler will be associated with wise counsellors and will be kept from errors in the practice of government. By his kindness toward inferior officers and employees, they will be stimulated to do good work. By his love of the people, the public virtue will be cultivated, and progress and happiness will prevail. By his encouragement of the industries, the nation will be wealthy and prosperous. By his hospitality toward foreigners, the nation will be well populated. And by his benevolence toward other states, the prestige and influence of his kingdom will extend far and wide, and international peace will be the result." [1]

In conclusion, the *Chung Yung* states that one who is virtuous will be sure to receive the appointment from God to reign over the kingdom. God creates and produces things and makes them useful and nourishing by various ways according to their own qualities. For example, the tree that flourishes is nourished while that which is ready to fall, is overthrown. It is the great process of biological growth, and holds good in human affairs. The virtuous will be used. A verse in the *Book of Poetry* which eulogizes the virtue of King Wên, illustrates this point:

> The admirable, amiable prince,
> Displayed conspicuously his virtue;
> He loved the people and the officers;
> He received the appointment from God.
> God protected him and assisted him;
> And decreed him the throne.
> Age and fame, emulation and dignity
> Were given him as regards.[2]

[1] *Chung Yung*, ch. xx, sec. 14.
[2] *Chung Yung*, ch. xx, sec. 2–5.

CH'ÊNG or Interpretation of Truth as the Fundamental of Good Government and Social Happiness

Among the necessary steps for good government and social happiness, cultivation of personality is the point from which to start. The responsibility for such a task is heavy, and its course is long. A thorough previous preparation is necessary; without such previous preparation there is sure to be failure.[1] The foundation of all previous preparations is *ch'êng* or "sincerity", which is the fundamental of good government and social happiness.[2] The virtue of sincerity is fundamental for the ruler in the cultivation of the support of his relatives, of his friends, of his superior officers, and that of his people. Natural sincerity or natural truth is the way of God. The attainment of sincerity or the interpretation of truth is the duty of man. There are five ways of obtaining the virtue of sincerity, namely, extensive study of that which is good, accurate inquiry regarding it, careful reflection upon it, its clear discrimination, and the earnest practice of it.[3]

One may be born with the virtue of complete sincerity. Through the virtue of complete sincerity self-perfection of personality is effected, the path of reason is directed, and the full development of one's nature results. Since one is able to develop his own nature, one can influence the nature of other men. Since one is able to develop the nature of other men, one can develop also the nature of all other things, animate or inanimate. Such a person would then have the ability to assist God in controlling social development. Since he is controlling social

---

[1] *Chung Yung*, ch. xx, sec. 16.
[2] *Chung Yung*, ch. xx, sec. 17–18.
[3] *Chung Yung*, ch. xx, sec. 16–19.

development his greatness can be compared with that of God Himself.¹

Generally men are not born with the virtue of complete sincerity. They can only acquire it by the constant pursuit of goodness. By means of the virtue of sincerity man becomes intelligent and wise. Intelligence and wisdom create actions and changes; and actions and changes constitute social development.²

The virtue of sincerity is all-inclusive. " Sincerity is the end and the beginning of things." The virtue of sincerity is not only to perfect one's self, but also to perfect other men and things manifests his wisdom. Both love and wisdom are virtues belonging to nature.³

In conclusion, the book of *Chung Yung* gives three illustrations of the perfect man's rule : the first is concerned with the virtue of the perfect men ; the second is concerned with the way of the perfect men in promoting good administration and universal happiness ; and the last is concerned with the outcome of the perfect man's rule.

First, the virtue of the perfect man. Only perfect men should rule. Because of his intelligence, brilliancy, wisdom, and learning he is fitted to exercise control ; because of his magnanimity, generosity, benignity, and mildness he is fitted to enforce laws and exercise forbearance ; because of his impulsiveness, courage, firmness, and endurance he is fitted to determine governmental principles ; because of his self-adjustment, graveness, rightness, and impartiality he is fitted to direct the people ; and because of his accomplishments, thoughtfulness, prudence, and sanity he is fitted to exercise discretion in political affairs. Thus, he is seen and the people all reverence him. He speaks and the people all believe him ;

¹ *Chung Yung*, ch. xxii.   ² *Chung Yung*, ch. xxiii.
³ *Chung Yung*, ch. xxv.

he acts and the people all are pleased with him. In other words, he is loved by the people.

Second, the way of the perfect man in promoting good administration and universal happiness. The way consists of three principles which are consequences of perfect sincerity. The first principle is that the virtuous man will adjust the great relations of mankind. To adjust human relations is regarded by Confucius and his disciples as one of the most important tasks of rulers. The relations consist of that between ruler and ruled, that between superior and inferior officers, that between father and son, that between husband and wife, that between brothers, that between friends, and that between neighbours. A clear definition of these relations is an absolute essential of good government. The next principle is that the perfect man will establish the foundation of humanity, that is, he will see that virtue of love prevails. The third and last principle is that the virtuous ruler understands the principles of universal development, the most important of which is that God creates and produces things. He makes them useful and nourishing according to the qualities of the things. Thus, the virtuous govern the kingdom according to the principles of universal development, the principles of nature, and the principles of perfect sincerity.

Third, the outcome of the perfect man's rule. In the first place, the faith of the people in their government will prevail. In the second place, the people will be stimulated to virtue, even without rewards or encouragement from the government. In the third place, the people will depart from the use of law and punishments. Lastly, the principle of innate order and social harmony will prevail ; and the whole world will be conducted into a state of happy tranquillity.[1]

[1] *Chung Yung*, ch. xxxi–xxxiii.

Doctrine of Chung Yung

Summary

The book of *Chung Yung* deals with the psychological aspect of political control. The fundamental contribution of *Chung Yung* to the field of political philosophy is the theory that to obtain the good life, the government must regulate the innate feeling of the people and the outward actions resulting from such feelings. In other words, to use the technical terms of the sociologists, the government must proceed to study individual attitude and endeavour to set up a new set of social values that will be most advantageous in bringing about political progress.

The thesis of *Chung Yung* is this: there is an ideal of perfection which is termed God's "nature". The ideal road to reach that destination is termed the "path of reason". The best method of studying this path of reason is "education", and the great object of education is "sincerity", or the interpretation of truth. "Sincerity" includes three great human virtues: love, wisdom, and courage. Having achieved the perfection of these three virtues the ruler reaches the state of *chung yung*. The words of *chung yung* signify a state of perfect harmony existing in the innate feelings of associated man, in social interactions of individuals, and in the interactions of innate feelings and socialized activities. Love is to enjoy *chung yung*; wisdom is to know *chung yung*; and courage is to practise without deviation the ways of *chung yung*.

Government is an agency for the socialization of the virtues that will lead to the state of *chung yung*. The practical principles of *chung yung* that should be applied in government may be outlined briefly: (1) government should be a process in which the better man assists in improving the inferior by control, by education, and by nourishment; (2) government should show reciprocal sympathy and mutual faith between rulers and ruled ; (3) rulers should have concordance in word and action ; (4) rulers should accommodate themselves to the conditions of the situations ; (5) the rulers should promote religion and filial piety to supplement political control ; and (6) there should be standard rules in the art of government.

The ruler should have nine standard rules, namely, cultivation of personality, honouring of men of virtue and talent, affection toward his noble relatives, respect toward his great ministers, kindness toward subordinate government officers and employees, the love of his people, the promotion of industries, hospitality toward foreigners, and benevolence toward foreign states, as the surest way to promote international peace. Finally, the book of *Chung Yung* concludes that " sincerity " is the directive force of all these dynamic political phenomena. Through the work of sincerity, and through it alone, political progress may be brought about.

CHAPTER XI

SOCIAL EVOLUTION

The meaning and importance of *I* : " Evolution " defined—
  The importance of the *Book of Change*.
The principle of change : Change as a cosmic and social
  process—Causation of change—The three social laws—
  The basis of the universe and the basis of society.
The principle of phenomenal imitation : *Hsiang* defined—
  Origin of civilization—Steps of social evolution—
  Progress *v.* evolution.
The principle of rational judgment : The utilitarian basis of
  Confucian ethics—The definition of *tz'ŭ*—The functions
  of *tz'ŭ*—The programme of *tz'ŭ*.
Summary.

THE MEANING AND THE IMPORTANCE OF *I*

By " evolution " I mean a series of changes in a particular class of phenomena. The term " social evolution " refers academically to the development of society from the lowest status of savagery to the highest status of civilization thus far obtained. Students of sociology have endeavoured to ascertain the universal laws of social evolution which laws constitute the basis of their descriptive and analytical study of the different types of social phenomena. Furthermore they have reduced the very vague concept of " social evolution " to the very concrete meaning of cultural development of particular social groups. Then laws of social evolution describe how the different groups of peoples have created, transmitted, perpetuated, and expanded their civilization, namely, their socially acquired ways of thinking, speaking, feeling, and doing.

Political Philosophy of Confucianism

The Confucian principles of social evolution constitute the foundation of the political and social philosophy of the Confucian School. Indeed, Confucius and his early disciples present all of the speculations concerning the state and society in terms of these principles which are found largely in the *Book of Change* or *I Ching*.[1] Confucius himself was very fond of the *I*. When he was about seventy, he made a statement, saying: "If I had some more years to finish the study of the *I*, I might be without great faults."[2] Indeed, the *I* is a book of social truths, a study of which would "acquaint us with the fundamentals of cosmic and social evolution, free us from faults of ignorance, and inspire us ideals of progress". The method of the book, however, is deductive, beginning with the abstract principles and later proceeding to their practical application. The *I* is considered by the Chinese scholars as being the most difficult book of all classics.

The Principle of Change

The first principle in the Confucian theory of general evolution is that of transmutation or change. According to the *I* there is nothing static in the universe: everything is changable; and the change is constant and continuous—an infinite process.[3] One day while standing by a stream Confucius observed

---

[1] For the historical account of the *Book of Change*, see G. G. Alexander: *Confucius, the Great Teacher*, pp. 190–9. Readers should be aware of the fact that the authenticity of the account Mr. Alexander related is not wholly acceptable. A good discussion of the *Book of Change* is found in Hu Shih's *Outlines of the History of the Chinese Philosophy*, vol. i, pp. 77–92. The author is much indebted to Dr. Hu's book in the interpretation of the Confucian theory of social evolution as contained in this chapter.

[2] *Analects*, bk. vii, ch. xvi.

[3] *Book of Change*, The Great Appendix, bk. i, ch. i.

SOCIAL EVOLUTION

that the waters flowed on indefinitely. "Alas," he said, "it passes on just like this, ceasing not day or night."[1]

The word "it" refers to the course of evolution, the idea being that everything in the universe evolves ceaselessly like water flowing in the stream. The present will soon become the historical past. One commentator says: "Nature moves without end; time passes with the days and months; and the seasons pass with summer and winter. Things grow in numberless varieties. Evolution continues day and night, without end."[2] Another commentator gives a similar interpretation of the Confucian saying in these words: "This is the course of nature. The past has passed and the future is succeeded by futures. Not for a single moment does it cease."[3]

Thus, according to the philosophy of the *I*, nature changes and evolves. It is dynamic. What then, is the explanation of this process of constant transmutation? The *Book of Change* replies that it is due to the contact of unequal natural forces. The very fact of inequality gives rise to tendencies to change.[4] At first there was but one "Grand Terminus",[5] which created two different elementary forces, a male, or *Yang*, and a female, or *Yin*.[6] The qualities of the male force are activity, inflexibility, hardness, and firmness. The qualities of the female force are inactivity, flexibility, softness, and gentleness. These two forces, naturally so unequal, have constant contacts

---

[1] *Analects*, bk. IX, ch. xvi.
[2] Ch'êng I's commentaries on the *Analects*, quoting practically from the *Book of Change*, The Great Appendix, bk. II, ch. v.
[3] Chu Hsi's commentaries on the *Analects*.
[4] *Book of Change*, The Great Appendix, bk. I, ch. i; bk. II, ch. i.
[5] In Chinese *T'ai Chi*. The *T'ai Chi* may be literally translated as the "Great Origin". Theologically, it means the Beginning, the Creator, or God.
[6] *Book of Change*, The Great Appendix, bk. I, ch. v.

and conflicts with each other. As a result of these contacts and conflicts, movements are created, and varieties are formed.[1] This is the Confucian explanation of the cosmos : everything is a creation of natural evolution from the interaction of unequal natural forces.

Then, the *I* laid down the principle that the trend of evolution is from the simple to the complex. " The Grand Terminus created two elementary forces. In turn these two forces produced four forms, which again produced the eight trigrams."[2] These eight trigrams, further, created sixty-four sexagrams. These sixty-four sexagrams are multiplied further into three hundred and eighty-four figures, and so on indefinitely.[3] Thus the interaction of simple forces produces complex phenomena ; and this process of differentiation and multiplication explains the universe. Differentiation and multiplication are changes ; and so the whole process of evolution is only a natural growth from the simple to the complex by means of differentiation and multiplication through contact and conflict of various natural forces of unequal qualities.[4]

The *Book of Change* further maintains that things at the beginning are easy to understand and control, since they are quite simple. The farther they are advanced in the process of natural evolution and the more complex phenomena they evolve, the harder it is to understand and control them.[5] Thus to seek the beginning, the simple, the easy, or the root cause is essential to the investigation of all universal

[1] *Book of Change*, The Great Appendix, bk. I, ch. i–ii, vi ; bk. II, chs. vi, xii.

[2] *Book of Change*, The Great Appendix, bk. I, ch. xi.

[3] Ch'êng I's Preface on the *Book of Change*, see also *Book of Change*, The Great Appendix, bk. I, ch. ix.

[4] *Book of Change*, The Great Appendix, bk. I, chs. i–ii, vi, ix–xi ; bk. II, chs. i, v–vi, x.

[5] *Book of Change*, The Great Appendix, bk. I, ch. i ; bk. II, ch. v.

phenomena, whether physical or social. All the complex phenomena can be reduced to oneness. They have one origin and can be reduced to something relatively simple. There are systematic interactions of phenomena, that is, cause and effect. Reasoning from the complex facts in the universe, we may discover basic principles. When we have discovered these principles, we may then predict future events.[1]

It is at this point that the *Book of Change* gives three important social laws. In the first place, he says that the wise man who understands the laws of evolution can predict future happenings, and that his power to predict enables him to control human affairs.[2] Science begins with the investigation of facts ; Confucius emphasized also the pursuit of knowledge from the investigation of facts. The *Ta Hsüeh* (The Great Learning) says : " The ancients who wished to cultivate a virtuous rule in the empire, first regulated well their own state. Wishing to regulate well their own states, they first secured happy homes. Wishing to secure happy homes, they first cultivated their persons. Wishing to cultivate their persons, they first rectified their minds. Wishing to rectify their minds, they first sought to be sincere in their thoughts. Wishing to be sincere in their thoughts, they first made an extensive pursuit of knowledge. Such extension of knowledge lay in the investigation of things." [3]

In the second place, in this complex process of natural and social evolution, there is system. Causation and consequences give rise to phenomena which pass from the simple to the complex, from the more comprehensible to the less comprehensible. Comprehen-

---

[1] *Book of Change*, The Great Appendix, bk. II, chs. v–vi, viii–ix.
[2] *Book of Change*, The Great Appendix, bk. II, chs. v–vi.
[3] The Text of Confucius, sec. iv.

sion of this system is of fundamental importance to social investigators.

In the third place, all happenings are not purely accidental, but rather the result of spontaneous development. There is a cause for all happenings, and the cause is historical. "Understand the past," says the *Book of Change*, "so you may judge the future."[1] Confucius says: "Study the antiquity, so that you may comprehend the new."[2]

The text of the *Book of Change* consists of two parts and sixty-four chapters. The first two chapters of Part I refer to heaven and earth, respectively; while those of Part II refer to husband and wife, respectively. Heaven and earth are the basis of universal phenomena; while husband and wife are the basis of the social system. In the universe heaven represents the male force, and the earth represents the female force. In society man represents the male force and woman represents the female force.[3] The *Book of Change* says that "There is an intermingling of the genial influences of heaven and earth, and transmutations in their various forms abundantly proceed. There is an intercommunication of seed between male and female, and transformations in their living types proceed".[4] Thus the Grand Terminus, which created the heaven and earth forces, is the foundation of the universe; and the family, which consists of husband and wife, is the basis of society and the foundation of the political state.

THE PRINCIPLE OF PHENOMENAL IMITATION

Changes, variations, differentiations, and multiplications take place not only in a more or less systematic

[1] *Book of Change*, The Great Appendix, bk. ii, ch. vi.
[2] *Analects*, bk. ii, ch. xi.
[3] *Book of Change*, Text, pt. i, chs. i–ii; pt. ii, chs. i–ii.
[4] *Book of Change*, The Great Appendix, bk. ii, ch. v.

and orderly manner, but also in accordance with the process of *hsiang*, which is fundamental to all transmutations. The title *I Ching*, as already suggested, is literally translated as the *Book of Change*; for *I* means change, and *Ching* means classic, canon, or book. In fact, the translation is not exact; it should read " Book of Evolution ", since the whole book is a consideration of cosmic and social evolution. Thus *I* is synonymous with evolution. Says the " Great Appendix " to the *Book of Change* : " What I mean by *I* (evolution) is *hsiang* (phenomena) ; what I mean by *hsiang* (phenomena) is *hsiang* (imitation)." [1] In another place, the " Great Appendix " says ; " *I* is creations out of creations." [2] Then a number of explanations and definitions of the terms *hsiang* and *hsiang* are given throughout the " Great Appendix ".[3] From these definitions, we may conclude that Confucius and his

---

[1] *Book of Change*, The Great Appendix, bk. II, ch. iii.
[2] *Book of Change*, The Great Appendix, bk. II, ch. v.
[3] The Great Appendix of the *Book of Change* (bk. I, ch. i), says : " The heaven is high ; the earth is low ; hence the settlement of the cosmos. There is the distinction between high and low, hence the organization of the matters (including men, animals, plants, and all cosmic matters). There is the regularity of the activeness and inactiveness, hence the distinction of the hard quality and the soft quality. Activities show certain definite tendencies, and matters exhibit varieties and types. There comes the good and bad. In the heaven there are phenomena (*hsiang*), and on earth there are forms. So we see the evolutionary transmutations ! " Thus *hsiang* is an observable or perceptible fact resulting from the evolutionary transmutations. Similar sense of the word is expressed in the statement that " good and bad is the *hsiang* of success and failure, repentance is the *hsiang* of sorrow and worry, transmutation is the *hsiang* of progress and retrogress, and softness and hardness is the *hsiang* of female and male forces " (bk. I, ch. ii). In bk. I, ch. vii, of the Great Appendix, the *Book of Change* says : " The wise man sees the facts in the universe and perceives in his mind the various models, then describes them through proper imitation. This is *hsiang*." See also bk. I, chs. x, xi, xii ; bk. II, chs. i, ii, iii, xii.

disciples regard evolution as a process of successive creations by means of phenomenal imitation.

What is meant by "phenomenal imitations"? Briefly speaking it is the creation of a thing in imitation of some external phenomenon. For example, let us hypothecate the phenomenon A. The thing B is created from the imitation of A. Thus A is the form or the model, and B is the substance. B is created from the imitation of A; C from B; and D from C. All things are thus created by some sort of imitation. At first there were only natural phenomena—such as heaven, earth, trees, plants, life, death, rain, sunshine, thunder, lightning, etc. Man, through his observation of natural phenomena, obtains certain concepts. It is in accordance with these concepts that he builds civilization.[1]

Again, the *Book of Change* says: "The *I* operates on a principle in accordance with universal phenomena, and reveals to us, therefore, the course of things in the universe. The wise man, looking up, contemplates the brilliant phenomena of the heavens, and looking down, he examines the definite arrangements of the earth. Thus he discovers the causes of darkness, or what is obscure, and the causes of light, or what is bright. He traces things to their beginning, and follows them to their end. Thus he discovers what can be said about life and death. He perceives how the union of essence and the breath of things, and the disappearance or wandering away of the soul produce the change of their constitution. Thus he discovers the characteristics of the anima and animus. Through the principle of evolution, the wise man comprehends natural transformation; and he uses them as a mould to make things by an ever varying adaptation. He comprehends the course of day and night and all other

[1] *Book of Change*, The Great Appendix, bk. I, chs. ii, iv, viii, x–xii; bk. II, ch. i.

connected phenomena. It is thus that his principles are spirit-like, unconditioned by place ; while the changes which he produces are not restricted to any form." [1] Thus all forms of culture are created by means of a process of phenomenal imitation. In addition to natural phenomena, human institutions and ideas may also be imitated and thus create other imitations. These inter-imitations and multi-imitations explain both natural and social evolution.

In pointing out the steps of social evolution, the *Book of Change* asserts that at the outset there are many varieties of natural *phenomena*. As these natural phenomena enter into human perception, there result *ideas and concepts*. Ideas and concepts are precedent to the existence of material forms. When ideas and concepts are reduced to material forms there are *definite things*. When these *things* are socially improved, regulated, and formulated we have *laws, standards, and institutions*. When these laws, standards, and institutions are carried out, operated, and generalized for all people, we have *achievements*. Then there is created an *ideal* or *spiritual state* in which achievements disadvantageous to man's life are eliminated, and in which those advantageous are universally accepted and preserved.[2]

Thus the *Book of Change* points out not only the steps of social evolution, but also the ethical elements of social growth. Social evolution, according to the *Book of Change*, may go one way or the other : it sees no distinction between good and bad. It is the duty of man to decide which is good and which is bad. Since all phenomena or institutions, whether good or bad, grow, it is the duty of man to preserve the good and eliminate the bad. Thus we are led to the important Confucian theory of rational judgment.

[1] *Book of Change,* The Great Appendix, bk. I, ch. iv.
[2] *Book of Change,* The Great Appendix, bk. I, chs. xi–xii.

Political Philosophy of Confucianism

The Principle of Rational Judgment

The last principle of evolution is that of rational judgment or *tz'ŭ*. While the process of phenomenal imitation is going on, many changes take place. Phenomena create substances, and substances lead to phenomena. Inter-imitation and multi-imitation produce types and varieties. Then there are some things that are disadvantageous and harmful to the existence and development of human life, and others that are advantageous and beneficial. Since these different phenomena occur or are produced, man must select, that is, preserve those which are advantageous and profitable, and eliminate those which are disadvantageous and unprofitable. Thus there is introduced the distinction between the good and bad.

The *Book of Change* says: "The sage ruler, observing the phenomena, gives distinctions between good and bad."[1] Again, "Good is a phenomenon of having succeeded to get, and bad is a phenomenon of having failed to get."[2] Here the social ethics of the Confucian School is placed upon a utilitarian basis. The life of man is the highest aim of society. Accordingly society should be so organized that the best type of life is promoted. Moreover, history and group experience teaches that certain qualities and activities are profitable to the development of the best life. On the other hand, there are other qualities and activities that are detrimental and harmful to the development of the good life. And so the former qualities and

[1] *Book of Change*, the Great Appendix, bk. 1, ch. ii. The words *chi* and *hsiung* mean good and bad rather than success and failure. According to the Great Appendix of the *Book of Change*, good and bad is the phenomena of success and failure. The idea is this: That which tends to give success in securing the good life of man is good, and that which tends to cause failure in securing the good life of man is bad.

[2] *Book of Change*, The Great Appendix, bk. 1, ch. ii.

activities are regarded as good, virtuous, and moral, and the latter as bad, evil, and immoral. It is, then, the duty of all men and women to study carefully the distinctions between these two types of social qualities and social activities. Such is the foundation of Confucian Ethics.[1]

The *Book of Change* defines *tz'ŭ* (rational judgment) as "each indicating a tendency".[2] There are varieties of phenomena in the universe. All varieties change, evolve, and develop. Each variety indicates a tendency either toward good or toward bad.[3] Man observes these tendencies and exercises his power of selection. Seeing that war tends to endanger human life, he concludes that war is bad and should be eliminated. Since peaceful co-operation tends to benefit the life of man, it is said to be good and should be promoted. This rational process of selection is *tz'ŭ*.

This touches the modern theory of social progress when "rational judgment" is a step following "phenomenal imitation" in the theory of evolution. According to modern theory, social progress consists of a social change toward an ethical goal. It is distinct from social evolution in that the latter consists of a series of social changes without being attended by ethical values. Social evolution may tend toward the better or toward the worse. It way be progressive or it may be retrogressive. The authors of the *Book of Change* point out that things in the universe are changeable, and then that things are created and changed through phenomena. The authors are not satisfied with mere evolutionary growth. They would not allow all things to grow unmolested ; wish only the good, moral, and profitable things to grow ; while

[1] Kung Yung-tai, "Commentaries on the Book of Change."
[2] *Book of Change*, The Great Appendix, bk. I, ch. iii.
[3] The words "good" and "bad" are used in the Confucian utilitarian sense.

the bad, immoral, and unprofitable things should decay. This is the idea of social progress.

All things are dynamic; they move and change and grow. Things are not bad in themselves. It is their actions and their tendencies that bring consequences and cause successes and failures, good and evil, gains and losses. In *tz'ŭ* (Judgment) there is a distinction between good and bad phenomena. It has two functions: Positively it encourages the people to do good because good will bring profit and success to their lives; and negatively, it teaches the people to do no evil, since evil will bring harm and failure to their lives.[1]

Finally, from the above discussion, it may be said that *tz'ŭ* consists of four distinct steps: (1) the presence of a group of phenomena, which includes models and matters, inter-imitations and multi-imitations; (2) the observation of the tendencies of these phenomena and the study of their consequences; (3) the drawing of distinctions between good and evil, and deriving definitions for them, good being that which is profitable to life, and bad being that which is harmful to life; and (4) the process of selection, that is, the adoption of the good and the elimination of the bad. This four-fold process is always present in evolution; and so we have at first natural and social evolution, then scientific investigation, ethical teachings, and finally, the concept of social progress or social improvement.

Summary

The theory of evolution is the foundation of Confucian political and social philosophy. Thus theory is extensively discussed in the *Book of Change*. Evolution, according to the *Book of Change*, consists of three

[1] *Book of Change*, The Great Appendix, bk. I, chs. viii, xii; bk. II, ch. i.

processes, namely, the process of transmutation, of phenomenal imitation, and of rational judgment. In the first place, all things natural as well as social, change incessantly. They change from the simple to the complex. Differentiation and multiplication goes on all the time. The "Great Appendix" says: "What I mean by change is phenomenon, what I mean by phenomenon is imitation." All things change and create in accordance with the process of phenomenal imitation. On the one hand, there is a model, a form, or a phenomenon. On the other hand, there is a substance, or a thing which is made in imitation of the model. Man, observing phenomena in his natural and social environment, obtains certain concepts, and then creates certain things by imitating the phenomena he observed. At first there are natural phenomena and there are then human ideals and ideas which lead to human achievements in conformity with nature. Thus all arts, all cultures, all civilizations, are created from a process of phenomenal imitation.

While this process of phenomenal imitation is going on, changes are many. Differentiation and multiplication of things produce varieties and types. Some are profitable and advantageous to the existence of man's life, while others are not. In order to bring about the greatest good in the life of man it is necessary to discriminate between that which is advantageous and that which is disadvantageous. So we regard the former as good and moral, and the latter as bad and immoral. Consequently man must select, that is, to preserve and develop the good, and eliminate the bad. We have morals, customs, and laws to enforce the distinction and the process of selection. This is done by human judgment through the reasoning power of man; and this is the theory of rational judgment.

CHAPTER XII
POLITICAL PROGRESS

International nature of Classical teachings.
The three stages of social development : The age of disorder—
    The age of small tranquillity—The age of great similarity.
Factors of progress : The *ching t'ien* system—Invention and
    eugenics—Government, justice, *Li,* and religion—
    Education and faith in progress.
Steps of securing progress : Essence of the political philosophy
    of the Confucian School summarized.
Summary.

INTERNATIONAL NATURE OF CLASSICAL TEACHINGS

Before considering the classical idea of progress, views of Confucius and his early disciples on international affairs should be briefly discussed. It is misleading to say that " Confucius makes no provision for the intercourse of his country with other and independent nations " ; or that " China was to him the ' middle kingdom ', ' The multitude of great nations ', ' All under Heaven ', and ' Beyond it were only rude and barbarous tribes ' ".[1]

One Chinese writer goes as far as to say : " Confucius has made many provisions for the intercourse of his country with other and independent nations ; ... and we can compile the International Law of Confucius even from the *Spring and Autumn* only. In Confucius' time, China was divided into many nations. The number of leading nations was twelve, and the total number of nations was over

[1] James Legge : *The Chinese Classics,* vol. i, pp. 107-9.

one hundred. Therefore, his country was not China, but Lu. Since Lu had intercourse continuously with other and independent nations, why should Confucius know nothing about them? These nations were called 'The multitude of Great States' and the 'Middle Kingdom'. This was the international society. and the term Middle Kingdom was like the term Christendom. Beyond this, there were at this time only rude and barbarous tribes, so far as the Chinese knew. This was the condition under which Confucius lived. By the term 'All under Heaven', however, Confucius really meant the whole world, and it included not only the multitude of great states, but also all the barbarous tribes. Although it was sometimes used to cover only the Chinese world, such a term, everyone can see, could never mean a national state. In fact, Confucius always keeps the whole world in his mind." [1]

The *Li Chi* says that "a ruler should look on 'all under heaven' as one family and on all in the 'Middle Kingdom' as one man".[2] This statement evidently means that the ruler should look upon the world as one family, and China as an individual in the family. It is significant to note that in this statement the early Confucians ignore the feudal national states, and that they look upon the entire international society of the independent Chinese states as a unit. Moreover, they treat the whole world as a unit, and China as only one of the many sub-units of the world unit.

The statement has another significant phase. In the Confucian Classics the word "family" indicates mutual affection, community of interests, mutual responsibility in the promotion of family welfare, and economic

[1] Chen, H. C., "Economic Principles of Confucius and His School," in *Columbia University Studies*, vol. xliv, pp. 16–17, note.
[2] *Li Chi*, bk. vii, sec. ii, 18.

communism. When *Li Chi* says that one should regard the world as a family and China as an individual, it means that nations should have affection, community of interests, mutual responsibility in the promotion of public welfare, and economic communism. All the family virtues should be developed as world virtues, and one should regard other peoples, races, and nations as he does his own family. Under the Confucian system the individual practically loses his individuality, and is subordinated to the interests of the family as a whole. Likewise an empire like China, much less the smaller national states at the time of the Confucian era, should not develop any sort of narrow national patriotism, but should subordinate itself to the interests of the whole world. Great indeed is the saying : " Within four seas, all are brethren." [1]

THE AGE OF DISORDER

In the Appendices of the *Book of Change* the origin of primitive culture and its progress toward a more enlightened civilization is discussed. In the stage of primitive culture the people arise from cosmic and social disorder ; the social mind was narrow ; and the economic life was crude. Due to the lack of transportation and communication, the people lived in isolated groups. There was no *li* or social propriety. Peaceful contact between groups was unknown—such contacts taking the form of war. Within the group the people were controlled by military force and there was no rule of virtue.

At later times, wise rulers arose. They undertook, on the one hand, to improve the economic life of the people by new inventions and division of labour, and, on the other hand, to enlighten the social mind and to

[1] *Analects*, bk. XII, ch. v.

cultivate social sympathy by the teaching of *li* and virtue. New inventions consisted of implements for fishing and hunting, agricultural implements, housing, weaving, marketing, bargaining, mining, systems of transportation and communication, domestication of animals, military equipment for self-defence, mechanics for handicrafts, household utensils, methods of burying the dead, language, social institutions, and the political state.[1]

The teaching of *li* and virtue consists of the worship of God, thanksgiving to nature, remembrance of ancestors, sacrifices to the heroes of society, and the institution of the rules of rectification to govern human relationships. Hence the social mind of the time was greatly broadened and civilization was advanced from the primitive state to a higher stage.[2] The sage rulers to whom the Confucian Classics frequently refer are the geniuses of the time or the creators of new civilizations.

The Stage of Small Tranquillity

The next higher stage of culture is the stage in which we now live; the stage of "small tranquillity". Referring to the social and political conditions of the period, the *Li Chi* says : " The kingdom is inherited through family. Each one regards as his parents only his own parents, and treats as his children only his own children. The wealth of each and his labour are only for his self-interest. Great men imagine it is the rule that their estates should descend in their own families. Their object is to make the walls of their cities and suburbs strong ; and their ditches and moats secure. Propriety and justice are regarded

[1] *Book of Change*, The Great Appendix, pt. ii, ch. ii.
[2] *Li Chi*, bk. VII, sec. i, 6–12.

as the threads by which they seek to maintain in its correctness the relation between the ruler and the minister ; in its generous regard the relation between father and son ; in its harmony the relation between elder and younger ; and in a community of sentiment the relation between husband and wife ; and in accordance with them they regulate consumption, distribute land and dwellings, distinguish the men of military ability and cunning, and achieve their work with a view to their own advantage. Thus selfish schemes and enterprises are constantly taking their rise, and war is inevitably forthcoming.

"In this course of propriety and justice, Yü, T'ang, Wên, Wu, Ch'êng Wang, and the Duke of Chou are the best examples of good government. Of these six superior men, every one was attentive to *li*, thus to secure the display of justice, the realization of sincerity, the exhibition of errors, the exemplification of benevolence, and the discussion of courtesy, showing the people all the constant virtues. If any ruler, having power and position, would not allow this course, he shall be driven away by the multitude who regard him as a public enemy. This is the stage of small tranquillity."[1]

To analyze this classical statement we will find in the stage of small tranquillity the following factors : (1) family as the basis of social and political organization, (2) private property, (3) the national state and the necessity of national defence, (4) war, (5) selfishness, (6) worship of military heroes and cunning diplomats, and (7) revolutions. In order to preserve possible harmony and obtainable order, the doctrine of rectification, the government of virtue, the principle of *li*, the institution of monarchical government, the theories of political democracy, punishment and justice, moral education, and the rules of benevolent politics

[1] *Li Chi*, bk. VII, sec. i, 3.

are applied by the best governments. Indeed, this stage is a stage of practical ideals and obtainable order.

The Stage of Great Similarity

The highest stage of civilization is the stage of "great similarity". The *Li Chi* describes the conditions of this stage as this: "When the great principle of the great similarity prevails, the whole world becomes a republic, possessing a common spirit. The people elect men of talents, virtue, and ability. Their words are sincere, and they cultivate universal harmony. Thus men do not regard as their parents only their own parents, nor treat as their children only their own children. A competent provision is made for the aged until their death, employment for the able bodied, and means of education for the young. The widowers, widows, orphans, childless men, and those who are disabled by disease are all sufficiently maintained. Each man has his proper work and each woman has her proper home. They produce wealth, disliking that it should be thrown away upon the ground, but not wishing to keep it for their gratification. Disliking idleness, they labour, but not alone with a view to their own advantage. In this way selfish schemes are repressed and find no way to arise. Robbers, filchers, and rebellious traitors do not exist. Hence the outer door remains open, and is not shut. This is the stage of great similarity." [1]

The stage of great similarity is a Confucian ideal. "Great similarity" means a state of perfect social equality and harmony. In the state of great similarity the whole world forms one single social organization, and the individual is the independent unit; both socialistic and individualistic characters reach the

[1] *Li Chi*, bk. vii, sec. i, 2.

highest point. There is no national state, and so there is no war, no need of defence, nor of "men of military ability and cunning". Men of talents, virtue, and ability are elected by the people, so that the people themselves are the sovereign, and monarchy does not exist. The family ceases to be the foundation of social and political organization. When the people "do not regard as their parents only their own parents, nor treat as their children only their own children", the modern relationships between husband and wife, between father and son, and between older and younger brothers would be absent. Everyone loves everybody else as his parent or his child or himself. There is no private property, no idle class, no inheritance and no selfish scheming.

In the state of great similarity the old, the unemployed, the widows, the widowers, the orphans, the childless, and the disabled are taken care of by society under a perfect system. There is absence of immorality and crime, and consequently no need for law, rites, justice, and police. Everyone is naturally as good as everyone else, and each has only natural love toward others. In short, in the state of great similarity there is the highest moral excellence and social communism. And then, the doctrine of rectification, the principle of benevolent politics, the rules of *li*, the esssence of political unity or unitary sovereignty, the theories of political democracy, and all other artificial institutions concerning social and political control are made useless. These rules belong to the state of small tranquillity only. The state of great similarity is the state of extreme social harmony and perpetual peace resulting from the fullest development of human nature. It is all natural, and is the ideal of political progress.

The theory of great similarity is quite utopian. It is being criticized that this theory is of Taoist authorship; such a criticism, however, has no textual ground. It is safe to state that such a utopian philosophy was voiced by early Confucianists who might have been influenced by Taoist thinking. At the same time a more practical system was devised to secure peace, order, happiness, and progress under the existing conditions of social and political development. This practical system is the system of small tranquillity. Yet in the process of political progress there must be ideals and values, so that the society may proceed in the rightful direction of self-development, and that it may acquire a larger and deeper political and social consciousness. For this reason there establishes in the *Li Chi* a set of political and social ideals, such as universal peace, universal brotherhood, absence of private property, absence of national states, moral perfection, and social communism.

Factors of Political Progress

So much for the general principles of political and social progress. In the Classics one may discover many practical factors that are contributive to progress. The first factor is the *ching t'ien* system by means of which social wealth may be equitably distributed and the economic well-being of the people thus promoted. The progress of the *ching t'ien* system, interpreted by a famous historian of the Western Han Dynasty, may be measured periodically by the length of one year, three years, nine years, eighteen years, twenty-seven years, and thirty years. Under this system, in the cultivation of three years the people have a surplus of food sufficient for one year. From this economic proficiency, the sense of pride and shame is developed; and quarrels and litigations do not exist. Therefore, every three years an examination of merit is given to the conditions of the people and the civil service.

In nine years, after three examinations have been held, the undeserving officials are degraded, and the deserving promoted. There is a surplus of food sufficient for three years, and the improvement of the life of the people is called " advancement ". In eighteen years there are two periods of " advancement ", and such a condition is called " peace ". The surplus of food is sufficient for six years. In twenty-seven years there are three periods of " advancement ", and this is called " extreme peace " ; and surplus of food is sufficient for nine years. Then virtue will prevail, and the government will reach a stage of perfection. These stages illustrate the improvement of social, economic, and political life, and the advancement of productive power, and the accumulation of social wealth, and so the *ching t'ien* has progressive features.[1]

The second factor in political progress is technical invention, which is the basis of economic progress. From the state of savagery when man wore leaves and feathers, ate raw meat and grass, and lived in caves or open air, human beings have achieved tremendous progress in material civilization by new inventions. To insure material progress technical invention should be promoted more and more by government.[2]

The third factor in progress is a peculiar theory concerning eugenics. According to Elder Tai's *Record of Rites*, the first thing in eugenics is the choice of the mother. Therefore, when the parents choose the wife of their son, they must select her from among those families which have had a high standard of morality for all generations. For this reason, the

[1] Pan Ku, *History of Han*, ch. xxiv.
[2] *Book of Change*, The Great Appendix, pt. ii, ch. ii.

daughter of a rebellious house, the daughter of a disorderly house, the daughter of a house which has produced criminals for more than one generation, or the daughter of a leprous house, or the daughter who has lost her mother and has grown old, should not be taken in marriage.

When a woman is pregnant, the rules are as follows: while sleeping, she should lie on her back; while sitting or standing the body should be in an upright position, and the weight evenly distributed. She should not laugh too loudly, nor eat food of bad flavours, nor anything which is not cut properly; nor sit down on anything which is not placed properly. The eyes should not see bad colours; the ears should not hear bad sounds; and the mouth should not utter bad words. She should read good poetry, and tell good stories. By these means the child will be physically, morally, and mentally excellent. Whenever a woman is pregnant, she must be very watchful in regard to the things by which the mind is affected. If she is affected by good things the child will be good; if by bad things, he will be bad. These are the rules of eugenics of the Confucian School.[1]

The fourth factor in progress is benevolent government. Inasmuch as government is the most important of human institutions, benevolent government is the most effective factor in bringing about rectification, popular education, economic prosperity, good civil service, scientific philanthropy, respect for homes, preservation of justice, liberty and democracy, safety and protection, economy and efficiency, universal peace, and extension of the government of virtue, all of which are contributive to social progress.[2]

The fifth factor in progress is criminal justice or punishment. By means of punishment the bad elements among the people are either reformed or

[1] Bk. XLVIII, lxxx.   [2] See *Li Chi*, bk. VIII.

eliminated. Punishment gives enforcement to the *li*; thus *li* applied the doctrine of rectification, and punishment enforces its application. The highest form of punishment is one that is exercised with love and wisdom, remedying the sources of evils and attaining to perfect goodness. The contribution of punishment to progress is that it encourages the good elements of society to promote goodness by eliminating the bad elements.[1]

The sixth factor in progress is the principle of *li*. By means of *li* man has developed the social mind from a state of crudeness and indiscrimination to a state of mutual responsibility and rectification. Moreover, through *li* society has passed from a state of disorder to a state of obtainable order.

Li makes two main contributions to progress. First, it defines social relationships; and thus individuals are enabled to know definitely what they should do. This social definiteness negatively prevents social indecision and unrest and positively promotes social harmony. Secondly, *li* regulates human feelings by means of the cultivation of good environment. Man is largely controlled by feelings and desires which often hinder the full play of the perfect moral nature of man. *Li* recognizes both human feelings and moral nature. It enables the individual on the one hand to develop his moral nature, and on the other hand, to satisfy his desires and feelings. A harmonious development of moral order is then made possible. For instance, food, drink, and sexual pleasures are among the strong desires of man. *Li* does not repress these desires in order to develop the moral nature: it regulates them by the rites of marriage, rites of district-drinking, rites of archery, and other rites; and these very rites cultivate virtuous character, such as sincerity,

[1] *Li Chi*, bk. I, III, IV, XVII.

love, and modesty. Thus the desires, passions, and feelings are satisfied ; and at the same time the moral nature of man has the opportunity of developing. When such harmony between the moral nature and the human desires is brought about, society will progress toward the ideal.[1]

The seventh factor in progress is music. Music in the narrow sense, according to the *Yüeh Chi*, included poetry, singing, dancing, and musical instruments. In the broader sense, in addition to these four forms of music, there are appreciation of the beauty of nature, harmony, or happiness between individuals, and all forms of public recreation. While *li* regulates human feeling through the cultivation of a good environment, *yüeh* or music harmonizes individual and group feelings, and cultivates a type of individual attitude that is most harmonious with the environment.[2]

The eighth factor in progress is religion. By means of religious sacrifices, man appreciates the gift of nature. Hence he develops many moral qualities such as being grateful, economical, and careful in using natural goods. Ancestor worship promotes human sympathy, love of fellow beings, love of civilization, love of fatherland, reverence to the old, kindness to the young, and a sense of responsibility to the family and to society in general. Worship of God brings about intelligent understanding of the laws of nature, of the relation between man and man, and of his own place in the cosmic development. In short, religious worship promotes love of God, love of man, and love of nature, all of which are fundamental in progress.[3]

The ninth factor is education. It trains the mind, body, character, and skill of the individual. Education

---

[1] *Li Chi*, bk. vii, sec. i, 4 ; ec. ii, 10–20 ; ec. iii, 1–10.
[2] *Li Chi*, bk. xvii, sec. 11–18.
[3] *Li Chi*, bks. IV, VII, XX–XXII.

does not include schooling alone; family discipline, hunting, walking, social meetings, and personal interviews possess great educational values. In other words, anything that would train the conduct and character of the individual, or that would increase one's knowledge and skill is a form of education. Furthermore, in education emphasis should be laid more on the training of the mind, character, and feelings than the increase in knowledge and skill. The fundamental value of education to progress is to make the democracy of the masses, not the aristocracy of the intellectuals or the virtuous, to understand and hence to move toward the social ideal. This is best explained by the words of the *Li Chi*: " When a ruler governs in strict accordance with law, and seeks for the assistance of the good and upright—this is sufficient to secure him a considerable reputation, but not sufficient to move the multitude. When he employs the virtuous and worthy, and adopts all the best views of the people everywhere, this is sufficient to move the multitude, but not sufficient to transform the multitude. If he wishes to transform the people and to perfect their manners and customs, must he not start from education?

" The jade uncut will not form a vessel for use; and if men do not learn, they do not know the way in which they should go. On this account wise kings, when establishing good governments for the people, should make education and schooling a primary object; as it is said in the 'Charge to Yüeh', the thoughts of the rulers from first to last should be fixed on education. However fine the viands be, if one does not eat, he does not know their tastes; however perfect the royal doctrine may be, if one does not learn it, he does not know its excellence." [1]

In other words, political progress has its foundation

[1] *Li Chi*, bk. XVI, 1–3.

in education. Without education, the mass of the people would be ignorant and would not know the importance of the royal doctrine and the direction of progress. Therefore good government alone, or a royal doctrine alone, would not be sufficient to secure political progress. Education must be its foundation.

The final factor in progress is the faith in progress itself. As a carriage cannot proceed without wheels, so man must have faith in order to progress.[1] On this account Confucius and his early school set up a great many social and political ideals for his people to follow—such as benevolent government,[2] the doctrine of royal supremacy,[3] the state of perfect music (*yüeh*), and the state of great similarity. There is one element common to all these ideals, that is, a state of perfect harmony and complete goodness wherein the completely ethical state is the ultimate goal of all political and social control. Then, according to Confucius, there is a road that leads to this ideal goal; and the entire political, social, and moral philosophy of Confucius is a body of practical suggestions for the cultivation of this " royal " road.

The fundamental factor of the cultivation of the " royal " road is education.[4] It is through education only that the people are able to follow the road. Thus, the immediate purpose of all social and political institutions—such as the state, government, family, *li*, music, morality, and religion—is education. Take the state for example. Confucius says the most important function of the State is rectification.[5] Rectification is an educational function. Indeed,

[1] *Analects*, bk. ii, ch. xxii.
[2] The doctrine of *wang chêng* was thoroughly discussed by Mencius.
[3] In Chinese *wang tao*.
[4] See *Chung Yung*, ch. i.
[5] The doctrine of *chêng ming*.

Political Philosophy of Confucianism

Confucius emphasizes the economic well-being of the people, the promotion of which forms the major part of government activities, and yet he says that the best way to govern the people is to enrich them; and after having enriched them, educate them.[1] In this statement the economic well-being of the people is only a means of giving to the people a surplus of energy and time to devote to education.

Elements of Progress

The book of *Chung Yung* devotes itself entirely to the point that the greatest factor in progress is faith in progress itself. In it, an ideal condition, is pictured together with many practical ways of attaining that ideal. The whole purpose of this book, as well as the whole purpose of the Confucian philosophy, is stated in a few words at the very beginning of the book of *Chung Yung*, in these words: "What God has endowed is called nature; an accordance with this nature is called the path of reason; the way to cultivate the path of reason is education."[2] Then, the main body of the book discusses solely the practical principles of *Chung Yung* in government. We may point the essence of the political philosophy of the Confucian School in these words: To achieve progress, there must be (1) a purpose or ideal, (2) a path of reason or a practical way toward that ideal, and (3) education as an agency to cultivate this path. The word education includes religion, *li*, rectification, school instruction, social education, moral environment, recreation, and the state. The state is only a means of the means to the ethical end; but it is the greatest means of all for seven reasons: (1) It is the central agency of universally free education;

[1] *Analects*, bk. xiii, ch. ix.   [2] Ch. i.

(2) political authority is necessary to promote rectification ; (3) the state is the greatest institution in the promotion of that economic well-being which gives the people a surplus of time and energy for educational activities ; (4) the state insures safety, protection, and peace, so that progress may be peacefully pursued ; (5) the state is the greatest institution in religious worship ; (6) the state is the most effective instrument for social betterment, for the application of *li*, and for the promotion of *yüeh* ; and (7) a government of virtue is itself an educational institution, teaching and nourishing the people.

Summary

According to the *Book of Records* and the *Li Chi*, one should regard the whole world as a family and China as a single individual in the family. The Confucian concept of progress is expressed in the *Li Chi*, which classifies the development of civilization into three stages. The first stage is the stage of disorder or savagery, characterized by the absence of *li*. The second stage is called the stage of small tranquillity. In this stage there are family, private property, national states, war, selfishness, militarism, cunning diplomacy, and revolution. It is in this stage that the principle of *li*, the principle of rectification, the principle of benevolent government, the principle of unitary sovereignty, the theories of political democracy, law and justice, and moral education are useful. It is accordingly a stage of attainable order and practical ideals, and it is the one in which we now live.

The highest stage of civilization is the stage of great similarity. It is a stage dominated by the ideals of cosmopolitanism, humanitarianism, and communism. In this stage there is no private property, no national state, no special family relationships, no war, no diplomacy or militarism, no crime and immorality. Hence all the practical ideals such as *li*, benevolent government, government of virtue, and the like, are useless. Everyone loves another as himself. There is absolute equality, social communism, universal brotherhood, and moral excellence. Indeed, the theory of the great similarity constitutes a purpose or a goal of political progress for the Confucian believers ; and the theory of small tranquillity is a practical suggestion for the realization of such a purpose.

From the Classics may be inferred a number of practical factors in political progress : (1) the *ching t'ien* system ; (2) technical invention ; (3) eugenics ; (4) benevolent government ; (5) criminal justice ; (6) the principle of *li* ; (7) music ; (8) religion ; (9) education ; and (10) faith in progress itself. To achieve progress there must be three elements : (1) an ethical goal ; (2) a path of reason ; and (3) education as an agency to cultivate the path of reason. The word education is used in a very broad sense. The state is the greatest means in the promotion of education, which in turn cultivates the path of reason leading to the ideally ethical goal.

Selected Bibliography

The following is a brief list of the most important books for studying social and political ideas of Confucius and his disciples :—

1. The Primary Source

Book of Poetry or *Shih Ching*, James Legge's translation given in *Chinese Classics*, vol. iv.

Selected Bibliography

Book of Records or *Shu Ching*, James Legge's translation given in the *Chinese Classics*, vol. iii.
Book of Rites or *I Li*.
Book of Change or *I Ching*, James Legge's translation given in the *Sacred Books of the East*, edited by F. Max Müller, vol. xvi.
Analects or *Lun Yü*, James Legge's translation given in the *Chinese Classics*, vol. i.
Ta Tai Li or the *Elder Tai's Record of Rites*.
Li Chi or the *Younger Tai's Record of Rites*, James Legge's translation given in the *Sacred Books of the East*, vols. xxvii and xxviii.
Great Learning or *Ta Hsüeh*, James Legge's translation given in the *Chinese Classics*, vol. i.
Chung Yung or *Doctrine of the Mean*, James Legge's translation given in the *Sacred Books of the East*, vol. xxviii.
Tso Chuan or *Tso's Commentary to the Spring and Autumn*.
Kung-yang Chuan or *Kung-yang's Commentary to the Spring and Autumn*.
Ku-liang Chuan or *Ku-liang's Commentary to the Spring and Autumn*.
Mencius or "Works of Mêng Tzŭ", James Legge's translation given in the *Life and Works of Mencius*.
Hsün Tzŭ or "Works of Hsün Ch'ing".
Êrh Ya or "Encyclopædia of Confucian Literature".
Lao Tzŭ's *Tao Tê Ching* or "Book on Reason and Virtue", translated by Paul Carus.
Liu Hsiang's *Shu Yüan* or "Park of Narratives".
Tung Chung-shu's *Many Dewdrops of the Spring and Autumn* or *Ch'un Ch'iu Fan Lu*.
Twenty-four Histories.
Kuo Yü or "National Discussion".
Chan Kuo Ts'ê or "Essays of the Period of Warring States".
Han Fei Tzŭ or the "Works of Han Fei".
Mo Tzŭ or the "Works of Mo Ti".
Kuan Tzŭ or the "Works of Kuan Chung".
Chuang Tzŭ or the "Works of Chuang Chou".
Chou Kuan or the "Official System of Chou Dynasty".
Lü Shih Ch'un Ch'iu or "Lü's Annals of Spring and Autumn".
Lun Hêng, or Wang Ch'ung's "Essays".
Chu Hsi's *Chin Ssŭ Lu* or "Records of Recent Thoughts".
Ssŭ-ma Ch'ien: *Shih Chi* or "Historical Record".

2. Secondary Sources (in Chinese)

Chang Ping-lin : *Essays on Chinese Literature (Kuo Ku Lun Hêng).*
Chang Hsüeh-ch'êng : *Interpretations of Literatures and Histories (Wên Shih T'ung I).*
Chin Shou-shên : *Explanation to the Examination of Spurious Literature, Ancient and Modern (Ku Chin Wei Shu K'ao Shih).*
Hu Shih : *Outlines of the History of Chinese Philosophy*, vol. i (*Chung Kuo Chê Hsüeh Shih Ta Kang*).
Ku Chieh-kang : *Discussion on Ancient Histories (Ku Shih Pien),* vols. i and ii.
K'ang Yu-wei : *Research on the False Classics of the School of Hsin (Hsin Hsüeh Wei Ching K'ao).*
Essay on Cosmopolitanism (Ta T'ung Shu).
Liang Ch'i-ch'ao : *History of Political Thought of the Pre-Ch'in Period (Hsien Ch'in Chêng Chih Ssŭ Hsiang Shih).*
Liang Ch'i-ch'ao : *Lectures on Philosophy and Sciences) Hsüeh Shu Yen Chiang Chi),* vol. i.
Liang Ch'i-ch'ao : *Explanations of Important Books and the Method of Studying them (Yao Ti Chieh Tzi Chi Ch'i Tu Fa).*
Liang Shu-ming : *Oriental and Occidental Cultures and their Philosophy (Tung Hsi Wên Hua Chi Ch'i Chê Hsüeh).*
Yü Yüeh : *Questionable Authenticity of Ancient Literature (Ku Shu I I Chü Li).*

3. Secondary Sources (in English)

G. G. Alexander : *Confucius, the Great Teacher* (1890).
H. C. Chen : " Economic Principles of Confucius and his School " in *Columbia University Studies*, vols. xliv and xlv.
M. M. Dawson : *The Ethics of Confucius* (1915).
Hu Shih : *The Development of the Logical Method in Ancient China* (1920).
Ku Hung-ming : *The Discourse and Sayings of Confucius* (1898).
A. W. Loomis : *Confucius and Chinese Classics* (1887).

INDEX

Administration, the nine standard rules of successful, 210–12
"Advanced scholar," 194
Age of disorder, 234–5
Age of great similarity, 237–9
Age of small tranquillity, 235–7
Agriculture, 140–2
Alexander, G. G., 220, 250
Analects, or *Lun Yü*, xiv ff., 2 ff., 16 ff., 27 ff., 44 ff., 63 ff., 90 ff., 106 ff., 130 ff., 161 ff., 175 ff., 203, 220 ff., 234 ff., 249
Ancestor worship, political significance of, 72–3
"Ancient literature," or *Ku Wên*, xiv, 17
Anti-Confucian movements, 6–7
Assyrians, the, xx

Background of Confucian thinking, Chap. I, Summary, 24–5
Bad government, four evils of, 109–11
Bashford, James W., 7, 250
Benevolent government: Definition, 105–6; the five principles of, 106–9; the rule of virtue as a requirement of, 111–14; the rule of love as a requirement of, 114–16; *Ch'êng* as the fundamental of, 214–16; as a factor of progress, 241–2
Book of Change. See *I Ching*
Book of Filial Piety. See *Hsiao Ching*
Book of Poetry. See *Shih Ching*
Book of Reason and Virtue. See *Tao Tê Ching*
Book of Records. See *Shu Ching*

Book of Rites. See *I Li*
Book of Shang Yang. See *Shang Chün Shu*
Borrowing authority, the practice of, xv

Carthaginians, the, xx
Chaldeans, the, xx
Chan Kuo Ts'ê, 249
Chang Chih-tung, ix
Chang Hsüeh-ch'êng, 250
Chang Hung, 2
Chang Ping-lin, 250
Change, principle of, 220–4; as a cosmic and social process, 221–2; causation of, 222–3
Ch'ao t'ing, or the "court", 27
Chen, H. C., 70, 233, 250
Ch'êng Hao, 16
Ch'êng I, 16, 17, 221, 222
Ch'êng T'ang, 180
Chi K'ang, 122
Ch'i, 2 ff.
Ch'i, prince of, 2 ff.
Ch'ien Hsüan-tung, 1, 17 ff.
Chi-lu. See Tzŭ-lu
Ch'in dynasty, xiii, 21
Ch'in Shih Huang Ti, xiii
Chin Ssŭ Lu, 249
China, xii ff., 61, 118
China's Only Hope, ix
Chinese, the, xvii ff.
Chin Shou-shên, xiii, 250
Ching or "classics", 14 ff., 92
Ching Tien Shih Wên or *Explanations to Classical Literature*, 15
Ching t'ien system: Described, 140–2; and education, 156–7; and local self-government,

251

INDEX

178-9, 189-93; as a factor of progress, 239-40
Ch'ing dynasty, 17 ff.
Chou, 184-5
Chou Kuan, xiii ff., 14 ff., 92, 249
Chou Li, 14 ff., 92, 249
Chou dynasty, ix, 8 ff., 15, 82, 86
Christ, 119
Christianity, xxi
Chronicles of An Yen. See *Yen Tzu Ch'un Ch'iu*
Chu Hsi, 111, 122, 221, 249
Chuang Tzŭ, xiii, xv, 249
Chuang Tzŭ, xiii, xv, 249
Ch'un Ch'iu Fan Lu, 55 ff., 249
Ch'un Ch'iu of Lu, 54. See *Spring and Autumn*
Chung Yung (*Book of*), 16 ff., 53, 64 ff., 112 ff., 137, 146, 193, 199 ff., 245, 249; contribution to political philosophy, 201-2; on political progress, 246-7
Chung Yung : Definition, 198-200; essential qualities of, 200-2; nature of, 202-6; the three virtues of, 205-6; practical application in government, 206-13; *Ch'êng* as the fundamental virtue, 214-16
Civilization, origin of, 226-7
Classification of books, 16
Classification of Classics, 18
Communism, 237-9
"Complete scholar," 194
Confucian "bill of rights", 110-11
Confucian Classics : the orthodox interpretation, 14; various groupings of, 14-18
Confucian concept of nature, 64-6
Confucian ethics, utilitarian basis of, 228-9
Confucian political philosophy : Contrast between western political philosophy and, viii; fundamental concept of, 49; essence of, 246
"Confucian village," 8
Confucianism : Defined, xvi; basic literature of, 14-25
Confucius : Life of, 1-8; his administration in the State of Lu, 3-6; postmortem honours of, 7-8; not a utopianist, 11-12; time of, 8-14; attitude of, toward irresponsible hermits, 11-14; relation to classical literature, 17 ff.; sensitive to natural phenomena, 65-6; on *li*, 90-3
Contrast between Western and Confucian political philosophy, viii
Corwin, Edward S., xi, xxii
"Country of *Li I*," 93

Dawson, D. D., 250
Democracy and representation, Chap. IX, Summary, 195-7
District drinking and archery, 151-4
Distinction between *ching* and *chuan*, 16
Doctrine of *Chung Yung*, Chap. X, Summary, 217-18.
Doctrine of the mean. See *Chung Yung*
Doctrine of rectification, Chap. III, 46-9; Summary, 59-60
Doctrine of *wang chêng*, 245. See *wang chêng* also
Duke of Ai, 128
Duke of Chou, xv, 20, 28, 54, 208, 236

Education : State provision of, 156; as a prerequisite of punishment, 165; or *chiao*, 201; as a factor of progress, 243-6

252

INDEX

Egerton, Clement, xxii
Egyptians, xx
Elder Tai's Record of Rites. See *Ta Tai Li*
Ellwood, C. A., xxi
"Eminent scholars," 194
Encyclopædia of Confucian Literature. See *Êrh Ya*
Êrh Ya, 16, 22, 249
Essays of the Period of Warring States. See *Chan Kuo Ts'ê*
Eugenics as a factor of progress, 240–1
Europe, 61, 119
Evolution: Definition, 219; steps in social, 227

Faith in progress, 246–7
Family and the State, 66–73; as the basic institution in human society, 66–7; as the foundation of the state, 67–8
Family Saying of Confucius or *K'ung Tzŭ Chia Yü*, 20
Ferguson, John C., xxii
"Five Classics" or *Wu Ching*, xiii, 14, 17
Five relations or *wu lun*, 29
"Forest of K'ung," 7
"Four Books" or *Ssŭ Shu*, 16, 17, 198
Four classes of people, 62
Functions of the state and government regulation, Chap. VII; Summary, 157–9

God or Heaven, 6, 31 ff., 74 ff., 166–8, 174 ff., 201 ff., 221 ff., 235 ff.
Government: Positive and negative functions of, 129; as the greatest of social institutions, 129; requisites of, 130–4; the eight functions of, 135–6; based upon natural laws, 182–3; by the consent of the governed, 180–3
Government regulation: Chap. VII; Summary, 157–9; of social wealth, 139–40
Great Learning. See *Ta Hsüeh*
Greeks, the, xx

Han dynasty, 14 ff., 53, 189
Han Fei Tzŭ, xv ff., 249
Han Fei Tzŭ, xv
Hegelian type of political thinking, xix
"Higher Criticism," xiii ff., 14 ff., 92, 199
Historical Record or *Shih Chi*, 1, 2, 8, 56, 249
Hsia dynasty, 86
Hsiang or phenomena, 225–6
Hsiang or imitation, 225–6
Hsiao Ching, xvi, 14, 16
Hsieh Wei-yü, xxii, 117
Hsü Hsin, xviii
Hsü, Leonard S., xxii
Hsün Tü, xviii
Hsün Tzŭ, xiii, 21, 24, 47, 48, 56, 166, 249
Hu Shih, viii ff., 20, 48, 54, 220, 250
Huan, 5
Huan of Ch'i, 54
Huang Ti, xv, 31
Human nature, 162–3
Husband and wife, 35, 37, 224–5

I the meaning and importance of, 219–20
I Ching, xiv, 14 ff., 30 ff., 44 ff., 63 ff., 92 ff., 116 ff., 143 ff., 164 ff., 187 ff., 220 ff., 235 ff., 248; importance of the book, 220
I Li, 15 ff., 92–3, 249
I Tung Tzu Wên, 20

Index

Imperialism, 119–220
Industrial and commercial regulation, 143–8
International ethics, six principles, 212–13
International nature of Classical teachings, 232–4
Invention as factor of progress, 240

Japan, 119
Jên chêng or *wang chêng* (benevolent government), 106, 182
Jên mu, 174
Justice. See Legal Justice

K'ang Yu-wei, xiii ff., 17, 250
Kao Yao, 164, 190
King, the, 77–82; as a model of the nation, 77–9; as the maker of laws, 79; and revolution, 79–80; ideal qualities, 80–2
King Hsiang of Liang, 181
King Mu, 167
Ku Chieh-kang, xiii ff., 19 ff., 22, 250
Ku Hung-ming, 118, 119, 250
Ku-liang, 1
Ku-liang's Commentary, 15 ff., 29, 249
Ku-liang Chuan. See *Ku-liang's Commentary*
Kuan Tzŭ, xvi, 249
Kuan Chung, xviii
Kung-yang, 1
Kung-yang Chuan. See *Kung-yang's Commentary*
Kung-yang's Commentary, 15 ff., 29, 141 ff., 191, 194, 249
Kung-po Liao, 6
Kung Yung-tai, 229
Kuo Ku Lun Hêng, 250
Kuo Yü, 15, 21, 249

Labour and immigration, 143–6
Lao Tzŭ, xviii, 2, 11, 249

Law and justice, Chap. VIII; Summary, 172–3
Legal Justice: Human nature, and 162–4; development of, 164–6; administration of, 164–7; and criminal punishment, 167–9; ideal system of, 169–70; sociological ideal of, 171; as a factor of progress, 241–2
Legalism: Limitations of, 125, 160–2; useful in the age of practical politics, 161–2; ultimate unnecessity of, 171
Legge, James, 33, 199, 232, 248–9
Li: Functions of, 90–1; its place in the development of civilization, 92–3; meaning and programme of, 93–4; and Yüeh, 94; practical application of, 95–6; constitutional significance of, 96–9; human nature and, 99–100; as a factor of progress, 242–3
Li Chi, xiv, 2 ff., 14 ff., 38 ff., 47 ff., 72 ff., 91 ff., 112 ff., 128 ff., 166 ff., 175 ff., 233 ff., 249
Liang Ch'i-ch'ao, xiii ff., 20 ff., 75, 93, 250
Liang Shu-ming, xxii, 250
Liberty, equality, and equity, 185–9
Lieh Tzŭ, xiii ff., 249
Liu Hsin, xiii, xiv, 23
Liu Jên-hsi, xxii
Local self-government, 189–93
Loomis, A. W., 250
Lou Teh-ming, 15
Love: As the highest ideal of government, 114; Confucius on the negative and positive rule of, 114–15; parental love *v.* political love, 115–16; romantic love *v.* political love, 116

Index

Lu, Prince of, 14 ff.
Lu, State of, 2 ff., 128, 233
Lü Shih Ch'un Ch'iu, 249
Lü's Annals of Spring and Autumn. See Lü Shih Ch'un Ch'iu
Lun Yü. See Analects

Machiavelli, xix
Machiavellian politics, xix, xxi
Many Dewdrops of the Spring and Autumn. See Ch'un Ch'iu Fan Lu
Medes, the, xx
Mencius, xiv, 28, 54, 57, 65 ff., 119 ff., 138 ff., 181 ff., 245
Mencius, 2 ff., 16 ff., 28 ff., 48 ff., 73 ff., 111 ff., 138 ff., 181 ff., 245, 249
Methodology in the art of government, 209
Middle Kingdom, 76, 232-3
Militarism, 116-18
Military dictatorship, 124-5
"Minister of Heaven," 176
Minister of State, 83-6
Mo Ti, xv, xviii
Mo Tzŭ, 249
"Model of virtue," 181
"Modern Literature or Chin Wên," xiv
Modern researches in ancient Chinese history, 17-24
Monopoly, 146-8
Muller, F. Max, 33, 249

Nature and political organization, 62-6
Nature or hsing, 201
National Discussion, See Kuo Yü
Nationalism, 118-19
Nei Ching, xv
Nietzschian philosophy, xix
"Nine Classics" of the Confucian School, 15

Official System of Chou Dynasty. See Chou Kuan
Organic theory of kinship, 78-9
Ou-yang Hsiu, 17, 20

Pan Ku, 240
Pao Hsi, 30 ff.
Park of Narratives. See Shu Yüan
Partisanship and favouritism in politics condemned, 185-6
Path of reason or tao, 201
Perfect man's rule, 215-16
Period of "Spring and Autumn", 9
Persians, the, xx
Phœnicians, the, xx
Place of the Confucian School in the history of political philosophy, xvii-xxi
Plato's Republic, 95
Poetry, 66, 150-1
Political confidence, 181-3
Political Progress, Chap. XII; Summary, 247-8
Political unity, 73-7
Political Unity and organization, Chap. IV; Summary, 87-9
Porter, Lucius, xxii
Princeton University, xi
Principle of benevolent government, Chap. VI; Summary, 125-7
Principle of change, 220-4
Principle of discrimination between tendencies, 45-6
Principle of imitation, 44-5
Principle of li, Chap. V; Summary, 103-4
Principle of ministerial responsibility, 84-5
Principle of phenomenal imitation, 224-7
Principle of rational judgment, 228-30

Index

Principle of social evolution, 220
Principle of spontaneous development, 43–4
Principles of family organization applied to state, 68–72
Principles of international ethics, 212–13
Progress: Factors of, 239–46; elements of, 246–7; v. evolution, 229–30, 234–9
Propriety, meaning of, 35
Psychological aspect of political control, 199–200
Public administration, rules of, 121–4
"Punishment of Lu," 167–9
Public opinion, 176–9

Record of Recent Thoughts. See Chin Ssŭ Lu
Recreation, state regulation of, 150–6
Rectification: Doctrine of, Chap. III; Summary, 59–60; definition, 46–7; as a factor of government, 47–9; three stages of, 49; practical programmes of, 49–59; criminal justice as the last step of, 164–6; as a factor of progress, 245–6
Relationships (*lun*), the concept of, 29
Relief and philanthropy, 148–50
Religion: As an agency of social and political control, 154–6, 208–9; as a factor of progress, 243
Righteousness, meaning of, 35
Romans, the, xx
"Royal Regulation" on judicial administration, 169–70
Rule of love, 114–16
Rule of virtue, 111–14, 160–2

Sacred Books of the East, 33, 249
"Select scholar," 194
Sense of shame, 161–2
"Seven Classics" of the Confucian School, 14
Shambaugh, Benj. F., xxii
Shang Yang, xviii
Shang Chün Shu, xiii, 249
Shantung Province, 2
Shê chi or the "altar to the spirit of territory and grain", 27
Shêng of Chin, 54
Shih Ching, xiv, 14 ff., 71, 92 ff., 115 ff., 141, 175 ff., 248
Shu Ching, xiii, 14 ff., 29 ff., 69 ff., 92 ff., 129 ff., 164 ff., 175 ff., 248
Shu Yüan, 55, 249
Shun, 31, 76 ff., 175, 189, 205, 208
Sincerity or *ch'êng*, 202, 214–16
"Six Classics" of the Confucian School, 22
Slavery, 187–8
Social development: Place of the state in, 29; three stages of, 234–9
Social evolution, Chap. XI; Summary, 230–1
Social justice, 186–7
Social disorganization, 61–2
Social happiness, the three principles of, 215–16
Social laws, the three, 223–4
Socialism, 237–9
Socialization, *ch'êng* as a factor of, 214–16
Socrates, x
Source material in historical research, xiii ff.
Sovereignty: Unitary, 73–7; location of ultimate, 74–5; Mencius' interpretation of the

256

Index

patriarchal theory of government, 75–7; concept of popular, 76–7; centralization of power, 77
Sphere of governmental authority, 134–9
Spring and Autumn, 1 ff., 14 ff., 26 ff., 53 ff., 92, 116 ff., 137 ff., 186 ff., 249
Ssŭ-ma Ch'ien, 1, 2, 8, 56, 249
Ssŭ-ma Kuang, 17
State: Functions of, Chap. VII; essentials and symbols of, 26–9; and the development of civilization, 33–7; and its origin, Chap. II, 30–3, 35–7, 41–2; justification of the existence of the, 37–41; as a means of the means to the ethical end, 246–7
State of Ch'i, 181
State of *li yüeh*, 133
State of Yen, 181
Su Hsiang, 2
Sung dynasty, 16 ff.
Sung, Prince of, 2
Symbols of the state, 26–7

Ta Hsüeh, 16 ff., 49, 59, 67 ff., 112 ff., 131 ff., 177 ff., 249
Ta Tai Li, 15 ff., 50–1, 92–3, 249
T'ang, 86, 236
T'ang dynasty, 14 ff.
Tang Tsu, 2
Tao Tê Ching, 11, 249
T'ao Wu of Ch'u, 54
Taoist influence on Confucianism, 10–12
Taxation, 131–9
Theory of educational representation, 193–5
Theory of five relations, 29
Theory of political stewardship, 174–6

Theory of revolution, 79–81, 183–5
Theory of social origin, 33–6
Theory of *ta t'ung* (great similarity), 146, 237–9
"Thirteen Classics" of the Confucian School, 16
"Three Commentaries" or *San Chuan*, 15 ff.
Three principles of social phenomena, 43 ff.
"Three Rites" or *San Li*, 15 ff., 92–3
T'ien hsia, meaning of, 39, 232–3
T'ien Tzŭ or "son of heaven", 74 ff.
Tithe, system of, 137–9
Ts'e She-he, 2
Tso Chuan. See *Tso's Commentary*
Tso's Commentary, 1 ff., 15 ff., 29, 75, 249
Tsung miao or "ancestral temple", 27
Tung Chung-shu, xviii, 55, 58
Tyau, M. T. Z., xxii
Tz'ŭ or "rational judgment": Definition, 229; functions of, 229–30; programme of, 230
Tzŭ-hsia, 124
Tzŭ-kung, 8, 13, 130
Tzŭ-lu, 6, 205
Tzŭ Ssŭ, 199

Van der zee, Jacob, xxii
de Vargas, Phillip, xxii

Wang An-shih, xviii
Wang Ch'ung's Essays or *Lun Hêng*, 249
Wang Mang, xiii
Wang tao or the "royal doctrine", 245
Wang Yang-ming, xviii
Wên, 53, 208, 236

257

Index

Wên Shih T'ung I, 250
Wên of Chin, 54
Women, political status of, 188
Works of Chuang Chou. See *Chuang Tzŭ*
Works of Han Fei. See *Han Fei Tzŭ*
Works of Hsün Ch'ing. See *Hsün Tzŭ*
Works of Kuan Chung. See *Kuan Tzŭ*
Works of Lieh Yü-k'ou. See *Lieh Tzŭ*
Works of Mêng Tzŭ. See *Mencius*
Works of Mo Ti. See *Mo Tzŭ*
Wu, 53, 184, 208, 236
Wu hsing or the " five elements ", 135
Wu lun, 29 ff.

Yao, 31, 75 ff., 175, 189

Yao Chi-hang, 17
Yen Chêng-tsai, 2
Yen Hui, 205
Yen Jo-chu, 17
Yen Tzu Ch'un Ch'iu, xiii, 249
Yin or " musical air ", 101
Yin and *yang* as cosmic forces, 70, 221
Yin dynasty, 86, 180
Yü the Great, xv ff., 54, 86, 236
Yü Yüeh, xiii, 137, 250
Yüan Shou, 74
Yüan tzŭ, 74
Yüeh Chi, 14, 103
Yüeh Ching, 14
Yüeh: *Li* and, 99–103; ideal of, 99–100; functions of, 100–2; social nature of, 102–3; as a factor of progress, 243
Younger Tai's Record of Rites. See *Li Chi*

For Product Safety Concerns and Information please contact our EU representative GPSR@taylorandfrancis.com
Taylor & Francis Verlag GmbH, Kaufingerstraße 24, 80331 München, Germany

www.ingramcontent.com/pod-product-compliance
Lightning Source LLC
Chambersburg PA
CBHW052218300426
44115CB00011B/1734